THE ATLANTIC LITERARY REVIEW

Quarterly

January-March & April-June 2005 Volume 6 Number 1-2

ATLANTIC
PUBLISHERS & DISTRIBUTORS

CONTRIBUTORS

Agrawal, Sadhana : Department of English, Govt. Maharaja Auto. P.G. College, Chhatarpur (M.P.), India. E-mail: dcharcha@sancharnet.in

Armellino, Elisa : Department of English, University of Turin, Turin, Italy. E-mail: elysarm@yahoo.it

Bhatt, Preeti : Department of English, Sant Jayacharya College, Jaipur, Rajasthan, India. E-mail: preetibhatt@datainfosys.net

Chakravarty, Saumitra : Department of English, V.V.S. First Grade College, Bangalore, India. E-mail: saumitra@postmark.net

Kazmi, S.N.R : Department of English Language and Literature, International Islamic University Malaysia, Gombak, 53100 Kuala Lumpur, Malaysia. E-mail: snasir30@hotmail.com

Khan, Jalal Uddin : Department of English, Department of Foreign Languages, University of Qatar, P.O. Box 2713, Doha, Qatar. E-mail: jukhan@gmail.com

Koopmann, Shari A. : Department of English, Valencia Community College, Osceola Campus 3-225, Florida, USA. E-mail: SKoopman@Valenciacc.edu

Krishnan, R.S. : Department of English, North Dakota State University, Old Main 103, Fargo, North Dakota 58105-5014, USA. E-mail: RS.Krishnan@ndsu.edu

Manohar, Murali : Department of English, University of Hyderabad, Gachibowli, Hyderabad, India. E-mail: dmbm_vs@yahoo.co.in

Mund, Subhendu : Department of English, BJB College (Autonomous), Bhubaneswar 751 014. Mailing address: 'Prabhamayee,' VI-M-37 Sailashree Vihar, Bhubaneswar 751 021, INDIA. E-mail: subhendu_mund@hotmail.com

Purkayastha, Tirthankar Das : Department of English, Vidyasagar University, Midnapore, West Bengal, India. E-mail: tirthankar11@rediffmail.com

Rollason, Christopher : 17 avenue Foch, F-57000 Metz, France. E-mail: rollason@9online.fr

Saranghi, Chhayakanta : Department of English, D.A.V. College, Titilagarh Dist. Bolangir, Orissa, India. E-mail: khansony@rediffmail.com

The Atlantic Literary Review

VOLUME 6 NUMBER 1-2 (JANUARY-MARCH & APRIL-JUNE 2005)

TABLE OF CONTENTS

Editors' Introduction

Five Years of *The Atlantic Literary Review*

The first number of *The Atlantic Literary Review* was dated July-September 2000, and so with the present issue our journal completes the first five-year cycle of its existence. We at *ALR* feel we have every reason to take pride in what we have achieved so far, and we believe we have established ourselves as a major and respected open forum for criticism in the field of English-language literary studies, especially though not exclusively in the areas of postcolonial literature and Indian Writing in English. We therefore invite our readers to accompany us for a moment, as we take stock and look forward to the future.

Let us start with what we are not. *ALR* is not a journal of literary theory, comparative literature, linguistics, translation studies, cultural studies or media studies. Nor are we an all-purpose literary journal. It is not our usual policy to publish book reviews or raw creative writing. What we are committed to is the dissemination of articles, written in English and not previously published, that fall within the field of literary criticism as commonly understood, relating to literature also written in English (our contributors may, of course, choose to incorporate elements from the other domains mentioned above in order to structure and articulate their readings of literary texts). Given these limitations (which remain on the broad side), both the articles' subjects and their authors may be from anywhere in the world, and indeed the greater the diversity the better. We have occasionally ventured into comparative studies to publish articles that place an English-language alongside a non-English-language work, or included texts on writers such as Rabindranath Tagore or Ngugi wa Thiong'o, who, though mainly not writing in English, are of undisputed importance for national or postcolonial writing in that language. However, in the light of the global reach of the English language and the multiplicity of literatures now existing in it, we feel our remit is already wide enough for a single journal.

ALR is published in New Delhi, India, and naturally a significant proportion of our contributors have been Indian and a large number of the articles published have focused on Indian Writing in English. At the same time, we pride ourselves on being a fully international journal, in ways that reflect the most positive aspects of globalisation. Our Editorial Advisory Board takes in academics and scholars of a wide variety of origins, and a similar diversity characterises both the origins of our contributors and the English-language authors written on. We are particularly pleased to have welcomed numerous contributors from the non-English-speaking world, notably though not exclusively from the scholarly communities of Spain, Italy and Finland. All major literary genres have been represented across our issues—novels, short stories, poetry, drama, travel writing, autobiography. In addition, we believe that our pages over the years have succeeded in achieving a fair gender balance, in terms of both contributors and writers studied: equal opportunities, in all senses, are present among our aims and goals.

As well as Indian Writing in English (both home-grown and diasporic), African and Caribbean literatures have featured strongly, reflecting the multipolar nature of the postcolonial phenomenon. Recent British, Irish, Canadian, Australian and New Zealand literature, too, have all been represented. Meanwhile, while our contributors' main focus has tended to be on contemporary writing, it has never been our position to neglect the older literary tradition, and challenging reappraisals of earlier, canonic writers have featured in our pages. We have also published a total of seven special issues devoted wholly or mostly to particular topics. These have included one single-author project (marking V.S. Naipaul's Nobel award), and the following more general subjects: Postcolonial Literatures: Globalisation of Discourses and National Identities; National Literatures in English and the Global Market; Past and Present in Post/Colonial Literatures; Diasporic Indian Fiction; Postcolonial Feminist Writing; and Indian Women's Short Fiction.

An idea of the flavour of *ALR* can be gleaned from a brief glance at the list of writers most featured in our pages over these five years, up to and including the present number. Indeed, it is worth enumerating the authors on whom we have published three or more essays (comparative articles included). Thus, we have featured 16 articles on V.S. Naipaul (8 in the above-mentioned special issue), 8 on Anita Desai, 7 on Salman Rushdie, 6 on Amitav Ghosh, 5 on Toni Morrison, and 3 each on Raja Rao, Shashi Deshpande, Manju Kapur, Arundhati Roy, M.G. Vassanji,

Wole Soyinka and William Shakespeare. Among the Indian writers spotlighted, we may note a certain balance between the India-resident and the diasporic, while the presence of Shakespeare is a reminder of our continued openness to the canonic.

ALR has always been and remains open to contributors of all methodological hues whose interests fall within our delineated sphere. All relevant information may be found on our website at: <http://atlantys.homeip.net/perso/atlanticliteraryreview/>, which we strongly encourage prospective contributors to explore. For the future, we hope to achieve even greater diversity, and will gladly welcome submissions on the better-known and emergent writers from the geographical areas less represented hitherto, not to mention new contributors from all parts of the globe. Finally, *ALR* is the product not just of its editors but also and above all of its contributors and readers, to whom we extend an open invitation to join us in dialogue on the future aims and directions of our journal, as it moves with confidence into the second half of its first decade. After five years, the work has, in a strong sense, only just begun.

— *Rajeshwar Mittapalli*
— *Christopher Rollason*
— *Dora Sales Salvador*

The Reversal of the Mother Goddess Image in Shakespeare's Tragedies

Saumitra Chakravarty

The view is often met that the world of Shakespeare's tragedies is an essentially masculine world where women are forcibly suppressed physically, sexually and psychologically. Hence it is a patriarchal world tending towards tyranny and power divorced from responsibility, often leading to a separation of the man from the mantle he inherits or usurps. It is a world of kings, generals, Machiavels, fathers, brothers and husbands and, therefore, a belligerent, hard and cynical one. Women who do gain a foothold in this world, at least temporarily, are women who have forcibly repressed their femininity. Lady Macbeth unsexes herself with the aid of the spirits of darkness, Portia slashes her thigh to gain access into her husband's confidence, Regan and Goneril assume the role of rebellious sons and unleash anarchy within the kingdom. The softer, feminine side of nature, the forces of innocence represented by the Ophelias and Cordelias, are deliberately sacrificed and silenced.

The purpose of this paper, however, is to expose the paradox of the situation by examining the role women *do* play in the tragedies despite assertions to the contrary. In the process, it is necessary to break down structured identities and defined parameters and above all to show that none of these equations are fixed.

Tragedy happens when certain factors spin out of control, when elements which the ruling powers that govern society or individual lives have officially distanced as the unacceptable 'other' encroach upon clearly defined peripheries. Let me briefly list the factors that led to the crystallization of an identity that was essentially white, English and male in the day of Shakespeare and his contemporaries. The Elizabethans and Jacobeans were great believers in 'degree,' under which everything from stars to rocks, from man to the basest forms of life, had its own fixed position in the structured hierarchy of the universe. The official declaration of James I, the sovereign was equated to God. In addition, the governing factors of that definition of an English identity were not only political and racial, but also religious and ethical. Stephen Greenblatt, in his essay "Shakespeare and the Exorcists," talks of the strategies that were part of an intense and sustained struggle in the late sixteenth and early seventeenth centuries in England to redefine the central values of society. At the heart of this struggle was the definition of the sacred, "a definition that directly involved secular as well as religious institutions, since the legitimacy of the state rested explicitly on its claim to a measure of its sacredness [...]. In early modern England rivalry among elites competing for the major share of authority was characteristically expressed not only in parliamentary factions but also in bitter struggles over religious doctrines and practice" (Greenblatt, 259). The boundaries of the sacred and the demonic or diabolical were redefined with the struggle between Catholics and Protestants in Tudor England, and, often, also between the religious proclamations of the ruling monarch and the lingering religious residue from an older faith in sections of the population. Anything beyond this pale was rejected as 'otherness' unacceptable to the concept of an ordered society. In this patriarchal set-up, as also Jews and Moors were alienated, women were either forced to embody the Elizabethan image of the chaste, obedient queen, wife, mother, sister and daughter, or were exposed and suppressed by outraged fathers as Ophelia and Cordelia were, or worse, were exorcised and burnt at the stake as witches. It is such a world then, that Shakespeare apparently represents in his tragedies.

However, it is also true that a certain fluidity was already creeping into this pre-defined set-up by the time Shakespeare composed his major tragedies. The voyages of discovery had opened up new social and cultural horizons and an awareness of them within the national consciousness, whether willingly or unwillingly. Burgeoning of trade had led to the change from a fixed feudal hierarchy to a more fluid capitalist one where capital could propagate a shift up the social order from *nobilitas minor* to *nobilitas major*, where money could fetch a citizen a baronetcy. Above all, it brought up a more multi-racial and multi-religious society to challenge the national identity, though racial and religious segregation continued. In other words, it was no longer possible to deny or ignore the identity of that 'other' in any stratum of society.

Tragedy is a recognition that the unpredictable, the unidentifiable, the untameable exists and can erupt without warning, wreaking havoc within the structured hierarchy and also within the human mind. It is cathartic because it invites us to recognise this paradox as being deeply rooted in the individual's psyche and therefore to control it. Roles can be reversed and the inherent associated functioning can be violated, leading to a fluidity that threatens to destabilize the order within the pre-defined system. It is a paradox that allows for such Manichean contradictions as light and darkness, fertility and barrenness, sacred and demonic, life and death, chastity and wantonness, to become interchangeable by relaxing their boundaries.

Since I am talking of the role of women in the tragedies and the power they can exercise over the patriarchy within which they function, let me begin by illustrating this paradox through an examination of the goddess cults in several ancient religions. In most European goddess cults, the mother goddesses are recognised as a triad, e.g. as the Celtic Macha in her three aspects of prophetess-warrior-matriarch, or the Greco-Roman triad of Persephone-Demeter-Hecate. However, none of these roles are unidimensional, and their influence upon an essentially patriarchal society appears to be multifaceted. In Celtic mythology, Daghdha the mighty one, must mate with the goddess of war, who is also the fertility symbol, in order to increase his potency. Macbeth himself is referred to as Bellona's bridegroom at the height of his valour and strength. Sex and war occur together in a number of Celtic legends. Medhbh of Connact is said to have controlled the armies of Ireland. No king could rule in Tara without having first mated with her. The king in myth must be married to his kingdom in a ceremony at which a libation may appear as an ugly hag, symbol of a desolate and bloodied kingdom. We recall Macbeth's meeting with the witches before his unrightful accession to the throne. In the Celtic legend, the ugly hag is transformed into a beautiful goddess when kissed by the rightful claimant to the throne. However, Macbeth was a usurper who still had the power to be a successful administrator, given his valour and strength, as Claudius tried to be in Denmark. Nonetheless, when the usurper turns bloody tyrant, the barren, destructive hag-like image assumes control and the forces of fertility gradually die away. In the Celtic myth, Daghdha the mighty one had as his symbol a club, one end of which kills and the other brings back to life, thus balancing the forces of destruction and re-creation. Similarly, in Indian goddess myths, Durga the ten-armed goddess, armed with the collective might of the male gods to destroy evil, is also worshipped in a harvest festival in autumn, with rituals which include both the shedding of sacrificial blood and the offering of *navapattrika*, symbolising nine fruits of the field. The imbalance in *Macbeth* is clearly seen, for while we have repeated references to the "seed" of Banquo, Macbeth talks of an "unlineal hand," a "barren sceptre," a "fruitless crown" (III.i), all images of infertility and desolation, though Scottish history does speak of sons of Macbeth, a fact corroborated by Lady Macbeth's words: "I have given suck, and know/ How tender 'tis to love the babe that milks me" (I.vii.). The earth cannot be regenerated till blood is spilt to drown the weed and water the real sovereign flower, in a therapeutic process required for the prosperity of the denuded kingdom of Scotland.

Turning to another aspect of the goddess myth, in the Persephone-Demeter-Hecate triad of Greco-Roman tradition, it is generally accepted that Persephone symbolizes virginal innocence, while Demeter, Earth-goddess and grain-giver, is a full-breasted and large-hipped symbol of fertility. Hecate, on the other hand, is barren, aged, shrivelled and associated with death, darkness and evil. However, a closer examination of their mythical roles in various aspects of the tradition may focus on the fluidity and interchangeability of their iconic status. Demeter the life-giver also ushers in the death-bringing forces of Winter in her terrible anger at the abduction of her daughter Persephone. Persephone herself represents innocence and chastity, violated by the "Host of many," as Pluto is referred to in the Homeric hymns. To my mind, Persephone also represents a repressed sexuality forcibly kept under control by her vigilant Earth-mother. She loses her innocence when she unwittingly pulls out the root of the narcissus blooming on the plains of Enna by the will of her father Zeus. The gateway to the underworld that she opens up in the process is like the genital orifice which leads her to sexual union with Pluto, son of Kronos and gives her a sense of power, as ratified by the repeated references to her as the "dread" Persephone throughout the *Iliad* and the *Odyssey*. This union which brings about her empowerment is sealed with her acceptance of the pomegranate which ensures her stay as Queen of the Underworld for at least one-third of the year.[1] In Shakespeare, the obvious Persephone-image of repressed sexuality occurs in Ophelia hemmed in on all sides by harsh, dominating and callous men and finally driven mad. Ophelia does not see herself as "monastery-bound" like the coldly chaste Isabella of *Measure for Measure*. The flowers she bedecks herself with in her madness reflect both her enforced virginity and her unconscious urge for sexual fulfilment. Thus on the one hand we have fennel[2] and columbines[3], while on the other we have the dichotomy inherent in the lines:

Fantastic garlands
Of crow-flowers, nettles, daisies and long-purples
That liberal shepherds give a grosser name
But our cold maids do dead men's fingers call them.
(*Hamlet,* IV.vi)

In the tragedies, female sexuality is not allowed to develop. Hamlet is more alarmed by his mother's desire for sexual fulfilment than by his uncle's treachery, and has an almost immature revulsion against such desires, as seen in his treatment of Ophelia. Desdemona breaks through her codified status of the "a maiden never bold" (I.iii) imposed upon her by her father and the state, by embracing a wild adventurous Moor and in so doing challenges the essentially white European Renaissance identity. It is ironical that the Moor himself should refer to her in the coldly chaste terms that he wished to promote and for which he strangled her without chance of self-defence: "Cold, cold, my girl!/ Even like thy chastity" (V.ii). In *King Lear*, female sexuality is demonised: "But to the girdle do the gods inherit/ Beneath is all the fiends" (IV.vi.).

The Mother Goddess is generally represented by fertility rites and harvest symbols and in ancient Stone Age icons, with large breasts, full hips and a pronounced vulva.[4] She is the Magna Mater, the Great Mother, Demeter-Ceres-Annapurna, who regenerates and fertilises the Earth. She is the benign counterpart of the destruction and dissolution threatened by the Terrible Mother. This last version of the triad may be found in Kali, whose lust for blood is magnified by blood-shot eyes, her garland of heads and her gory tongue, and in Hecate, of shrunken body and shrivelled breasts, associated with death and the ghosts of the nether world. Kali also represents untamed sexuality, as seen in her image astride Shiva, her consort, and in the sacrificial offerings of blood, flesh and wine. In Indian mythological terms, this tension inherent in the two versions of the Great Mother may be identified as the contrast between fertility and destruction, "Anna-purna" and "Anna-rikta Bheeshana." This contrast is also seen in the *Rg Veda*, between Usas, light-and life-bringer and Nirrti, death-bringer. Usas is often represented as a cow that yields her udders for the benefit of mankind (*Rg Veda*, 3:58, 4:5), like Prithvi in the *Atharva Veda* (12:1). Nirrti, on the other hand, in scattered references in the *Rg Veda*, is associated with death and destruction and, in the *Taittriya Upanishad*, as a dark force, dressed in dark clothes, receiving dark husks as her share of the sacrifice. David Kinsley, in his book on Hindu goddesses, says that Kali's shocking appearance puts dharma in perspective and is realized as "a threat to society's feeble attempts to order what is essentially disorderly: life itself" (Kinsley, 129). However, the *Devi Mahatmya* shows how when Durga, the embodiment of Beauty and Power, is attacked by Canda and Munda, her face darkens to an inky hue ('masheevarnamabhuttada') with anger, and suddenly Kali emerges from her forehead, wearing a garland of human skulls and wielding a skull-topped staff (*Devi Mahatmya*, VII.vi). More important is the assumption in the *Devi Mahatmya* that when Durga and her fierce band of Matrkas cannot contain the uncontrollable fertilization process in the demoniac orgy unleashed by Raktabija, it is Kali who stems the process by sucking the blood from the demon's body (*Devi Mahatmya*, VIII. 52-54, 57). Thus there is blood-letting as well as blood-sucking, both recognisably therapeutic in their own ways. The spilling of blood is also recognized as a necessary process to purge the land and regenerate it, as earlier mentioned in this essay.

Just as destruction and recreation are interchangeable in ancient myths, the symbols of barrenness and fertility are constantly switched in Shakespearean tragedy, thus changing what is potentially life-giving into a death-bringing process. Though Lady Macbeth has often been referred to as the fourth witch in the play, contributing to her Hecate-like image, there are ample references to her as a fertility symbol as well, in the breast and milk images: "I have given suck […]" (I.vii); "Come to my woman's breasts […]" (I.v) Thus, while Lear curses his treacherous daughters with barren wombs and destroyed seed, Macbeth invokes the blessing of fertility on his wife: "Bring forth men-children only" (I.vii). Ironically, he himself is destined to die at the hands of one who has symbolically circumvented the usual channel of birth. Similarly, there are references to the "milk of human kindness" (I.v.) and the "sweet milk of concord" (IV.iii.). The breast image of overflowing milk representing prosperity is reversed in *Richard II*, when York chastises the Duchess for breeding traitors:

Thou frantic woman, what dost thou make here?
Shall thy old dugs once more a traitor rear?
(*Richard II*, V.iii.)

In *Macbeth*, life-giving and life-rearing in the womb, breast and milk images are swiftly turned into death-bringing ones which irrevocably denude Lady Macbeth of her essential womanliness, when she invokes the "murdering ministers" of the nether world to take her milk for gall and promises to dash out the brains of her suckling child. In so doing she exchanges her Demeter-role for a Hecate-like one. In the Hindu scriptures, while Prithvi the Earth-goddess oozes life-giving nectar from her breasts, Bhairavi the destroyer smears her breasts with blood. Within the text of the play of course, the obvious parallel to the mother's reversed role of destruction occurs in the sow that has eaten her nine farrow, referred to in the apparition scene.

The juxtaposition of life and death in the womb and breast images is also seen in Cleopatra's comparison of the asp to a babe suckling at the breast:

> Peace, peace!
> Dost thou not see my baby at my breast
> That sucks the nurse asleep?
> (*Antony and Cleopatra*, V.ii)

This woman of waning lip and eye seems to surmount age and consequent termination of fertility and rides forth surrounded by Caesarion and all the unlawful issue that the aged pair have produced between them. In fact the play seems to defy what might have been its association with the aging third of the Greco-Roman triad of goddesses by its repeated images of fertility like "the fire that quickens Nilus' slime" (*A&C*, I.iii) or "The higher Nilus swells/ The more it promises" (II.vii), and Cleopatra is but a serpent of old Nile. The images of uncontrolled fertility contrast starkly with the discipline and rationality embodied by the stern Roman culture, which ironically seems to place the widow Octavia in a barren, shrivelled Hecate-like role in Antony's eyes. In *Julius Caesar,* Calpurnia's barrenness is publicly flaunted by Caesar at the feast of Lupercal.

Coming to Hecate, whose name means "influence from afar" in Greek, she represents the last and the most barren and aged of the triad of goddesses. Demonised by Christianity and by Greek patriarchs, she is associated with evil, black magic and the netherworld, to be worshipped at three-way crossroads at night. She was one who could coerce the gods at will, like Kali dominating the prostrated Shiva and unlike Durga, who, though an embodiment of female power, symbolises the amalgamated strength of the male gods. In *Macbeth,* Hecate represents an avenging force that will ultimately bring the wayward son to his downfall when her female subordinates have been lax or unwilling. However, as mentioned by Hesiod, Hecate was originally a moon goddess, who did some good by reporting the abduction of Persephone. In the original triad, she was represented as a wise old woman. In *Macbeth*, too we have lingering echoes, as in the reference: "Upon the corner of the moon/ There hangs a vaporous drop profound" (*Macbeth*, III.v.). Further, as in the life-giving, life-taking breast images in the play, there is also a paradox inherent in Hecate and her witches. For while the witches are generally represented as withered, wild, bearded women with skinny lips and bony fingers, antithetical to the images of femininity discussed so far, there are hidden references to the sexual power they wield over their male victims.[5] The apparition scene in Act IV represents a wild orgy, where decency, reason and order are dissolved to give way to primal chaos, in much the same way as Egypt overpowers Rome in *Antony and Cleopatra*. In *Macbeth*, the forces of darkness, here embodied by an uncontrolled feminine presence, overtake the structured patriarchal society of Scotland. Lady Macbeth, who has herself exchanged her Demeter role for a Hecate-like one, anticipates this orgy in her taking of wine, her drugging of possets (to induce a swinish sleep) and her reference to "the receipt of reason/ A limbeck only" (*Macbeth*, I.vii). The masculine valour of Bellona's bridegroom already having succumbed to the power of his wife, he is now overwhelmed by the enormity of feminine forces till he acknowledges their power to strike at the very pillars of civilisation:

> Though you untie the winds, and let them fight
> Against the churches; though the yesty waves
> Confound and swallow navigation up;
> Though bladed corn be lodg'd and trees blown down
> Though castles topple on their warder's heads [...]
> (*Macbeth*, IV.i)

These forces are a reminder that what is distanced by a well-ordered structured society as the 'other,' exists and lurks around the fringes of that society, ready to strike at will. The virtuous Banquo confesses to wicked dreams that abuse the curtained sleep. The darker face of the feminine is often represented in a succubus image that can seduce men in their sleep, and provoke erotic dreams and nocturnal emissions in men to propagate their own demonic species.[6] The *Book of Isaiah* associates Lilith, Adam's first wife who represents unfettered sexual dominance and power, with demons, owls and jackals, nocturnal creatures who strike unexpectedly "to lead astray the spirit of knowledge" (*Isaiah*, 34:14). In *Macbeth*, the overtaking of the tragic hero by dark feminine forces is anticipated by the sailor of Act I Scene iii, who will be drained as dry as hay:

> Sleep shall neither night nor day
> Hang upon his penthouse lid.
> He shall live a man forbid [...]

He is a man, in other words, who loses his masculine identity and falls victim to the female succuba.

Joyce Carol Oates, in an essay on *King Lear*, says: "When the feminine or maternal is not objectified, it begins to take on too powerful an essence. It 'haunts' the conscious mind. Denied finite objectivity, the feminine is inflated out of all proportion to an individual's ability to contain it, just as any unconsolidated, unvoiced yearning becomes inflated and deadly, threatening to crowd consciousness out altogether" (Oates, 23). The feminine factor in tragedy therefore represents the unconscious, the untameable, the unpredictable forces of existence. Man, in the ordered, rational superstructure that he carefully constructs around himself—in the "queenless" kingdoms of Lear, Duncan, Malcolm, or in those where the queen is allowed to play little or no part, like Claudius, Caesar's or the later Macbeth's—is really in a state of somnambulism. His inability to recognise the feminine force, to acknowledge it and thereby confront the chinks in his social and psychological armour, endows him with what is essentially a false sense of security. This makes him all the more vulnerable. Lear's definition of his own rising hysteria: "O how this mother sucks up towards my breast/ Hysterica Passio" (II.iv) reveals a man divided within, lost in his battle to crush the forces of the feminine. Othello, "whose subdu'd eyes,/ Albeit unused to the melting mood,/ Drops tears as fast as the Arabian trees/ Their med'cinal gum" (V.ii.), and Macduff, who must bear his loss like a man but also feel it like a man, are also strong men on their way to recognising the feminine factor of existence which they had, in their prime, sought to suppress.

The ancient Greeks acknowledged the innate power of feminine forces and the necessity to control the dominance of the male in social and political life. In Homer's *Odyssey*, Book X, the "dread Persephone" gives judgement even in death only to the Theban Teiresias, the blind soothsayer, who is essentially androgynous and therefore more complete, "that he alone should have understanding, but the other souls sweep shadow-like around" (*Odyssey*, 159). The male Roman priests of Magna Mater were required to castrate themselves in her cave temples, so that the land could be given a new lease of life. It is the function of tragedy to recognize the essential duality of existence, to break down the rigid dichotomy between the norm and the exception, between the pre-defined identity and the alienated 'otherness,' and excavate the paradoxes within.

Notes

1. It is possible to compare with the image of Shodasi, in Hindu mythology, the most youthful version of the Mahavidyas, the Devi's incarnations in the *Devi-Mahatmya*, who is seen as a girl of sixteen astride the prone body of Shiva, with whom she is having intercourse on a pedestal made up of the male pantheon of Brahma, Visnu, Rudra and Indra. The *Devi-Mahatmya* consists of 700 mantras on Sri Durga, contained in thirteen cantos of the *Markandeya Purana* (LXXXI to XCIII).
2. Stephen Greenblatt, (in "Shakespeare and the Exorcists" 262), talks of the *benandanti*, members of a northern Italian folk cult who went forth seasonally to battle with *fennel stalks* against their enemies the witches. If the *benandanti* triumphed, the harvest would be good. Later the Inquisition pronounced the witch-fighting benandanti themselves as witches and had them persecuted. Fennel stalks may then be taken as symbols of fertility.
3. Queen Elizabeth I propagated her image as the Virgin Queen by associating herself with flowers that symbolised chastity and virginity (the eglantine, the wild white rose).
4. Among the *pithas* where parts of Sati's body is supposed to have fallen after the Daksha Yagya in Hindu mythology, the Kamakshya pitha is where her yoni or sexual organ is worshipped in stone smeared with red paste, symbolizing menstrual blood.
5. The Greeks performed the Eleusinian Mysteries in the Temple of Demeter, essentially recognizing the ambiguity of existence. This worship was not only a propitiation of the Earth Mother by fasting and purification, it also involved a ritualistic descent into the underworld to bring renewed life back out of the jaws of death. The characteristic feature was a pig sacrifice. Since pigs were associated with fertility and potency, it was believed that mingling their blood with the seeds of grain would increase the yield of the harvest. In the apparition scene in *Macbeth*, the blood of the sow is mixed in the cauldron with other poisonous or nocturnal animal parts, thus mingling the life-giving and the death-bringing.

6. In the Talmud, it is said that after separation from Eve for 130 years, when her son Cain caused death in the world, Adam fathered evil spirits, which happened as a result of 'wet dreams.'

Works Cited

Greenblatt, Stephen. "Shakespeare and the Exorcists." In Shakespeare's *King Lear*. Ed. Frank Kermode. London: Macmillan, 1992.

Homer. *The Complete Works of Homer*. New York: Modern Library, 1950.

Kinsley, Davis. *Hindu Goddesses: Vision of the Divine*. Delhi: Motilal Banarsidass Publishers, 1998.

McEachern, Claire, ed. *The Cambridge Companion to Shakespearian Tragedy*. Cambridge: Cambridge UP, 2002.

Oates, Joyce Carol. "'Is This the Promised End?': The Tragedy of King Lear." *Journal of Aesthetics and Art* (Fall 1974).

Shakespeare, William. *The Globe Illustrated Shakespeare: The Complete Works*. Ed. Howard Staunton. New York: Gramercy Books, 2001.

The Markandeya Purana. Trans. Swami Jagadeeshwarananda. Chennai: Sri Ramakrishna Math, 2001.

Willis, Roy, ed. *World Mythology: The Illustrated Guide*. London: Duncan Baird Publishers, 1993.

Zimmerman, Susan, ed. *Shakespeare's Tragedies* (Contemporary Critical Essays, New Casebooks). London: Macmillan 1998.

Manfred as a Key Byronic Text

Jalal Uddin Khan

English Romantic poetry is highly autobiographical. Byron's is no exception being, among other things, an expression of the characteristic traits of his personality—proud, reckless and egotistical disregard of others and sad, melancholy reflections about human destiny and human history. Critical of contemporary conventions, Byron is in search for a perfect ideal not possible in human life. Born in a line of Byrons, all known for their wild character, he was the only child of his parents, born with a defective foot, but he grew up to be a handsome young man.[1] No wonder he had a number of scandalous affairs, including the incestuous one with his half-sister Augusta Leigh, which contributed to the break-up of his marriage, seriously damaging his social reputation and causing him to leave England in 1816, never to return again, till his death in Greece in 1824 at the age of 36.[2]

This sense of self-exile combined with the pride of noble birth and contempt for ordinary humanity is reflected in Byron's heroes, who are actually dramatic projections of the moods of his ego, obsession, isolation and cynicism. His choice of setting in the wild and stormy aspects of nature provides a fitting background to his turbulent personality and that of his characters. He was called "the Napoleon of London drawing rooms" and "the last Promethean," comparing himself to a volcanic eruption in view of his passionate ambition and tragic destiny to ruin all he came near. He is considered the most European of all the English Romantic poets not only because of his extensive European tours and cosmopolitan connections but also his similarities with his elder and younger contemporaries on the continent, Goethe and Leopardi, respectively.

Similarly, Byron is considered the least Romantic of all English Romantic poets. One of the reasons is that he admired the eighteenth century Augustan satire and the neoclassical elegance of form and style, although he himself did not care much for the art of diction in his poetry. He did not like the elder generation of his fellow Romantic poets (Wordsworth, Coleridge, and Southey), whom he bitterly attacked as inferior and insufficient because he thought they were confined to small lakes and ponds and hills of the English Lake District as opposed to the oceans and seas across the continent through which he would extensively travel. His sense of rebellious pride and freedom was unlikely to find home in the tame and tranquil surroundings of the Lake poets. With no sympathy for the Wordsworthian sense of the moral and benevolent nature, Byron developed his particular attitude to the wild and stormy from his boyhood. In *Hours of Idleness* (1807), his first volume, he speaks of the inspiring mountainous scenery and:

> [...] the freeborn soul,
> Which loves the mountain's craggy side,
> And seeks the rocks where billows roll.[3]

Expressing his dislike of flat country, he wrote to Augusta: "Level roads don't suit me." His Childe Harold says that to him "High mountains are a feeling, but the hum / Of human cities torture" (*Childe Harold's Pilgrimage, CHP*, III, 682-83).

However, in his own way, Byron too, like other Romantics, was conscious of human imperfections in the world of reality; but, unlike them, he gives a satirical portrait of such imperfections, constantly mocking at them and searching for an impossible ideal of perfection. It was precisely against such an obsessive search that Madame (Germaine) de Stäel, who was regarded as the mistress of the age, warned Byron when she attempted, without success, to effect a reconciliation between him and his wife, saying: "You ought not to have declared war on the world. It's an impossibility [...] I tried it myself when I was young—but it's impossible."[4]

Manfred is Byron's first dramatic work—"a dramatic poem," as he called it in its subtitle, suggesting that it is a combination of lyric and drama like the later *Prometheus Unbound (A Lyrical Drama)* by Shelley. By describing the piece as "metaphysical" in nature, Byron suggests that it is a closet drama of strange and inexplicable ideas, meant for reading, not for the stage. The quotation from *Hamlet* prefacing the poem ("There are more things in heaven and earth, Horatio,/ Than are dreamt of in your philosophy") also suggests the conception of incomprehensible things beyond the bounds of ordinary, general human philosophy and the amazing power of the human mind to conceive of things normally inconceivable. That there is a great influence of Shakespeare's play on Byron's is made clear not only by the above extract but also, as it will be shown below, throughout the rest of *Manfred*. Byron himself knew that he was writing something wild and strange. "God help me," he wrote to his publisher, "if I proceed in this scribbling I shall have frittered away my mind before I am thirty. But it is at times a real relief to me."[5] Like the earlier *Childe Harold*, especially Canto III, and *The Prisoner of Chillon*, *Manfred* is highly psychological, "at core 'mental,' a psychomachia, in which the allegory is one of the individual in quest of self-definition."[6] All three works, Byron's most cohesive set, according to the critic Frederick W. Shilstone, are "a sustained examination of the autonomous life and mind," exploring the issues of "philosophical exile" and "the mind's ability to forge myths as well as to debunk them."[7]

The time and circumstances of the composition of *Manfred* are significant. It was begun in late 1816, when Byron was in exile following a series of events that, according to John Clubbe, formed "the crisis of 1816" and constituted "the central traumatic experience in Byron's life."[8] Finished the following year in Italy, its composition was immediately preceded by Byron's getting to know Goethe's *Faust* via Matthew Lewis, the author of the Gothic novel *The Monk*, who was visiting him in Geneva in the summer of 1816.[9] Both in its setting (Manfred's Gothic castle in the high mountains of the Swiss Alps) and its content of strange and scary excesses of supernatural, ghostly nature, it is Byron's most Gothic work. Perhaps the poet took the name of the title character from the evil Manfred, one of the major characters in the first true Gothic novel, Horace Walpole's *The Castle of Otranto* (1765). It is also possible that he took the name from the 13th century young king of Sicily, Manfred, who was a natural son of Emperor Frederick II and who in many ways seems to resemble both Byron and his hero.[10]

It was in the same summer, on the stormy night of 16 June 1816 and the following night, that Byron and the rest in the group of exiles (the rest being Byron's personal physician John William Polidori, Shelley and his wife Mary, and her stepsister Claire Clairmont, who was Byron's former mistress) had their famous ghost-story sessions during which all were prompted to come up with their own ghost stories. On the following night Byron recited Coleridge's *Christabel*, having a highly embarrassing yet subsequently creative impact on Shelley and Mary. The immediate results of Byron's instigation, "We will each write a ghost story," were an undeveloped and lost story by Shelley based on the experiences of his early life, *The Vampyre* by Polidori, a fragment of a tale by Byron himself, and Mary Shelley's *Frankenstein: or, The Modern Prometheus*, which had of course a longer and more complex genesis with more developments to follow in the activities of the group during the week following the evening of 16 June.[11]

If the main character of Polidori's tale, Lord Ruthven, may have been based, as some critics think, on Byron, the first-person narrator of Byron's fragment seems to have been based on Polidori, while its main character Augustus Darvell—a remarkable man "of considerable fortune and ancient family," "a being of no common order," "a prey to some cureless disquiet," with "peculiar circumstances" and "irreconcilable contradictions" in his life, who "had already travelled extensively"—is an autobiographical projection of the poet himself, to be developed within a few months into the autobiographical Manfred. *Manfred* is indeed a product, just as is *Frankenstein*, of the influence of the discussions they all had that summer on "various philosophical doctrines," including, following the Promethean myth of the creation of man from clay and the more recent (late 18th century) experiments of the natural scientist Erasmus Darwin, "the nature of the principle of life, and whether there was any probability of its ever being discovered and communicated" by reanimating a corpse or by manufacturing and then bringing to life the component parts of a creature.[12]

This is clearly evident in Manfred's wonderful self-disclosure to the Witch of the Alps, in which he states that while he held slight communion with ordinary humanity and in fact hated being a human being of "all clay" himself:

My joy was in the Wilderness, to breathe
The difficult air of the iced mountain's top, [...] to plunge
Into the torrent, and to roll along
On the swift whirl of the new breaking wave [...]
To follow through the night the moving moon,
The stars and their development; or catch
The dazzling lightnings till my eyes grew dim;
Or to look, list'ning, on the scatter'd leaves,
While Autumn winds were at their evening song.
These were my pastimes, and to be alone; [...] *And then I dived,*

In my lone wanderings, to the caves of death,
Searching its cause in its effect; and drew
From wither'd bones, and skulls, and heap'd up dust,
Conclusions most forbidden. Then I pass'd
The nights of years in sciences untaught [...] I made
Mine eyes familiar with Eternity [...] and with my knowledge grew
The thirst of knowledge, and the power and joy
Of this most bright intelligence [...] (II.ii. 62-96, emphases mine)[13]

Manfred's long and laborious cultivation of his "sciences," that is, occult bodies of knowledge, not only enables him to raise spirits and have power over them, just as the fourth-century neo-Platonic philosopher Iamblichus, as he mentions, could call up Eros and Anteros, gods of love and unreturned love respectively, from the hot springs at Gadara in Syria, but also experiment with dead tissues in an effort to discover the principle of life and death. He is asking the Witch if it is in her power to "wake the dead" or make him dead. Ultimately he discovers that even the "long pursued and super-human art" of his occult "sciences" fails to bring him his long-sought forgetfulness, and that he is forced to live in despair for ever.

Under the impact of the Alps, Byron used strange and wild materials in *Manfred*, although it may also have some Wordsworthian elements of deep calm and solitude present in his other contemporary compositions.[14] Whatever action it has mostly consists of dialogues with powerful supernatural spirits including the Witch of the Alps, Arimanes, Destinies, and Nemesis, and only a few human characters (a pastoral chamois hunter living in the higher regions of the Alps; an old abbot who represents organised yet weak and ineffectual Christian religion; and two other minor characters, Herman and Manuel). Obviously, there is what Ryan Hunter calls "a sort of three-tier hierarchy;" with the "sublime pagan or polytheist figures" easily dwarfing the Christian abbot in power and influence but themselves being subordinate to the yet greater power of the individualist human will embodied in Manfred.[15] But Hunter fails to see that there is actually a four-tier hierarchy, with Manfred himself being subject to a controlling, invisible, overseeing power suggested several times in the play—by the spirit of his star, which both "obeys and scorns" him and which is "Forced by a power (which is not [his])" to appear at his call; by the incantational voice ("By a power to thee unknown"); and by Manfred himself when he is about to jump from a high cliff ("There is a power upon me which withholds/ And makes it my fatality to live").

The mountainous and misty landscape with crags, cliffs, cataracts, precipices, avalanches, and woods and valleys, both in the higher and the lower Alps, at all times of the day (midnight, morning, noon), not only provides a sensational setting for the strange and uncommon nature of the plot, but also serves the function of symbolically reflecting the restless agitation in Manfred's mind. The remarkable scenery described by Byron as "rocks, pines, torrents, glaciers, clouds, and summits of eternal snow far above them" is a fitting background against which, Watson says, "Byron's conception of the powerful mind on the mountain summit receives its most extended expression."[16] Acknowledging that the poem as a whole drew its inspiration from the Alps, Byron himself said, "It was the Staubach and the Jungfrau, and something else, much more than Faustus, that made me write *Manfred*."[17] Yet Manfred is very much a Faustian figure—highly proud, extremely independent, individualistic, and lonely, musing in despair and melancholy and invoking dark, evil spirits through magic conjurations.[18] As Howard Nelson argues, "Like Goethe's *Faust*, which Byron had just read, *Manfred* is concerned with man's struggle against the universe."[19] Like Faust, Manfred has been left dissatisfied by his scholarship in philosophy and science. Both are overreachers and both use the means of sorcery and magic to overreach themselves, although the knowledge of the occult ultimately proves to be futile. Both either confront or are tempted by the forces of good and evil struggling for the control of their respective souls.

However, there is one major difference: while Faust sells his soul to the devil in order to gain humanly impossible unlimited power, the very idea of such subjection is anathema to Manfred, who says to the evil spirits just before his death:

> My past power
> Was purchased by no compact with thy crew
> But by superior science—penance—daring—
> And length of watching—strength of mind—and skill
> In knowledge of our fathers—when the earth
> Saw men and spirits walking side by side,
> And gave ye no supremacy. (3.4.113-19)

Manfred never seeks to enter into any agreement that will make his soul yield to the devil:

> Byron's great invention is to have Manfred, unlike Faust, disdainfully reject the offer of a pact with the powers of darkness. He thereby

> sets himself up as the totally autonomous man, independent of any external authority or power, whose own mind, as he says in the concluding scene, generates the values by which he lives "in sufferance or in joy," and by reference to which he judges, requites, and finally destroys himself.[20]

Among the other differences, while Faust seeks omnipotence to be able to do whatever he likes, Manfred seeks death and forgetfulness. While Faust is set on the course which actually takes him to his tragic loss of self-control, masterminded by Mephistopheles, Manfred remains the master of his fate throughout, and meets his tragic end on his own terms, not those of the devil. Whereas Faust has a brief period of deceptive worldly enjoyment followed by intense and unbearable suffering in death, Manfred is past the stage of worldly bliss, only to continue in his pain and despair, to be relieved in death. For Faust, it is utter damnation and hellfire in the religious sense; for Manfred, it is a matter of his own raging in his own mind with no care for religious sanction or the consequences of religious transgression. In other words, Manfred begins where Faust ends. Manfred is also a figure like Ahasuerus, "the legendary Wandering Jew who, having ridiculed Christ as he bore the Cross to Calvary, is doomed to live until Christ's Second Coming."[21] His condition of longing for a death that is denied him is modelled on the legend of the Wandering Jew, so repeatedly treated in Romantic literature.

Manfred seems to be guilty of some mysterious crime, which has been the cause of his being an outcast, living in proud isolation but tormented by endless remorse. He expresses a sense of unbearable burden upon his conscience from the very beginning:

> My slumbers—if I slumber—are not sleep,
> But a continuance of enduring thought, [...] in my heart
> There is a vigil, and these eyes but close
> To look within. (I.i. 3-7)

Alone at midnight in his Gothic castle in the mountains, Manfred recounts, like Marlowe's Faustus, his mastery of the various fields of knowledge, which he says has been of no avail to him. Even though a human being, he has no human emotions of fear, love, hope or dread, and therefore remains unaffected by the ways of mankind with no interest whatsoever in their concerns and pursuits:

> Good, or evil, life,
> Powers, passions, all I see in other beings,

Have been to me as rain unto the sands,
Since that all-nameless hour. (I.i. 21-24)

In fact, he is even hostile to anything that is human. Like Faustus, the mortal Manfred then sets his course on the forbidden quest and invokes the powerful elemental spirits to help him out of his crisis. These polytheist pagan spirits—seven of them, being, in order of appearance, those of the air, mountains, oceans, earth, winds, night, and Manfred's own star—are of "the unbounded universe, [...] to whom the tops/ Of mountains inaccessible are haunts/ And earth's and ocean's caves familiar things" (I.i.29, 32-34). They are proudly aware of their immortal and eternal state of being, the seventh being the most interesting of them all in view of the fact that it is the spirit of Manfred's guiding star, under whose influence he was born and which thus rules his destiny. This seventh spirit provides the complex history of that star and its chequered course in the space (which actually reflects Manfred's own in life), from its smooth origin before the earth to how it later became:

A wandering mass of shapeless flame,
A pathless comet, and a curse,
The menace of the universe;
Still rolling on with innate force,
Without a sphere, without a course,
A bright deformity on high,
The monster of the upper sky! (I.i. 117-23)

All the spirits, however, regardless of their formidable power, still have to yield to Manfred, who, in the forcefulness of his spirit of independence and determination, dominates them and makes them serve him as he wishes. They are ready to offer him everything (power, kingdom, pleasure, wisdom, long life) except what he seeks—forgetfulness of what pains him, which they know but which he would not utter. As superhuman beings, to whom past, present and future are the same, they do not have any knowledge or idea of death, memory, recollection, and forgetfulness. As such, it is beyond their power to provide Manfred with what he so desperately longs for—oblivion—which is possible, they suggest, only when he dies. As they stress upon their fine quality of glorious otherworldliness and thereby try to undermine Manfred's mortal status by calling him "a child of clay" and "a worm," Manfred asserts his supremacy by being sarcastic and scornful about them and by describing himself in terms of the extraordinarily noble and heroic elements of his favourite deity—Prometheus, a favourite with other Romantic liberals as well, including Shelley:

> Slaves, scoff not at my will!
> The mind, the spirit, the Promethean spark,
> The lightning of my being, is as bright,
> Pervading, far darting as your own,
> And shall not yield to yours, though coop'd in clay! (I.i. 153-57)

As the spirits are about to be dismissed for having been of no use, Manfred asks them to appear in the physical forms of their choice. When the most powerful of them, the seventh, appears in the shape of a beautiful female figure, Manfred rushes forward to embrace it only to see it mysteriously vanish, causing him to fall senseless.[22] This figure, probably representing "the ideal of the beautiful and good that Manfred had pursued in his uncorrupted youth" may be "a simulacrum of Astarte," to appear later in Act II.[23] According to the "elderly and wise" Manuel, one of Manfred's long-time dependants, who plays a role like that of the chorus in ancient Greek tragedy or the blind octogenarian Tiresias in the Oedipus myth, one Lady Astarte was:

> The sole companion of his wanderings
> And watchings—her, whom of all earthly things
> That lived, the only thing he seem'd to love,—
> As he, indeed, by blood was bound to do [...] (3.3.43-46)

That Manuel's testimony is authentic can be concluded from the fact that he had been in the service of the Manfred household even from before the birth of Manfred and knew both him and his father so well that he could distinctly contradistinguish between them in "mind and habits":

> I served his father, whom he nought resembles [...]
> Count Sigismund was proud,—but gay and free,—
>
> A warrior and a reveller; he dwelt not
> With books and solitude, nor made the night
> A gloomy vigil, but a festal time,
> Merrier than day; he did not walk the rocks
> And forests like a wolf, nor turn aside
> From men and their delights. (3.3.15, 19-25)

Sigismund was therefore exactly opposite to Manfred, thus confirming, as many other evidences in the play do, the latter's complete separation from his family tradition and other legacies of human nature in general.[24]

In order for those earlier "jocund times" to return to the Manfred castle in which, Manuel claims, "some strange things" have recently been happening, the current chieftain, Manfred.

It seems Manfred has committed some grave sin with relation to Astarte. The nature of the sin is only suggested, never clearly disclosed. The voice in the Incantation confirms the spell of the curse Manfred has been under and the hellish suffering he is destined to suffer without end. That there is a curse upon him is alluded to several times—by the incantatory voice ("Hath baptized thee with a curse"), by the spirit of his own star (quoted above), by himself in the opening soliloquy and invocation ("And feel the curse to have no natural fear"; "By the strong curse which is upon my soul"), and later with the chamois hunter beside him ("A blighted trunk upon a cursed root") and in his dialogue with the Witch of the Alps ("Then cursed myself till sunset"). The reference by the voice in the Incantation to him being one of the "brotherhood of Cain"—Cain, who murdered his brother Abel—suggests that Manfred may have killed someone closely related to him (Astarte) or may have contributed to her being killed.

The following morning Manfred is about to take his own life by plunging from a crag in the Jungfrau. His excellent Hamlet-like existentialist monologue as he contemplates suicide is worth quoting in length:

My mother Earth!
And thou fresh breaking Day, and you, ye Mountains,
Why are ye beautiful? I cannot love ye.
And thou, the bright eye of the universe,
That openest over all, and unto all
Art a delight—thou shin'st not on my heart [...]
Beautiful!
How beautiful is all this visible world!
How glorious in its action and itself;
But we, who name ourselves its sovereigns, we,
Half dust, half deity, alike unfit
To sink or soar, with our mix'd essence make
A conflict of its elements, and breathe
The breath of degradation and of pride,
Contending with low wants and lofty will
Till our mortality predominates,
And men are—what they name not to themselves,
And trust not to each other. (I.ii. 37-47)[25]

The notion that humans are "half dust, half deity" implies that if they could only change their "half dust" part into something divine, they would be entirely divine in status with all the potential of a super-deity.[26] It is this burden of mortality, which Byron describes in *Childe Harold* as "a fleshly chain," "this degraded form" and "the clay-cold bonds which round our being cling" (Canto III, ll. 685, 697, 699), from which Manfred longs to escape to become a pure soul as he hears the echoing pastoral music of the mountain shepherd and "the sweet bells of the sauntering herd" in the distance:

> Oh, that I were
> The viewless spirit of a loving sound,
> A living voice, a breathing harmony,
> A bodiless enjoyment—born and dying
> With the blest tone which made me! (I.ii. 53-56)

Manfred's pattern of thought here and later in the "We are the fools of time and terror" soliloquy anticipates Keats's 'Ode to a Nightingale' and Shelley's 'To a Skylark,' both of which foreground the contrast between body and soul, human and natural, and the pure principle and permanence of joy as represented by the bird-song and the transitoriness and ephemerality as represented by the condition of human mortality.

On the eye-witness account of the pastoral chamois hunter (one who hunts for chamois—rare goatlike antelopes found in the high Alpine ranges), Manfred is a lordly figure in dress and appearance: "Thy garb and gait bespeak thee of high lineage" (II.i. 7), with "his air/ Proud as a free-born peasant's" (I.ii. 63). He is, though, a man of "strange words and some half-maddening sin/ Which makes [him] people vacancy" (II.i. 31-32). He does not live a healthy life as he suffers from prolonged sorrow and unrest. Hardly of middle age, he describes himself as "gray-hair'd with anguish" as if he were a kind of desolated ("blasted," "blighted," "barkless" and "branchless") pine in winter, with a sense of the hours torturously dragged into ages (I.ii. 66, 73). It is not only that nothing can give him relief but also that everything becomes a projection of his disturbed mind, autobiographically supported by Byron's own experience. "Neither the music of the Shepherd, the crashing of the Avalanche, nor the torrent, the mountain, the Glacier, have for one moment lightened the weight upon my heart," Byron wrote, "nor enabled me to lose my own wretched identity in the majesty, the power and the Glory, around, above, and beneath me."[27]

In his restless misery Manfred is about to jump to death from a perilous peak when the chamois hunter, who would not have his "pure vales" stained with Manfred's "guilty blood," suddenly seizes him from behind to prevent him from his attempted suicide, helps him with his staff and girdle to secure a sure footing, and leads him away to his cottage down the Bernese Alps. Offered drinks of "an ancient vintage," Manfred sees only blood at the brim:

> I say 'tis blood—my blood! the pure warm stream
> Which ran in the veins of my fathers, and in ours
> When we were in our youth, and had one heart,
> And loved each other as we should not love
> And this was shed: (II.i. 24-28)

Manfred's terrified reaction is yet another evidence that he is totally cut off from his forebears. It seems he had loved and destroyed a young lady related to him by blood. The chamois hunter offers to guide him to his lordly castle down below in the lower valleys as he tries to comfort him by suggesting "The aid of holy men and heavenly patience" (II.i. 34), which Manfred declines in his habitual scornful manner:

> Patience and patience! Hence—that word was made
> For brutes of burthen, not for birds of prey;
> Preach it to mortals of a dust like thine—
> I am not of thine order. (II.i. 35-38)

Manfred may be suffering endlessly with the consciousness of "the fierce thirst of death," yet he feels extremely superior to the rest of the humanity to whom he is misanthropically averse. He can bear what others may not even dare to dream or what would make others perish in their sleep. In the wretched contemplation of his terrible actions his time seems to have prolonged into ages, empty and endless, yet heavy and unavoidable:

> [...] actions are our epochs: mine
> Have made my days and nights imperishable,
> Endless, and all alike, as sands on the shore,
> Innumerable atoms, and one desert,
> Barren and cold, on which the wild waves break,
> But nothing rests, save carcasses and wrecks,
> Rocks, and the salt-surf weeds of bitterness. (II.i. 52-58)

To a simple villager like the chamois hunter, Manfred's ability to capture his own state of mind in such a penetrating self-analysis is nothing but madness. Unlike Manfred's aristocratic yet wandering, feeble, weary-of-life tottering persona seeking death as he suffers from the inescapable burden of consciousness, the chamois hunter, much older than him, represents the common virtues of average humanity: innocence, steadiness, domestic peace and happiness, rest, warmth, guidance, and continuity through generations. Manfred gives a full picture of him as

> [...] a peasant of the Alps—
> Thy humble virtues, hospitable home,
> And spirit patient, pious, proud, and free;
> Thy self-respect, grafted on innocent thoughts;
> Thy days of health, and nights of sleep; thy toils,
> By danger dignified, yet guiltless; hopes
> Of cheerful old age and a quiet grave,
> With cross and garland over its green turf,
> And thy grandchildren's love for epitaph; (II.i. 63-72)

One of the most interesting things about *Manfred* is that it contains more pastoral elements than any other work by Byron. Since Byron was hardly a pastoral poet, there are not too many such elements in his works in the first place. Unlike Wordsworth, he was not much attracted to the solitude of nature, country life—idealized or realistic—or the simplicities or adversities of country people. Yet, as noted above, not only is the chamois hunter an interesting pastoral character but also the deep quiet of nature as expressed (through many soliloquies, monologues and apostrophes) in *Manfred* is informed by a sense of the Wordsworthian pastoral idealism. Also, as observed in note 11 above, Byron was reading Wordsworth about the same time as the composition of both *Manfred* and *Childe Harold's Pilgrimage III*, the only other comparable poetical work in matter of pastoral interest in Byron. In this contemporaneously written travelogue, nature and people along the banks of the Rhine are described in an idealized manner, the latter being seen as happy and carefree such that even an exile can find it comforting to be in the midst of such a scene. Byron's reflection, we remember, was in direct response to his own exile from England, from whose civilised community he had just run away with the result that he had now an opportunity to practically test out Wordsworth's proposition about the value of the common or natural man in a natural setting. Byron's Alpine journal of the time also bears out this realization of a pastoral existence as represented by shepherds in their mountain pastures.[28]

Ironically, while Manfred sees all the good qualities of ordinary settled life in the chamois hunter, none of them would matter to him, whose "soul was scorch'd already!" He denies that he wreaked any revenge on his enemies; instead, he pleads guilty as follows:

My injuries came down on those who loved me—
On those whom I best loved: I never quell'd
An enemy, save in my just defence—
My wrongs were all on those I should have cherished—
But my embrace was fatal. (II.i. 84-88)

In his proud isolation and independence, Manfred not only utterly rejects the chamois hunter's offer of prayer for him wishing the restoration of his being through penitence but also, having generously recognised his pity for him by a gift of gold, asks him not to follow him any more.

So far neither Manfred's communion with the "abstruser powers" nor his contact with common humanity has been of any assistance to him. He retires, at about noontime, into the "sweet solitude" by a cataract in a lower valley in the Alps, enjoying the lovely sight of the arch created by the rays of the sunbow of the torrent. This provides the ideal condition for him, as a "Son of Earth," to invoke the spirit of the place—the beautiful Witch of the Alps—by playfully flinging some water in the air and muttering the adjuration for her to appear beneath the arch. She is described in terms of her "hair of light,/ And dazzling eyes of glory," her "calm clear brow" reflecting her "serenity of soul,/ Which of itself shows immortality" and her "celestial aspect" far superior to "the beauties of the sunbow which bends o'er thee." The Witch thus becomes one of the most significant characters to whom Manfred unlocks most of what he calls his "idle attributes" and his "heart's grief":

From my youth upwards
My spirit walk'd not with the souls of men,
Nor look'd upon the earth with human eyes;
The thirst of their ambition was not mine,
The aim of their existence was not mine,
My joys, my griefs, my passions and my powers
Made me a stranger; though I wore the form
I had no sympathy with breathing flesh
Nor midst the creatures of clay that girded me
Was there but one who—but of her anon. (II.ii. 50-59)

Despite the fact that Manfred hardly held any communion with human beings, it is implied that there was one with whom he had a dangerous relationship and whom he had badly harmed. That the sin was atrocious in nature is hinted at when he says:

I have not named to thee
Father or mother, mistress, friend or being,
With whom I wore the chain of human ties;
If I had such, they seem'd not such to me—
Yet there was one—(II.ii. 100-04)

Clearly, the memory of a woman haunts him with her physical and spiritual resemblance to him. Like him she also had a power to grasp the mystery of the universe but with a characteristic difference:

She was like me in lineaments—her eyes,
Her hair, her features, all, to the very tone
Even of her voice, they said were like to mine;
But soften'd all, and temper'd into beauty;
She had the same lone thoughts and wanderings,
The quest of hidden knowledge, and a mind
To comprehend the universe: nor these
Alone, but with them gentler powers than mine,
Pity, and smiles, and tears—which I had not;
And tenderness—but that I had for her;
Humility—and that I never had,
Her faults were mine—her virtues were her own—
I loved her, and destroy'd her. (II.ii. 105-17)

She was destroyed not with his "hand" but with his "heart," which:

[...] gazed on mine, and withered. I have shed
Blood, but not hers—and yet her blood was shed—
I saw—and could not staunch it. (II.ii. 119-21)

By all indication it seems that Manfred was guilty of incest. He honestly admits she was "a sufferer for my sins" (II.ii. 197). Such an admission unmistakably suggests a nobility of character far above ordinary humanity. He continues to give lyrical expression to the painful state of his mind in a poetry rich in imagery:

My solitude is solitude no more,
But peopled with the Furies; I have gnash'd
My teeth in darkness till returning morn,

> Then cursed myself till sunset [...] the cold hand
> Of an all-pitiless demon held me back,
> Back by a single hair, which would not break.
> In phantasy, imagination, all
> The affluence of my soul—which one day was
> A Croesus in creation—(II.ii. 130-42)

Manfred's terrible suffering forces him to pray for madness as a blessing or plunge deep into fantasy:

> But, like an ebbing wave, it dash'd me back
> Into the gulf of my unfathom'd thought. (II.ii. 143-44)

Yet his sense of pride is so frightening that when the Witch of the Alps demands his allegiance as a condition for her help with the fulfilment of his wish for death or forgetfulness, she is scornfully rejected:

> I will not swear—obey! and whom? the spirits
> Whose presence I command, and be the slave
> Of those who served me—Never! (II.ii. 158-60)

Left alone in the evening, Manfred soliloquises on the sorrows of life and dread of death, in a way reminiscent of Hamlet, and decides to try his science of black magic one more time, this time to call up the dead to find out what it is that is so dreadful about death. His rare admission that he fears death and that he trembles at the prospect of facing the spirits of the dead who might disclose strange secrets puts a human face on him. As he nears death, he realizes that its cold fact and its mystery are better left without being delved deep into, lest his fears about what is inevitable prove overwhelming.

At last Manfred enters the hall of the most powerful, presiding spirit of darkness and evil, Arimanes, who is on his throne beside a globe of fire at the summit of the Jungfrau. The name derives from Ahriman, the evil principle in the dualistic Zoroastrian religion. All the attendant Spirits, Destinies, and Nemesis, who remain ever-ready to fulfil Arimanes' commands to his complete satisfaction, speak in one voice in glorifying him hailed and worshipped as "Sovereign of Sovereigns," "Prince of Earth and Air" and "Prince of the Powers invisible." All this provides yet another opportunity for Manfred to assert his towering superiority. In keeping with his proud determination and stark independence, Manfred refuses to comply with the demand that he, a worm-like crouching mortal creature of clay, must bow down and prostrate himself before the

"Great" Arimanes. That he is an exceptional human being is testified to not only by the second spirit, who becomes distinguished in his knowledge of Manfred as a master of occult sciences and hence "of great power and fearful skill," but also the first Destiny, who becomes even more individualised in her brilliant characterization of Manfred thus:

> This man
> Is of no common order, as his port
> And presence here denote; his sufferings
> Have been of an immortal nature, like
> Our own; his knowledge and his powers and will,
> As far as is compatible with clay,
> Which clogs the ethereal essence, have been such
> As clay hath seldom borne; his aspirations
> Have been beyond the dwellers of the earth,
> And they have only taught him what we know—
> That knowledge is not happiness, and science
> But an exchange of ignorance for that
> Which is another kind of ignorance.
> This is not all—the passions, attributes
> Of earth and heaven, from which no power, nor being,
> Nor breath from the worm upwards is exempt,
> Have pierced his heart; and in their consequence
> Made him a thing, which I, who pity not,
> Yet pardon those who pity [...]
> No other Spirit in this region hath
> A soul like his—or power upon his soul. (2.4.51-72)

According to the testimony of yet another Spirit, Manfred would have made "an awful spirit" had he been one of them. Though an ill-fated and gloomy figure, he remains the supreme master of his fate, rejecting to kneel down before anything except his own despair and desolation or before anybody except "the overruling Infinite—the Maker" (2.4.47) to whom, he claims, even Arimanes himself is subject. As with his earlier human fear of death or of facing the dead, this also is a remarkable moment of admission of faith, religious and spiritual in nature, by Manfred, who is characteristically too overconfident and self-conceited in his blasphemous projection of himself to recognise any controlling power over him. In a moment he will also declare that compared with his own power "there are/ Powers deeper still beyond" (2.4.76), which he is seeking in order to obtain what he wants. He also believes that whatever he is "rest[s] between Heaven and myself" (3.1.53), describing the setting sun as the "earliest minister of the Almighty" (3.2.11). These moments establish, in a noble and dignified manner, that Manfred does indeed have a sense of religious faith, however unorthodox and thinly pronounced it may be.

Manfred asks Nemesis, the goddess of retribution for the sin of excessive pride known as *hubris* in Greek, to call up the dead, particularly the phantom of Astarte, "one without a tomb." With permission from Arimanes, Nemesis makes Astarte's spirit appear, but both Arimanes and Nemesis fail to make her speak, which makes them realise the limits of their power. While she would not yield to their command, she would respond, at least briefly, to her lover Manfred. In contrast with her who in death has lost her "living hue" and looks pale and feverish ("a strange hectic—like the unnatural red/ Which Autumn plants upon the perish'd leaf"), Manfred suffers a state of life-in-death, which is much worse:

Astarte! My beloved! speak to me:
I have so much endured—so much endure—
Look on me! the grave hath not changed thee more
Than I am changed for thee. Thou lovedst me
Too much, as I loved thee: we were not made
To torture thus each other, though it were
The deadliest sin to love as we have loved.
Say that thou loath'st me not—that I do bear
This punishment for both—that thou will be
One of the blessed—and that I shall die,
For hitherto all hateful things conspire
To bind me in existence—in a life
Which makes me shrink from immortality—
A future like the past. I cannot rest [...]
And I would hear yet once before I perish
The voice which was my music—Speak to me!
For I have call'd on thee in the still night,
Startled the slumbering birds from the hush'd boughs,
And woke the mountain wolves, and made the caves
Acquainted with thy vainly echoed name [...]
Yet speak to me! I have outwatch'd the stars,
And gazed o'er heaven in vain in search of thee.
Speak to me! I have wandered o'er the earth,
And never found thy likeness—Speak to me!

Look on the fiends around—they feel for me:
I fear them not, and feel for thee alone—(2.4.118-47)

The spirit of Astarte foretells Manfred's death the next day: "To-morrow ends thine earthly ills" and disappears without saying anything else, meaning that his questions whether he is forgiven and whether they would meet again go unanswered. Despite the ambiguity of the situation, Manfred seems to have obtained some peace of mind. Mythically, Astarte, also known as Ashtoreth, is a Semitic goddess of love, fertility and maternity, hence of productive powers, the Eastern equivalent of the Greek goddess Aphrodite. The character who bears this name thus stands in ironic contrast to the suffering hero who has been condemned to utter loneliness, emptiness and isolation.

The element of incest in *Manfred* may be taken as Byron's veiled confession of his relationship with his half-sister. However, it should be taken into account that the theme of incest was common in contemporary Gothic fiction as well as in the works of many other writers of the time, such as Goethe, Chateaubriand, Scott, and Shelley. Thus, the character of Manfred is a unique creation combining literary and autobiographical elements with those of heroic defiance and single-minded independence and rising to a level of imaginative power and conception at which it becomes its author's "supreme representation of the Byronic hero." Nietzsche recognized that Byron anticipated his own idea of the superman "who posits for himself a moral code beyond the inherited standards of good and evil" and claimed that the character of Manfred was greater than that of Goethe's Faust.[29]

Back at his castle on an evening of "inexplicable stillness," as he puts it, Manfred is greeted by an old abbot whose function, like that of the Good Angel and the Old Man in the tragedy of *Doctor Faustus*, is to try to get Manfred back to the way of religious solace and comfort. The fatherly abbot tells Manfred that it is unfortunate that people everywhere speak ill of him because of his communion with evil spirits instead of his being an inheritor of the good name of his noble ancestors, held in high esteem for centuries. The abbot, who by virtue of his age and religious calling claims that he has come to save his "son" Manfred and not to torment him by "prying into his secret soul," advises him to seek "penitence and pardon," to have "higher hope and better thoughts," and to repent and reconcile himself with heaven through the church. All the abbot's earnest pleadings for "atonement" and "auspicious hope" for the "blessed place" to succeed "earthly errors" are scornfully rejected: "I shall not choose a mortal/ To be my mediator" (3.1.54-55). Manfred does not believe that there is any power in religious practices and rituals to lighten the agony or:

The innate tortures of that deep despair,
Which is remorse without the fear of hell,
But all in all sufficient to itself
Would make a hell of heaven—can exorcise
From out the unbounded spirit, the quick sense
Of its own sins, wrongs, sufferance, and revenge
Upon itself; there is no future pang
Can deal that justice on the self-condemn'd
He deals on his own soul. (3.1.70-78)

In any case, whatever the power of religious institutions and beliefs may be, it is already too late for Manfred to repent and reconcile himself with heaven. Speaking in the same figurative language that Byron uses to record his mixed feelings yet great admiration for the fallen Napoleon, whom he describes as "the Lion" among the "Wolves" of the tyrannous kings (*CHP*, III, 169-70), Manfred too calls himself a lion of untameable nature, in proud and splendid isolation.[30] Like Napoleon, Manfred too, as the Witch of the Alps describes him, is "a man of many thoughts,/ And deeds of good and ill, extreme in both,/ Fatal and fated in thy sufferings." Yet, as Shilstone argues, there is a significant difference between Manfred and Napoleon.[31] Manfred, who seems to have learnt the lesson of the failure of fame, would not, therefore, hanker after it by ruling and serving at the same time as Napoleon did. For him, to rule and to serve at the same time for the sake of fame is an unacceptable "living lie," and as such he would never become the leader of the ordinary masses, who are dismissed as mere flocks of sheep or packs of wolves:

Who would become
A mighty thing amongst the mean, and such
The mass are; I disdained to mingle with
A herd, though to be leader—and of wolves.
The lion is alone, and so am I. (III.i. 119-23)

In fact, there is a strong presence of Napoleon and Napoleonic elements of tyranny, flight and despair in *Manfred*, thus completing as well as complicating the identification of the two heroic characters. Napoleon is held responsible for "the blood of a million" and "a nation's destruction," and his escape from his captivity is directly alluded to in the song of the first Voice exactly in the middle of the play, thus undercutting any efforts at complete identification between him and Manfred.[32]

Being singularly uninterested in life, Manfred finds desolation everywhere and describes the course of his existence in terms of the hot desert wind called the Simoom, which:

> [...] sweeps o'er
> The barren sands which bear no shrubs to blast,
> And revels o'er their wild and arid waves,
> And seeketh not, so that it is not sought,
> But being met is deadly [...] (3.1.130-33)

Strikingly echoing Manfred's own understanding of himself and humankind—an understanding, as mentioned earlier, similar to Hamlet's—the abbot, despite being rebuffed, does not want to give up on such "a noble creature," who:

> Hath all the energy which would have made
> A goodly frame of glorious elements,
> Had they been wisely mingled; as it is,
> It is an awful chaos—light and darkness—
> And mind and dust—and passions and pure thoughts,
> Mix'd, and contending without end or order,
> All dormant or destructive: he will perish,
> And yet he must not; I will try once more,
> For such are worth redemption; and my duty
> Is to dare all things for a righteous end.
> I'll follow him—but cautiously, though surely. (3.1.160-71)

On his reappearance as Manfred nears his death, the abbot reiterates that Manfred is a noble spirit, wandering but "not yet all lost." But Manfred knows it is too late and asks the abbot to go away. In his last moment—like that of Faustus but without Faustus' searing agony—both the abbot and Manfred see the fearful fiend of death—"the spirit or deity presiding over a human being from birth"—appear to take Manfred's soul away. It rises as a "dusk and awful figure":

> Like an infernal god from out the earth;
> His face wrapt in a mantle, and his form
> Robed as with angry clouds [...]
> His sight may shock thine old limbs into palsy [...]

Ah! he unveils his aspect; on his brow
The thunder-scars are graven; from his eye
Glares forth the immortality of hell—(3.4.62-68, 76-78)

Manfred, true to his nature as always, is not afraid and asserts his independence:

I have commanded
Things of an essence greater far than thine,
And striven with thy masters [...]
Away! I'll die as I have lived—alone. (3.4.84-86, 90)

More demons appear, as Mephistophiles and his followers do in Marlowe's *Faustus*, to summon and establish their claim upon Manfred. Despite the abbot's interference, they claim Manfred to be theirs only to be defied and dismissed as "greater criminals," having no right to punish him:

I stand
Upon my strength—I do defy—deny—
Spurn back and scorn ye! (3.4.119-20)

Manfred asserts himself for one more time before he breathes his last, claiming that the evil spirits have no power over him, that they can never possess him and that there is nothing they can do to help mitigate his inner torture. In what is yet another echo of Satan's argument,[33] Manfred says:

The mind which is immortal makes itself
Requital for its good or evil thoughts—
Is its own origin of ill and end—
And its own place and time—its innate sense,
When stripp'd of this mortality, derives
No colour from the fleeting things without,
But is absorb'd in sufferance or in joy,
Born from the knowledge of its own desert.
Thou didst not tempt me, and thou couldst not tempt me;
I have not been thy dupe, nor am thy prey—
But was my own destroyer, and will be
My own hereafter.—Back, ye baffled fiends!
The hand of death is on me—but not yours! (3.4.138-41)

As the demons disappear, Manfred expires, in presence of the old abbot, in the same tower where he studied his art. In his final moment he asks, in an extraordinary gesture of human bonding, for the hand of the abbot whose selfless efforts to redeem him have been rebuffed again and again. The fact that only the abbot is allowed to be there by his side at the moment of his death suggests not just the human element but also the positive and benign influence of religion on Manfred, however meagre that may be. His final words are an assertion of what Byron later claimed to be "the whole effect and moral of the poem": that it is "not so difficult to die"—an assertion in line with the earlier Byronic heroes such as the corsairs who also speak of death without fear. It is obvious that death comes to Manfred as a relief rather than a punishment.

The theme of death, which is of utmost importance in *Manfred*, was previously explored by Byron in *The Prisoner of Chillon*, where Bonnivard, resigned to his fate, would not seek relief from increasing despair in death because of his faith. Manfred, on the other hand, not only seeks relief in death but also dies a death completely on his own terms, consciously driving away all kinds of influences, religious, supernatural or otherwise. As Shilstone puts it, "In undertaking that investigation, *Manfred* culminates the works of 1816 and their exploration of Byron's exiled consciousness and in addition makes a final statement on the fate of the Byronic hero."[34]

According to Shilstone, *Manfred* presents "a moment of intense mental apprehension through the manipulation of characters, both natural and supernatural, that symbolize the forces operating within and upon Manfred's mind."[35] Comparing Byron's play with Aeschylus' *Prometheus Bound*, John Clubbe writes: "Both plays concentrate on mental rather than on physical action: Prometheus literally does not move on stage, Manfred moves only to find new settings and beings to counterpoint his mind's conflict. Only he has a life of his own; the other characters hardly exist except as projections of his moods."[36] Genre-wise, *Manfred* may be no more than a dramatic monologue which, as Blackstone thinks, "catches the hero in a moment of crisis,"[37] but its greatness lies in the way that moment of crisis is captured and made to provide an opportunity to deal with a number of complex and metaphysical themes containing most if not all the essential elements of a Byronic character. As a dramatic poem on a critical state of the hero's mind, the poem achieves the feat of brilliantly dramatising a range of varying moods, feelings and emotions yet expressing them in a reflective poetry of great lyrical heights. It is not easy to dramatise, describe and meditate all at the same time especially when there is nothing much—in the form of clashes and confrontations, external or internal, public or domestic—to build on. Only a poet of great power intensely experiencing the imaginative and psychological depths of his mind in a burning state of sensation or consciousness can do so. *Manfred* is therefore a key Byronic text picking up many of the characteristic ideas from his earlier poems and thus containing the key elements in the spectrum of Byronic perceptions, from heroic to scornful, intended to assert the independence of the Byronic mind. To quote Shilstone once again, it is "the ultimate act of summary and conclusion in Byron's struggle to define the imperative of the self and how it can oppose the myths of tradition, the end of a lengthy chapter in the poet's canon that has stretched from the earliest lyrics to the productions of 1816."[38]

Notes and References

1. Byron's father was a Captain in the army, who came to be known as "Mad Jack" for his extravagant nature, squandered away all his wife's property, and fled from his creditors to France in 1791. His grandfather, Admiral John Byron, was called "Foul Weather Jack." His grand-uncle, the "Wicked Lord," was the fifth Lord in line, upon whose death, childless, in 1798, Byron succeeded as the sixth Lord. Byron's mother, Catherine Gordon, was a hot-tempered woman.
2. Byron had a boyish passion for his young kinswoman Mary Chaworth. He had married Isabella Milbanke in 1815, who left him after the birth of their only daughter, Augusta Ada. Following his incestuous relationship with his half-sister Augusta Leigh, he left England with his mistress Claire (originally Jane) Claremont, who was stepsister to Mary Shelley and who became the mother of his (Byron's) daughter Allegra. Subsequently they fell out of love when he fell in love with Countess Teresa Del Gambey and lived with her till his departure for Greece in 1823.
3. Byron, "I Would I Were A Careless Child," *Hours of Idleness*, in *Complete Poetical Works* (Oxford: OUP, 1961).
4. Quoted in Howard Nelson, "The Thinking Man's Lake," *Horizon* 6.4 (Autumn 1965): 75.
5. Quoted in Nelson.
6. Frederick W. Shilstone, *Byron and the Myth of Tradition* (Lincoln and London: U of Nebraska P, 1988) 3.
7. Shilstone 100, 136. He also mentions *The Giaour* as "largely concerned with different ways in which the mind can perceive reality."
8. John Clubbe, "'The New Prometheus of New Men': Byron's 1816 Poems and

Manfred," *Nineteenth-Century Literary Perspectives: Essays in Honor of Lionel Stevenson*, ed. Clyde de L. Ryals, et al. (Durham, N.C.: Duke UP, 1974) 23.

9. The nature of Byron's knowledge of Goethe's *Faust*—whether he actually read it in English translation or in the German original—should be made clear here: to quote *The Norton Anthology of English Literature*, 6th ed., vol. 2, 513: "Byron denied that he had ever heard of Marlowe's *Doctor Faustus*, and because he knew no German he had not read Goethe's *Faust*, of which part I had been published in 1808. But his friend Matthew Lewis had read parts of *Faust* to him in extempore translation during the summer of 1816, just before the composition of *Manfred*, and Byron worked his memories of this oral translation into his own drama in a way that evoked Goethe's admiration."

10. The historical King Manfred had a stormy relationship with the Pope, was excommunicated, was reported to have been a noble and magnanimous, but strong and assertive character, and was renowned for his physical beauty and intellectual attainments. Both politically and personally he lived a short but turbulent life of 34 years only, very much like Byron, so much so that he was the subject of a number of plays.

11. For the relevant details of the ghost-story sessions, see Mary Shelley's 1831 "Introduction" to the revised third edition of *Frankenstein*, also included in *The Norton Anthology*, 847-51. Although nothing is known about what P.B. Shelley began and abandoned it, according to Nora Crook (in her edition of *The Novels and Selected Works of Mary Shelley*, vol. 1 [London: William Pickering, 1996] 1, 178), "Shelley's 1816 verse fragment beginning 'A shovel of his ashes took' has been identified as a vestige of his attempt." On her part at first Mary was uninspired. By hearing *Christabel* Shelley became so distraught that he thought Mary was the evil Geraldine and ran out of the room in fear. On the night of 22 June, the group discussed various philosophical doctrines, including the principle of life and whether it could ever be discovered and whether scientists could galvanise a corpse or manufactured humanoid. When Mary went to bed, she had a nightmarish dream described in the second part of her Introduction, according to which from the next morning she started developing the frightful yet powerful ideas of her dream with the opening lines of Chapter IV of *Frankenstein*: "It was on a dreary night in November [...]." She completed the novel in May 1817; it was first published anonymously on 1 January 1818. See also Polidori's *Diary,* and Kim W. Britton's online links to *Manfred* and *Frankenstein.*

12. See Mary Shelley's 1831 Introduction to *Frankenstein.*

13. All quotations from *Manfred* are taken from *The Norton Anthology* (cf. note 9 above).

14. Most of the third canto of *Childe Harold*, the whole of *The Prisoner of Chillon*, and several love poems addressed to Augusta were also composed

at this time, when Byron, under the influence of Shelley, had an opportunity to read Wordsworth's nature poetry under the sign of the quiet and sublime. As such, these works by Byron are deeply coloured by the Wordsworthian elements of meditation, contemplation, description and conversation.

15. Ryan Hunter, "Individualism and Religion in Byron's *Manfred*," <www.ualberta.ca/~rhunter/manfred.htm>.
16. *The Works of Lord Byron: Letters and Journals*, vol. III, ed. R.E. Prothero (London, 1898-1901) 352; J.R. Watson, *Picturesque Landscape and English Romantic Poetry* (London: Hutchinson Educational, 1970) 176.
17. *The Works of Lord Byron: Letters and Journals*, vol. V, 37.
18. The other literary ancestors of Manfred include the Gothic villains, Prometheus, and Satan.
19. Nelson 75.
20. Introduction to *Manfred*, in *The Norton Anthology* 514.
21. Introduction to *Manfred*, in *The Norton Anthology* 513.
22. The scene reminds us of Marlowe's Faustus embracing the phantom of Helen, which is actually a devil in Helen's form and which thus seals Faustus' death and damnation for ever. In Ingmar Bergman's *Wild Strawberries*, one of the death images is a dream figure that crumbles when the hero Isak Borg touches it.
23. *The Norton Anthology*, 519, note 7.
24. Shilstone 154.
25. Compare Hamlet's glowing Renaissance tribute to man, the earth and the sky (*Hamlet*, II.ii, 310ff):

    "[…] this goodly frame the earth [...] this most excellent canopy the air [...] this brave overhanging firmament, this majestical roof fretted with golden fire [...]. What a piece of work is a man, how noble in reason, how infinite in faculties, in form and moving, how express and admirable in action, how like an angel in apprehension, how like a god: the beauty of the world; the paragon of animals […] "Despite his eloquent tribute to fellow human beings, Hamlet does not forget the reality of the human condition, which he describes as a "quintessence of dust" with the vast space around him as "a sterile promontory" and "a foul and pestilent congregation of vapours."
26. Byron states the same idea in "Prometheus":

    "Man is in part divine,
    A troubled stream from a pure source;
    And Man in portions can foresee
    His own funereal destiny;
    His wretchedness, and his resistance,

And his sad unallied existence:
To which his Spirit may oppose
Itself—an equal to all woes,
And a firm will, and a deep sense,
Which even in torture can descry
Its own concentred recompense,
Triumphant where it dares defy,
And making Death a Victory."
[...] actions are our epochs: mine

27. *The Works of Lord Byron: Letters and Journals*, vol. III, 364.
28. Shilstone 127.
29. Nietzsche, quoted in *The Norton Anthology* 514.
30. Byron frequently expresses his complex range of feelings about Napoleon as a great hero and at the same time as an evil, Satanic power in his letters and journals. He wrote a number of poems on Napoleon following his fall. In *Ode to Napoleon Buonaparte*, he describes Napoleon as one who was "yesterday a King/ And now [...] a nameless thing," who taught others the lesson of the futility of ambition, who was "The Desolator desolate!/ The Victor overthrown!/ The Arbiter of other's fate/ A Suppliant for his own!" In *Childe Harold's Pilgrimage*, I (52-53), Napoleon is represented as "the Scourger of the world," "Gaul's Vulture" and the author of "one bloated Chief's unwholesome reign;" in *CHP*, III (19-20, 36-39), Napoleon is portrayed with many of the characteristics of the Byronic hero. He was a "fallen despot" yet "the greatest, nor the worst of men,/ Whose spirit antithetically mixt/ One moment of the mightiest, and again/ On little objects with like firmness fixt,/ Extreme in all things! hadst thou been betwixt,/ Thy throne had still been thine, or never been;/ For daring made thy rise as fall." In his fierceness Napoleon was "the Thunderer of the scene," who shook the world, which seemed to tremble even at his fall. "Conqueror and captive of the earth," he was "more or less than man—in high or low,/ Battling with nations, flying from the field;/ Now making monarchs' necks thy footstool, now/ More than thy meanest soldier taught to yield." He was "the loftiest star," who could "crush, command, rebuild" an empire yet not control his own "pettiest passion"; he was deeply skilled in men's spirits but he could neither look through his own spirit "nor curb the lust of war." He was flattered and then abandoned by Fate; he was Fortune's "spoil'd and favourite child."
31. Shilstone, 156. For a detailed discussion, see Simon Bainbridge, *Napoleon and English Romanticism* (Cambridge: Cambridge UP, 1995).
32. Napoleon escaped from his captivity on the island of Elba in March 1815. After his defeat at Waterloo, he was imprisoned on another island, St. Helena, in October 1815.

33. Satan's claim is that "The mind is its own place, and in itself/ Can make a Heaven of Hell, and a Hell of Heaven" (Milton, *Paradise Lost*, I, 254-55). Also I. 252 and III. 73.
34. Shilstone 153.
35. Shilstone 153.
36. Clubbe 38.
37. Bernard Blackstone, *Byron: A Survey* (London: Longman, 1975) 231.
38. Shilstone 153.

□

STATEMENT ABOUT OWNERSHIP AND OTHER PARTICULARS OF

The Atlantic Literary Review

FORM IV

(See Rule 8)

Place of Publication	:	New Delhi
Periodicity of the Publication	:	Quarterly
Printer's Name	:	Manish Kumar
Nationality	:	Indian
Address	:	B-2, Vishal Enclave New Delhi 110027
Publisher's Name	:	Manish Kumar
Nationality	:	Indian
Address	:	B-2, Vishal Enclave New Delhi 110027
Editor's Name	:	Rajeshwar Mittapalli
Nationality	:	Indian
Address	:	# 202, Vasista Apartments, Nakkalagutta Hanamkonda-506001 Andhra Pradesh
Names and addresses of individuals who own the newspaper and partners or shareholders holding more than one per cent of the total capital	:	K.R. Gupta B-2, Vishal Enclave New Delhi-110027

I, Manish Kumar, hereby declare that the particulars given above are true to the best of my knowledge and belief.

Sd/-

Date : 01st January, 2005

MANISH KUMAR
Publisher

The Music of Dionysus: Religion and Drama in Tagore's *Mukta-dhara* and Soyinka's Adaptation of *The Bacchae*

Tirthankar Das Purkayastha

In his article "Third-World Drama: Soyinka and Tragedy," Andrew Gurr speaks of the 'stasis,' the inviolate order of cosmic harmony, that tragedy upholds. This, Gurr argues, should render the Third World, governed as it is by an urgent drive for 'progress,' particularly uncongenial to the Tragic Muse. Gurr studies the conservative moorings of Wole Soyinka's plays in the Yoruba myths of Ogun and Obatala in the light of the Brechtian formulation that drama should be "an affair for philosophers, but for such philosophers who wished not just to explain the world but to change it."[1] Religion, Gurr argues, seeks to explain the flaws that contribute to human tragedy without trying to discover the means by which these flaws could be remedied. The sense of waste, which the spectacle of tragic suffering might generate in the mind of an audience, is accommodated, in the end, in the 'quietist wisdom' of religion. "This again is stasis," writes Andrew Gurr, "acceptance of an ordained status quo."[2]

This argument, valid in the context of a hiatus between life and art, however, ignores the subtle and insidious ways in which drama can sometimes become, even while remaining rooted in a traditional world-view, a radical instrument of change. While focusing on the traditional elements in Soyinka's plays, Gurr is reticent about the struggle between tradition and the human imperatives implicit in some of them. As Philip Brockbank has demonstrated, the hero of *The Strong Breed* does not merely 'accept' the role of a carrier but succeeds through his death, undertaken to save a child, in transforming that role. If the purpose of the ritual is to make the scapegoat bear the burden of the community's afflictions, Eman's death fulfils that purpose in a way never envisaged by those responsible for it. "The victim has moved humanity a step forward," writes Philip Brockbank, "for the ugly victimization of Eman, the enlightened school-teacher trying to save an imbecile child, works ironically in the manner of a carrier-ritual; the sick dogs will in time be ready for a fresh start."[3]

The present paper is focused on Soyinka's English-language adaptation of *The Bacchae* by Euripides, and seeks to reread this play alongside *Mukta-dhara* ('Free Current') by Rabindranath Tagore (the latter originally written in Bengali). It is not my purpose to assume indebtedness on either side. Despite his famous poem on Africa, in which the Indian poet resents the colonial oppression of the African people, Tagore did not live to witness the resurgence of the African nation and its struggle to put an end to apartheid. Soyinka, on his part, also does not seem to have been influenced, even remotely, by the Indian philosophy of life. It still seems intriguing to note some correspondence between these two plays, traceable, ultimately, to a faith, shared by the two poets, in the ultimate triumph of the human spirit over the deadening powers of tyranny. Tagore wrote his play in 1922 (it is considered by many to be the best among his symbolic plays), soon after his return from a visit to Europe, at a time when the Indian struggle for independence was in full swing. Originally titled *Path* or *Road*, the play deals with the misguided effort on the part of a king to harness the forces of nature, to the detriment of a people dependent on her bounties. The obvious ecological concerns which this issue involves are given cosmic significance by referring to Lord Siva as the fountain-head of all nature's blessings. By presuming to dam up the river, the tyrannical ruler discriminates in favour of his own people against their neighbours who depend on its water for their agriculture. Unlike the god in Soyinka's play, Lord Siva never appears in person on stage. He nevertheless is a living presence, whose symbol is the trident at the temple-top that looms, throughout the play's action, threateningly across the western sky. The trident and the machine or the engine-tower, which also menacingly rears its head against the sky, represent the polarities of nature and human skill on which the ideological conflict mainly turns. With the dam having proved an instrument of oppression in the hands of a callous tyrant, the waters of the spring pressing against its walls come automatically to symbolise Dionysian energies straining at the leash. While Soyinka calls his play, quite appropriately, 'a communion rite,'

Tagore's, by contrast, is centred on its hero, on whose self-sacrifice depends the salvation of his people.

It was on being commissioned by the National Theatre at the Old Vic in London in 1973 that Soyinka set himself the task of adapting the Euripidean tragedy to the political realities of Nigeria. His play reflects his bitter memories of having to contend with Nigerian military rulers to prevent the setting up of the separatist state of Biafra in the 1967-1970 civil war, and of being made to undergo two years' solitary confinement. "It is against this slice of contemporary reality," writes Albert Hunt, "that Soyinka's version of Euripides must be seen."[4] The emphasis in Soyinka's play is laid, unmistakably, on the tyrannical nature of Pentheus, whose struggle with Dionysus is not so unequal as it is in Euripides's play. As distinct from his counterpart in the original play, who is "too pitiably weak to fight,"[5] Pentheus in Soyinka is a brutal tyrant, whose "militaristic [...] bearing" is manifest from the very beginning of the play. There is nothing in Euripides to suggest Pentheus' cruel treatment of his slaves, which finds such pointed emphasis in Soyinka's reference in the stage directions to Pentheus's palace being "lined by the bodies of crucified slaves mostly in the skeletal stage." It is clear from its description of the sweating labour of the slaves 'flailing and treading' that it is on the relationship between the ruler and the ruled that the play will remain focused. The Slave-leader, who shows from the beginning a capacity to look beyond his present state of abject servitude ("When the present is intolerable, the unknown harbours no risks"—Soyinka, *Bacchae*, 240), sees the violent end of Pentheus as a kind of poetic justice:

Old Slave: [...] Oh this is a heartless
Deity, bitter, unnatural in his revenge.
To make a mother rip her son like bread
Across a banqueting board! I pity her.
Leader: Who pities us? When the mine-prop falls and pulps
Our bones with mud, who pities us? When harvest
Fails, who goes without? And you, if you had
Died at the feast of Eleusis, would Thebes
Have remembered you with pity? (300)

The 'sympathetic' portrayal of Dionysus as a being of 'divine self-assurance' is likewise attuned to the play's purpose to suggest that all tyrannies are 'unnatural.' Unlike in Euripides's play, Dionysus is here motivated not so much by a spirit of vengeance as by a god-like wish to reform a wayward son. Pentheus is characterised by pride and a wilful blindness. "Use your eyes, Pentheus" (259), says Tiresias to make the king see the folly of denying the power of a god whose authority is beyond all dispute. The king is lonely and his rule is propped up by force rather than genuine loyalties. Agave remains so blissfully absorbed in the esoteric cult of Dionysus that she remains virtually alienated from her son until she finds herself slipping, unwittingly, into the role of a priestess performing the ritual slaughter:

Herdsman: Well then—and may the god of oaths protect me—
Our herds of cattle had just climbed a hill
Grazing as they went—the dew was wet upon the grass,
The sun being hardly warmed up that early hour—
Well, by chance I stumble on this meadow, and in it
Find a scene just like a painting on a vase—motionless
Three rings of women—fast asleep. (278)

The son's separation from his mother signifies his wilful severance of the umbilical chord that linked him to the mainsprings of life. It is this life-denying aspect of him that Kadmos tries, in vain, to rectify: "You are born of earth yourself—remember that" (258). The women's surrender to the primal impulses has not resulted in licentiousness, as the herdsman hastens to testify, as the restraint is imposed from within, and not from without.

Soyinka's version of the play "gets even closer than Euripides," remarks Brockbank, "to the pathos and absurdity of human ordinariness."[6] The play depicts its slaves as being deprived of the reassuring presence of the hills of Cithairon, which are never completely out of sight in Euripides as an emblem of an alternative mode of existence. The Slave-leader has only a vague remembrance of a life beyond the city walls, while Pentheus, on his part, confesses to having never stepped beyond the city. The ecstasy brought about by the drinking of wine is interpreted by the Slave-leader as a sign of the imminent collapse of the barrier, not only between reason and instinct but also between ruler and ruled.

Leader: [...] There is heaven in this juice. It flows through my lips and I say, now I roll the sun upon my tongue and it neither burns nor scorches. And a scent-laden breeze fills the cavern of my mouth, pressing for release. I know that scent. I mean, I knew it once. I live to know it once again.

Herdsman: I think I understand you. Forget it friend. (236)

There is an insistence, here, as also in Kadmos' admonitions quoted above, on the perversion of a wilful turning away from what constitutes the real source of Pentheus's 'earthly' power. If Kadmos finds his words falling on deaf ears, Dionysus's attempt to rouse Pentheus's self-knowledge, by holding out his hand like a mirror before his eyes, also yields no result. It is, however, the tyrant's essential kinship with his own people, so perversely repudiated by him, that uniquely qualifies him for the role of the scapegoat, to be killed, in the play's *dénouement*, as part of the 'communion-rite.'

The custom in Pentheus's reign of using the slaves as scapegoats for the ritual cleansing of the state is, as K.E. Senanu has put it, 'a perversion of religion' which is also "the most radical form of tyranny."[7] As Euripides makes no mention of this ritual, its significance for Soyinka's play is immense. Tiresias attributes to it the growing resentment among the slaves, which he hopes to mollify, however temporarily, by taking the role upon himself. But his decision, as he confesses before Dionysus, is prompted as much by political foresight as a desire for self-renewal:

> Yes, there was hunger. Thirst. In this job one lives half a life, neither priest nor man. Neither man nor woman. I have longed to know what flesh is made of. What suffering is. Feel the taste of blood instead of merely foreseeing it. Taste the ecstasy of rejuvenation after long organizing its ritual. (243)

Tiresias is not just old but part of the system. His dance in honour of Dionysus, performed prematurely, must, therefore, seem ludicrous. Dionysus, however, assures him the promise of an epiphany, gets fulfilled in the end.

The ending, however, turns out to be a miracle or a series of miracles. That Soyinka intended it to be regarded as such is evident from the two tableaux introduced into his version of the play. The first image is that of a bridegroom forfeiting his bride by participating in a vulgar dance with a serving woman, under the influence of wine, much to the chagrin of the aristocratic in-laws. The bridegroom soon reveals his Dionysian fawn-skin hidden beneath the wedding garments. The second image is that of Christ, his halo replaced with the thorn-ivy crown of Dionysus, turning water into wine. While the first image involves transgressive violation of hierarchies, the second one presents God as the contriver of all such miracles. Despite the god's assurance that the spectacle is a mere illusion that Pentheus need not take too seriously, it appears in hindsight that it foreshadows the latter's ineluctable destiny. Led by the temptation to watch the orgies of the Maenads, the female worshippers of Dionysus, on the sly, Pentheus takes draughts of wine and wears the costume of a woman. This, in Soyinka's play, implies much more than mere overthrow of inner resistance. It turns Pentheus into a comic spectacle by robbing him precisely of that by which he has laid such huge store—his manliness:

> What! Dress myself as a Maenad? A woman?
> Make the throne a laughing-stock in Thebes? (288)

The Chorus, consisting of Bacchantes and slaves, watches Pentheus being tricked up like a scapegoat and brings home to the audience, through its poetry of dew-soaked nights and ovarian silences, the cosmic significance of the sacrifice:

> Slave: For there are forces not ruled by us
> And we obey them
> Trust them. Though they travel inch by inch
> They arrive.
> Old Slave: Dionysus? Or—Nothing.
> Not even a word for these forces.
> They lack a name. We will call them
> Spirits.
> Gods.
> Slave: Principles,
> Elements,
> Slave: Currents,
> Laws, Eternal Causes.
> Slave: But they are born in the blood
> Unarguable, observed and preserved before time [...] (292)

Led by Dionysus, Pentheus goes to meet his death. As he watches, from a tree-top, the Dionysiac rites being performed by his mother along with other women, she herself, urged by the god, pounces on him in a fit of frenzy and tears him limb from limb. Rejoicing over her success in killing what she supposes to be a mountain-lion, she holds aloft the severed head of her son on a thyrsus for all to see. It is only after Kadmos has made her take a closer look at her trophy that the truth begins to dawn on her, enabling her, gradually, to come to terms with the inevitable:

> Kadmos [The cry is wrung from him]: Why us?

Agave [Her hands are on Pentheus's head, about to lift it. Quietly]:
Why not? (307)

Soyinka makes a departure from Euripides in turning the play's ending into a moment of joy, "a communion-rite," "from a threnos of lamentation to a muted celebration, including a sudden recognition or an epiphany."[8] The stage is filled, as Soyinka puts it in the stage-direction, 'with the god's presence.' There follows mystical revelation of the deeper significance of the sacrifice. The jets of blood leap up through every orifice of the severed head before turning miraculously into wine, signalling the renewal of life or rebirth for all who have survived. "Slowly, dream-like," Soyinka adds in the stage directions, "they all move towards the fountain, cup their hands and drink." The miracle is wrought by a god who is beyond the "limitations of being human."[9]

If the role of the human agency has been reduced to the minimum in Soyinka's version of the Euripidean tragedy, it is embodied exclusively in the figure of a martyr in Tagore's *Mukta-dhara*. Abhijit, the protagonist of the play, has been brought up as a prince within the royal family, but by the time the play opens the king has already declared him to be a rebel, opposed to the royal policy of exploiting the subject people of Shiv-tarai in the interest of Uttarakut, the king's own country. In one of the earliest and most famous readings of this play, Edward Thompson speaks of its highly allegorical presentation of some of Tagore's political convictions, but, in his eagerness to uphold the universal relevance of the message, plays down Tagore's withering scorn for the exploitative policies of the British Empire:

> His deep distrust of *all* government by machinery and of *all* prostitution of science to serve violence and oppression, his hatred of a slavish system of education, his scorn of race-hatred and of *all* politics which seek to make one tribe dependent on another instead of risking the gift of the fullest freedom, his certitude that it is in freedom that God is found—all these are so prominent that each may with justice be claimed as the play's message.[10] (italics mine)

It goes without saying that Tagore never allowed his vision to be circumscribed by narrow nationalist ideologies, but it is equally true that India's ongoing struggle for Independence provided him with an immediate context for exploring the universal struggle of the human spirit against all kinds of bondage. "Both the personality and the words of Dhananjaya," as K.R. Kripalani has noted, "are a remarkable anticipation of the shape that the struggle for Indian Independence was to assume later under the leadership of Mahatma Gandhi."[11] King Ranajit's avowed aim is to prevent Shiv-tarai from becoming economically self-reliant and it is this that provokes Abhijit's indignation:

Uddhav. The Maharaja says that by clearing the Nandi Pass you have knocked the bottom out of Uttarakut's rice-bowl!

Abhijit. I have saved Uttarakut from the wretched fate of being forever a parasite on Shiv-tarai. (Tagore, *Mukta-dhara*, 30)

Bibhuti, the royal engineer, is as indifferent as the king himself to what the withholding of water might mean to the farmers: "I had no time to think of whether some farmer's paltry maize crop would die" (12).

Abhijit has set his face against everything that binds man and robs him of his freedom. His own imprisonment thus becomes equivalent to the building of the dam, but even before he becomes, literally, a captive in the hands of the king, he complains of invisible fetters:

Somewhere or other in the external world, God writes for us the secret mystery of each man's spirit. Mukta-dhara is His word to me, bearing the secret of my inner being. When her feet were bound in the iron fetters, I was startled out of a dream. I realized the truth—the throne of Uttarakut is the dam which binds my spirit. I have taken the road in order to set it free (27). His emancipation signals the hour of fulfilment of his life's mission.

The identity of a Crown Prince, which lies like a burden on Abhijit's shoulders, however, entails a moral responsibility that goes well beyond his official role. The marks of an "imperial destiny" (19) that Ranajit claims to have noticed on the foundling's forehead prove true in a manner hardly anticipated by the king. The knowledge that he was never born a prince but was borne by some vagrant mother by the springs of Mukta-dhara has a liberating effect on Abhijit's mind, enabling him to be united spiritually with all creation. The Machine affronts his sense of beauty, just as the tyrant's depredations hurt his sense of fair play. In a passage of great charm, he describes the ugliness of the machine which strikes him as an embodiment of human insolence: "And that is why I cannot endure that monster, that mutes the music of earth and guffaws with its iron fangs at the sky. I love this Paradise, that is why I shall fight its demons" (28). The machine in itself is only a neutral instrument of power and to attribute to it the monstrosities of its owner Tagore would consider to be as foolish as blaming a palm tree for a drunkard's drunkenness.[12] Abhijit's crusade is thus waged not so much against the Machine itself as against the tyrannies of which it has become a symbol.

The characters of Amba and Batuk are introduced to suggest that deaths have occurred in the past to realize the king's ambition. While the former bewails the loss of her son, the latter bemoans the death of two 'lusty' grandsons of his. The king wants all such deaths to be regarded as acts of sacrifice made in the larger interest of his realm. However, these deaths, like the ritual flagellation of the slaves in Soyinka's play, are endured by the unwilling victims of the king's tyranny:

Batuk. [...] They all say my two grandsons are fortunate to have given their lives.

First Citizen. Well, that is not untrue.

Batuk. Not untrue? When no life springs from the life laid down? When death is the only fruit of death? It is utter loss. Bhairav will never endure it. (26)

Abhijit, on the other hand, dies willingly to set free the waters of the spring. The supreme moment of self-sacrifice is anticipated in the messenger's covert reference to the 'cracks' that remain invisible to all but "the god of destruction" (13). As Abhijit strikes at its weakest spot, the dam gives way, unleashing the stream which carries away his lifeless body. As the news of his death arrives, the stage is filled with the noise of the rushing water which Dhanajaya, the Ascetic, is quick to identify with the cosmic dance of Lord Shiva:

Deep in my being, fierce and fleet,
Dance his footsteps, dance his feet. (70)

Despite the concern with the evils of tyranny that both plays have in common, neither seems to put its faith *exclusively* in the human initiative to end them. Abhijit's decision to lay down his life does not seem to have been arrived at through a reasoned analysis of the pros and cons but is an intuitive one, traceable to his symbolic kinship with Nature. If Dionysus has been identified, in Soyinka's play, with Ogun, "elder brother to Dionysos," as Soyinka puts it in his Acknowledgement,[13] Tagore's play identifies Nature with Bhairava, that is, God in His fearsome aspects. With Tagore, however, it is an article of faith that one must strive, individually, to conquer fear so that a mass movement, when it does take place, can be a positive affirmation of the human spirit. The significance of Abhijit's self-sacrifice lies precisely in its subjecting the human will that might fritter itself out in an aimless pursuit of violence to the Will of God:

Ganesh. We came to seek our Yuvaraja. We shall never find him now.

Dhananjaya. Nay, you have found him. He is yours forever now. (71)

In a speech, delivered to welcome Gandhi as an apostle of non-violence, Tagore had pointed out his country's debt to Christianity: "There is in Christianity the great doctrine that God became man in order to save humanity by taking the burden of its sin and suffering on Himself, here in this very world, not waiting for the next [...]. And to our great good fortune, Gandhiji was able to receive this teaching of Christ in a living way."[14] As noted earlier, it is mainly in the speeches of Dhananjaya that one finds the Gandhian philosophy of non-violence being articulated. It, however, remains for Abhijit to translate that philosophy into action.

The remarks of Andrew Gurr cited at the beginning of this article are based on the premise that all progress should be linear and that the triumph of God must imply the triumph of the *status quo*. This line of interpretation is akin to that advanced by Augusto Boal that sees the restoration of harmony in a tragedy as part of a strategy of containment, "the most perfect artistic form of coercion."[15] Seen from this perspective, Soyinka's play might appear to encourage abdication of all moral responsibility in the name of faith. That, to say the least, would be to grossly misread the play. It is mainly by transforming the play's ending to a ritual that Soyinka succeeds in making the Euripidean drama of God's dealing with man intelligible in terms of the Yoruba interpretation of history.

Distinguishing the Greek gods from the Yoruba deities, Soyinka writes in his *Myth, Literature and the African World* about the former's aloofness from the mortals, whose aberrations they punish despite their own proneness to similar moral lapses. In the Yoruba metaphysics, by contrast, the deities remain enmeshed in a process of reparation that covers all creation for any wrong committed at any point of time. Thus Obatala, guilty of having created deformed creatures with fingers rendered unsteady by the taking of too many draughts of wine, is made to undergo imprisonment which he, however, endures with the characteristic calmness of mind. More significant, however, is the role of Ogun, whom Soyinka describes as "a combination of the Dionysian, Apollonian and Promethean principles,"[16] in the context of Yoruba cosmogony. It is Ogun, of all deities, who undertakes the perilous journey across the gulf that separates the gods from man, thus exposing himself to the howling winds that threaten to tear him apart, were it not for his great power of Will. Ogun's saga is one of repeated adventures undertaken by the deity for the sake of his votaries. Presumably, it was the consideration of the part played by Dionysus in Euripides's play that might have led Soyinka to accept the Old Vic proposal in the first place.

It is this notion of the interpenetration of the divine and the human, the mystical and the mundane, in the ritual experience of the Yoruba community that needs to be kept in mind while watching Soyinka's version of the Euripidean tragedy. One can do worse than quote a passage from Soyinka to grasp the nature of participation in ritual drama:

> The actor in ritual drama [...] prepares mentally and physically for his disintegration and re-assembly within the universal womb of origin, experiences the transitional yet inchoate matrix of death and being [...]. Tragic feeling in Yoruba drama stems from sympathetic knowledge of the protagonist's foray into this psychic abyss of the re-creative energies.[17]

The involvement of the community ensures the effective bridging of the gulf separating it from the cosmic powerhouse of primal energies. The modern attempts to rationalise, in terms of psychoanalysis, the hypnotic spell of ritual experience fail miserably, as Soyinka has insisted, to grasp the sense of a cosmic totality underlying the Yoruba world-view:

> The community emerges from ritual experience "*charged with new strength for action*" because of the protagonist's Promethean raid on the durable resources of the transitional realm; immersed within it, he is enabled empathically to transmit its essence to the choric participants of the rites—the community. Nor would we consider that such a communicant withdraws from conscious reality, but rather that his consciousness is stretched to embrace another and primal reality.[18] (emphasis added)

From the perspective of Yoruba mythology, the Dionysus of Euripides's play becomes Ogun, the hero-god, his intervention in mortal business being seen not as a form of divine punishment for a human aberration but as an emblem of "the constant regenerative process of the universe."[19] If a tyrant's pride is something that calls for remedy, the passivity or weakness of his subjects is no less so. The description of Ogun in the Yoruba mythology as a god who swims in blood is suggestive of the sanguinary means by which a revolution may sometimes be effected. But the idea of a radical breach between the present and the future that 'revolution' implies in modern terminology is alien to the Yoruba world-view that sees the past, the present and the future as a seamless unity.

The Euro-American convention of separating the stage into a self-contained realm of aesthetic experience, away from the quotidian world of the spectators, must, therefore, prove inadequate in embracing the myriad levels of existence that ritual drama simultaneously inhabits. To regard Pentheus's death merely as the handiwork of a deity who has somehow taken it into his head to punish his aberration is, therefore, in the perspective of the Yoruba world-view, a typical case of philosophic myopia. By transforming the play's ending into a ritual, Soyinka situates his play, or rather his version of the Euripidean play, firmly within the tradition of African ritual drama. It may be pertinent, in this context, to recall the words of Kimberley W. Benston on the movement, observable in Modern Black Drama, "from *mimesis*, or representation of an action to *methexis* or communal "helping out" of the action by all assembled. It is a process that could be described alternatively as a shift from *drama*—the spectacle observed—to *ritual*—the event which dissolves traditional divisions between actor and spectator, between self and other."[20]

It cannot, however, be said of Tagore's play that the divine intervention in the mundane strivings of the exploited people of Shiv-tarai goes much beyond the level of abstract conceptualisation. The fact that Tagore belonged to the monotheistic creed of the Brahmo-community may have hindered him from viewing Lord Shiva in his incarnation of a phallic symbol of the regenerative forces of nature, an aspect that Soyinka, incidentally, connects with the vanished culture of a traditional society:

> And before that oriental twin-brother of Christianity—Buddhism—attenuated and circumscribed Asiatic thought, Lord Shiva drove his passionate course through earth, uniting all the elements with his powerful erection which burst through to the earth's surface, split in three and spurted sperm in upper cosmos.[21]

The relevance of Lord Shiva in Tagore's play about man's struggle to liberate the elemental forces of nature from the tyranny of man-made laws is not hard to see. Tagore, however, chooses to focus on the etymological meaning of Shiva as an embodiment of goodness, and bypasses the pagan associations of the fertility cult.

It should, however, be added in conclusion that, although *Mukta-dhara* remains a play within the Indo-European dramatic tradition of mimetic representation of the hero's individual destiny, it nonetheless, by laying its scene of action in the outdoors, and amid a vast concourse of men, a motley crowd consisting of teacher, pupils, labourers, artisans and devotees, focuses on the life of the community as distinct from that of its aristocratic rulers. Without speaking directly or in overt political terms of a possible mass uprising, it does invoke the forces of Nature that shape the lives of men. In dramatic terms, it employs the mythic pattern of divine intervention in a moment of spiritual or cultural crisis. There is, in the hymns of praise sung by the devotees, an acknowledgement of God's overseeing presence. Without the centrality of a ritual, however, Lord Shiva remains a mere symbol, and, despite the optimistic view of man's future as a function of God's will, the image of Lord Shiva in Tagore's play can be regarded only as a vague anticipation of Soyinka's vision of Ogun as an embodiment of 'primal energies' propelling the community to its desired goal.

Special Note

The quotations from the plays are taken from:

1. Wole Soyinka, *The Bacchae of Euripides. A Communion Rite,* in *Collected Plays 1* (Oxford: Oxford UP, 1973).
2. Rabindranath Tagore, *Mukta-dhara,* in *Three Plays*, *Mukta-dhara*, *Natir Puja, Chandalika,* trans. Marjorie Sykes (1950; Oxford: Oxford UP, 195) 4.

Notes and References

1. Andrew Gurr, "Third-World Drama: Soyinka and Tragedy," *Critical Perspectives on Wole Soyinka*, ed. James Gibbs (London: Heinemann, 1980) 140.
2. Gurr 143.
3. Philip Brockbank, "Blood and Wine: Tragic Ritual from Aeschylus to Soyinka," *Shakespeare in the Twentieth Century*, *Shakespeare Survey 36*, ed. Stanley Wells, et al. (Cambridge: Cambridge UP, 2002) 13.
4. Albert Hunt, "Amateurs in Horror," in Gibbs, ed. *Critical Perspectives on Wole Soyinka* 113.
5. H.D.F. Kitto, *Greek Tragedy: A Literary Study* (1939; London and New York: Routledge, 1997) 377.
6. Brockbank 16.

7. K.E. Senanu, "The Exigencies of Adaptation: The Case of Soyinka's *Bacchae*," in Gibbs, ed. *Critical Perspectives on Wole Soyinka* 109.
8. Senanu 109.
9. Kitto 380.
10. Edward Thompson, *Rabindranath Tagore, Poet and Dramatist* (Calcutta: Oxford UP, 1926, rpt. Calcutta: Rddhi, 1979) 271.
11. Introduction to Marjorie Sykes' translation of *Mukta-dhara* (see above) 5
12. The analogy is suggested in Tagore's *Letters from Russia*, Letter No. 05, dated 1 Oct. 1930.
13. Soyinka, 'Acknowledgment' to *The Bacchae*, in *Collected Plays 1* (see above).
14. Tagore, in *A Tagore Reader*, ed. Amiya Chakravarty (New Delhi: Rupa & Co., 2003) 271.
15. Quoted in *Shakespearean Tragedy*, ed. John Drakakis (Longman: London and New York, 1992) 6.
16. Soyinka, *Myth, Literature and the African World* (Cambridge: CUP, 1976) 26.
17. Soyinka, *Myth, Literature and the African World* 30-31.
18. Soyinka, *Myth, Literature and the African World* 33.
19. Soyinka, *Myth, Literature and the African World* 18.
20. Quoted in T.V. Prakash, "Across the Atlantic: Wole Soyinka 'meets' Ed Bullins," *The Atlantic Literary Review* 1.1 (Jul.-Sept. 2000): 61-76 (70-71).
21. Soyinka, *Myth, Literature and the African World* 3.

□

Paradigm Lost: Mediation, Narration, and Vision in V.S. Naipaul's *A Bend in the River*

R.S. Krishnan

No writer in modern times, barring, perhaps, Salman Rushdie, has drawn so much attention, laudatory as well as critical, as V.S. Naipaul. For instance, A. Sivanandan notes: "I never liked Naipaul. I could never read him without a sense of self-betrayal, I could not enter into his stories without being turned off from myself [...]. I first encountered Naipaul—a fellow colonial who knew my condition better than I did, described it with a fine and acute understanding, and then delivered me up to my subjugation in the pursuit of his own deliverance."[1] Edward Said, while acknowledging Naipaul as a gifted writer, is no less critical:

> Two things need to be said about the small band whose standard bearer Naipaul has become [...]. [I]n presenting themselves as members of courageous minorities in the Third World, they are in fact not interested at all in the Third World—which they never address [...]. Naipaul's accounts of the Islamic, Latin American, African, Indian and Caribbean worlds totally ignores a massive infusion of critical scholarship about those regions in favour of the tritest, the cheapest, and the easiest of colonial mythologies about wogs and darkies.[2]

Indeed, most recently, Paul Theroux, the erstwhile disciple of Naipaul, contends, of Naipaul's dismissal of writers such as E.M. Forster, R.K. Narayan and others, that "there is a pattern in Naipaul's attack—in almost every case the writers he attacks have been associated with him by critics under labels like 'colonial,' 'Commonwealth' or 'exiled.'"[3] In his defence, however, a critic such as Sara Suleri argues that "Naipaul's mature writing no longer conceives of the literary as a recourse from the political, but instead internalises the imperial tradition represented by both modes into a dazzling idiom that no longer needs to indicate the referents of its discourse. As a consequence of this condensation, such a language will never clearly identify the object of its indictment."[4]

While it is not uncommon for writers to be the object of such criticism, and even if, in Naipaul's case, such cavils may be attributed as the prevailing view of the Left, the charges have less to do with the aesthetics of his work than with his legitimacy as a postcolonial writer. In some of his earlier non-fiction works, most notably *The Middle Passage* (1962), *An Area of Darkness* (1964), and *In a Free State* (1971), Naipaul is viewed as having little patience with claims for indigenous cultural history or the struggle of emerging countries freed from colonialism to forge a national identity of their own. For instance, in *The Middle Passage* the shock of West Indians at Naipaul's peremptory dismissal of any culture or history indigenous to the West Indies or South America was only exacerbated by the work's enthusiastic reception in the West. Even *In a Free State*, ostensibly a "postcolonial" work because it focuses on the implications of history and culture to "half-formed societies" in the wake of the collapse of empire, contains enough ambiguities to allow for a reading that raises questions concerning Naipaul's stance as a postcolonial writer. As one critic notes: "Far from making him a cultural hero, however, the nature and impact of his work has been such as to make him among the most problematic, if not actually disliked, of Caribbean authors."[5] Indeed, Derek Walcott's couplet in his poem "The Spoiler's Return" would seem to sum up Naipaul's reputation in the Caribbean: "I see this island, and I feel to bawl,/ 'areas of darkness' with V.S. Nightfall."[6]

A case in point is Naipaul's 1979 novel, *A Bend in the River*. There is general agreement that in writing *A Bend in the River*, as Michael Gorra notes, "the paradigmatic text is of course *Heart of Darkness*, in which Africa becomes a metaphor for man's original state even as it also provides a metaphor for the darkness of the human heart."[7] Naipaul's novel, however, was preceded by three other works, all of them responses to Conrad's *Heart of Darkness*: Chinua Achebe's *Things Fall Apart* (1958), Ngugi's *The River Between* (1965), and El-Tayib Salih's *Season of Migration to the North* (1969). *Things Fall Apart* and *The River Between* examine the effect of colonial ideology and hegemony on native customs and culture, whereas Salih's *Season of Migration to the North* goes out of its way to draw attention to its deliberate transposition, reversal and reinscription of Marlow's journey into the heart of darkness.[8]

While Achebe, Ngugi and Salih appropriate Conrad's topoi to interrogate colonial ideology through the prism of cultural nationalism, Naipaul's fictional foray into Conradian territory raises interesting questions as to his ideology of containment and narrative strategy. It is my contention that *In A Bend in the River* Naipaul's sophisticated irony underscores, rather than ameliorates, the inherent nihilism of his postcolonial outlook.

In *Black Skin, White Masks*, Frantz Fanon states: "Every colonized people [...] every people in whose soul an inferiority complex has been created by the death and burial of its local cultural originality—finds itself face to face with the language of the civilizing nation; that is, with the culture of the mother country. The colonized is elevated above his jungle status in proportion to his adoption of the mother country's cultural standards."[9] The ambiguity of Naipaul's response to the paradigm of *Heart of Darkness* allows the possibility of reading *A Bend in the River* as Naipaul's tacit allegiance to his "mother country's cultural standards."

Naipaul sets *A Bend in the River* in an unnamed, but newly independent African state governed by a dictator, the "Big Man," whose claims to lead the newly created nation rest on his assertion of championing peace and social justice by arousing the nascent nationalism of his people. The resulting conflict between the "Big Man" and the revolution of the "Liberation Army" out to oust him forms the crux of the novel, in which the narrative voice belongs to Salim, an Indian merchant who moves inland from the east coast of Africa where he had spent his childhood, in order to improve his economic opportunities, by taking the position of manager of a convenience store. In redrawing the map of the journey taken by Conrad's protagonist, Naipaul has his narrator move from the "bush" to the city, from the African village to the "New Domain," from Africa to Europe.

Salim is the putative observer of the unfolding history of Africa, with claims to historical objectivity since, as he says, "[F]rom an early age I developed the habit of looking, detaching myself from a familiar scene and trying to consider it as from a distance." In introducing himself, he states: "My own pessimism, my insecurity, was a more terrestrial affair. I was without the religious sense of my family. The insecurity I felt was due to my lack of true religion [...]" (16). He has "no family, no flag, no fetish [... He] could be master of [his] fate only if [he] stood alone

[...He] could no longer submit to fate. [His] wish was not to be good, in the way of [his] tradition, but to make good."[10]

At the outset, Salim locates his narrative within the triangulation of Third World politics, colonial legacy, and mediated history:

> Of that whole period of upheaval in Africa—the expulsion of the Arabs, the expansion of Europe, the parcelling out of the continent—that is the only family story I have. That was the sort of people we were. All that I know of our history and the history of the Indian Ocean I have got from books written by Europeans [...]. If I say these things it is because I have gotten them from European books. They formed no part of our knowledge or pride. Without Europeans, I feel, all our past would have been washed away, like the scuffmarks of fishermen on the beach outside our town. (11-12)

Both the language and imagery suggests a *textual* rather than a *cultural* site, in which Salim is both outside of history and an outsider himself: he has no idea when his family had come to Africa, and the "past was simply the past" (11). And since all his "knowledge" comes from European books, his sense of history is not anchored in any cultural context.

As a trope, this textual site is most significantly demonstrated when Salim views the misquoted Latin inscription among the ruins at the bend of the river, "Miscerique probat polulos et foedera jungi," the colonial steamship company's memorial to its own inviolability, proclaiming proudly that the gods favor the coming together of countries and peoples, the ideology of the colonial enterprise enshrined for posterity.

Salim notes that "the steamer monument had been knocked down," as if "to wipe out the memory of the intruder" (26). When Salim realizes the inscription's error, a misreading which foreshadows his own affair with Yvette, whom he also misreads, he both marvels at and is appalled by the way the imperial powers have manipulated the past in the service of their rule: "I was appalled. Twisting two-thousand-year-old words to celebrate sixty years of the steamer service from the capital! Rome was Rome. What was this place? To carve words on a monument beside this African river was surely to invite the destruction of the town" (63). Salim realizes that the ruins were built on a lie—a misquotation that paradoxically refutes even as it confirms its colonial ideology, and also harks to Salim's own fears of "black men assuming the lies of white men" (16). This subtle allusion to Marlow's initial response to Kurtz's treatise, "The

Suppression of the Savage Customs" and his later recognition of its disjunction to Kurtz himself, is only one of Naipaul's many re-presentations of Conrad in the novel.

Salim's affair with Yvette, the European wife of Raymond, the "Big Man's" Belgian "historian," culminates in his beating her and, finally, spitting between her legs. Salim's beating of Yvette suggests the recognition of his own predicament, for her vulnerability only reinforces the dissolution of the distinction between Africa and Europe, between "bush" and civilization, between the various "lies." Indeed, Salim's representation of his relationship with Yvette is significant for the way in which it is couched in a language he appropriates from colonial discourse, contiguous with his own sense of textual history. His "fantasies," says Salim, "were brothel fantasies of conquest and degradation, with the woman as the willing victim, the accomplice in her own degradation. It was all that I knew" (174). The parallel scene outside the house of a mob beating a policeman, even as Salim wreaks violence inside, both prefigures and underscores the dissolution of the larger social and political order.

Naipaul seems to view the degeneration of politics and social order in newly-made societies as a concomitant of liberation movements. As Salim observes at the outset of the novel, "the country, like others in Africa, had its troubles after independence," and that "too many of the places [...] are full of blood" (3). If Naipaul's ideological orientations in *A Bend in the River* seem much more swayed toward the view of disorder as an unavoidable corollary of contemporary liberation movements in the Third World, this seems to be particularly underscored in his portrayal of the Big Man.

We are told that he "was creating modern Africa. He was creating a miracle that would astound the rest of the world. He was by-passing real Africa, the difficult Africa of bush and villages, and creating something that would match anything that existed in other countries" (100). But this "miracle" falls into ruin, meeting much the same fate as the grandiose inscription among the ruins. As the narrator explains, "You took a boy of the bush and you taught him to read and write; you levelled the bush and built a polytechnic and you sent him there. It seemed as easy as that, if you came late to the world and found ready-made those things that other countries and peoples had taken so long to arrive at—writing, printing, universities, books, knowledge" (102-03).

The Big Man's political career is a studied attempt at imitating the power he sees in the West, but the trappings of his political power—European-built planes, prominently posted photographs of himself printed in Europe, having Europeans as advisors—are as alien to the African experience as the water hyacinth that relentlessly covers and devours the river and which, Salim notes, "the people still called [...] 'the new thing' or 'the new thing in the river' and which to the people was 'another enemy' [and was] tearing away bush from the heart of the continent and floating it down to the ocean, incalculable miles away" (46).

The "New Domain" becomes, with its modern luxurious buildings, a European model with Western values, the black man imitating the white man's "lies." As Salim notes, "If it was Europe that gave us [...] some idea of our history, it was Europe [...] that also introduced us to the lie. Those of us who had been in that part of Africa before the Europeans had never lied about ourselves [...] we were people who simply did what we did. But the Europeans could do one thing and say something quite different; and they could act in this way because they had an idea of what they owed to their civilization" (16-17). The implication is that Africa, and by extension the Third World, cannot preserve its traditions and culture and, in fact, the colonised repudiate their own sense of nationhood and end up mimicking their erstwhile colonisers' culture, thus perpetuating the "lies."

The Liberation Army that opposes the Big Man's efforts clothes its rhetoric in the traditionalism of Africa, but its efforts are equally inimical to native culture. When the Big Man nationalises the businesses of foreigners, he delivers them to his supporters, not to the people. TheoTime, to whom Salim's store is delivered, tells Salim: "The revolution ha[s] become [... a] little rotten. Our young people [are] becoming impatient [...]. We have to absolutely radicalize. We were expecting too much of the President. No one was willing to take responsibility. Now responsibility has been forced on the people" (256). But TheoTime, as an African, "would have liked to live out his role in fact—to take over the running of the shop, or to feel (while enjoying his storeroom life) that he was running the shop. He knew, though, that he knew nothing; and he was like a man enraged by his own helplessness. He made constant scenes. He was drunken, aggrieved and threatening, and as deliberately irrational as an official who had decided to be *malin*" (262). As for the revolution itself, the Liberation Army is "going to kill everybody who can read and write, everybody who ever put on a jacket and tie [...]. They are going to kill and kill. They say it is the only way, to go back to the beginning before it's too late" (275). As if to underscore the irony, "the rage of the rebels [against the Belgians] was like a rage against metal, machinery, wires, everything that was not of the forest and Africa" (86).

The answer to the issue of stability seems neither to lie with the natives nor the Europeans. Raymond, the president's Belgian advisor, the ideal European intellectual "Africanist" who had "made Africa his subject," but who has "less true knowledge of Africa, less feel for it, than Indar or Nazruddin, or even Mahesh" (181-82). Indar, Naipaul's Third World intellectual, who had studied in London and returned to teach in the New Domain, tells Salim: "We have to learn to trample on the past [...] the world is in movement, and the past can only cause pain" (141). Third World people, according to Indar, "have no means of understanding a fraction of the thought and science and philosophy and law that have gone to make that outside world [...]. It never occurs to us that we might make some contribution to it ourselves" (143).

Those who believe in the Africa of the "bush" and the "village," and might have made some "contribution," cannot save themselves, much less their country, from the chaos into which it descends. Neither Ferdinand, the posturing new African man, nor his mother Zabeth, with her primitive faith, nor Father Huismans—whose collection of native masks, symbolic of a once ordered and structured society, end up, after his murder, as part of a gallery of primitive art in the US—can thwart the cultural and political entropy that seems to be Africa's fate.

Sara Suleri argues that Naipaul's "highly sophisticated ironizing of imperial mythmaking" often obscures "the [...] brilliance of *A Bend in the River* [...] his most sustained revision of [...] *Heart of Darkness*." Else why, Suleri asks, "Given Naipaul's self-consciousness as a writer [...] he should deliberately choose the idiom of self-punishment; why need he so deeply implicate the writer in his construct of historic disarray?"[11]

It is precisely this "highly sophisticated ironizing" that also allows for the ideological elision in the dialectical interplay between political content and aesthetic quality of the work. For one thing, Naipaul does not make clear who the narrator is addressing, since at the outset, the novel posits an ideological dimension that is striking in its pessimistic view of newly independent colonies: as Salim says at the beginning, "The world is what it is; men who are nothing, who allow themselves to become nothing, have no place in it" (3).

For all his claims to objectivity, both Salim's sense of history and his knowledge of the world are rooted in the text rather than in culture, and are Eurocentric rather than African. In a revealing moment, he confesses that he finds Father Huismans' Africa "of bush and river [...] different from mine. His Africa was a wonderful place, full of new things" (62) but then, Father Huismans "had his own idea of Europe, his own idea of his civilization" (63), an ambivalence that reflects Salim's own. Furthermore, the incongruity of Salim's astute observations of people, events, and the history of Africa and his lack of formal education (like Indar), raises legitimate questions regarding his narrative authenticity, since he had left school after "sixteen" and read only encyclopaedias and science magazines. As a sophisticated commentator on political issues, as a parser of Raymond's writings, as a nuanced historian of culture and society, Salim occupies a narrative niche that is neither that of an ironist/satirist nor that of a chronicler. Indeed, his ideological framework seems to impinge on his ironic stance. In response to a question from Ferdinand, Salim says:

> [I]n my wish not to give him political satisfaction, I had indeed said what I intended to say [...]. When we wanted to speak politically, when we wanted to abuse or praise politically, we said 'Americans,' 'the Europeans,' 'the white people,' 'the Belgians' [...]. The 'they' we spoke of in this way were very far away, so far away as to be hardly white. They were impartial, up in the clouds, like good gods. We waited for their blessings, and showed off those blessings [...] as though we had been responsible for them. (44-45)

This may be the ironist at work, or the chronicler of Africa's past, but in whatever case the inescapable fact remains that Salim's frame of reference, for all his avowed objectivity, implicitly acknowledges the difficulty for the non-Westerner of writing an "objective" history of his culture and society. Naipaul's "first person narrator," as one critic points out, "operates through a filter of disingenuousness and naiveté so embedded in his discourse that his overview of the events of his 'African' life is always couched in the discoveries of his ignorance."[12]

For Salim—who at the beginning of the novel declares that he has no culture, identity, family, flag, or religion—the failure or absolute destruction of culture in Africa, and by extension, the Third World, is less the product of the colonial system than it is of cultural nationalism, which tries to bring the past of the people to the present. The conclusion he comes to is that Africa is not only exiled from its past and tradition, but also from the future, since neither the nationalism of the Big Man nor the traditionalism envisioned by the Liberation Army has succeeded.[13] For Salim, a return to civilisation is impossible, and the "bush" remains the "abhorred condition of humanity—disorderly, overgrown, and untended, unpruned by the careful shears of civilization. It is above all a state of mind […] a mind whose history has been sheared away."[14] Salim's decision in the end, to "rejoin the world, to break out of the narrow geography of the town, to do [his] duty to those who depend on [him]," must be weighed against his action: "Naipaul's narrator tells his story with the self-consciousness of a Marlow, but finally exits like a latter-day Kurtz, to take refuge in a union with his 'Intended,' the daughter of Nazruddin, who lives, of course, on Gloucester Road in London."[15]

At the end of *Heart of Darkness*, Conrad, however complicit in his discourse,[16] describes Marlow sitting Buddha-like, away and apart from his immediate audience, signalling his discernment of the "truth" of his African experience. Whereas Marlow's storytelling relies on his audience's acuity in recognising, and validating, his claims regarding the European view of Africa and his particular concern for savage regression—potentially in himself and effectually in Kurtz—in *A Bend in the River*, however, Salim is too complicit in his own narrative and too Eurocentric in his history, to make his objective stance believable or his history authentic. What is implied instead is that efforts at coming to terms with revising and renarrating the past are doomed to failure, since neither the colonial past nor the postcolonial future offers any hope. Naipaul cannot but conceive of a postcolonial condition, and its representation in text, as anything but "permanently disabling, because of the disorder and inauthenticity imposed by the center on the margins of empire."[17] As Irving Howe insightfully observes:

> Naipaul offers no intimations of hope or signals of perspective. It may be that the reality he grapples with allows him nothing but grimness of voice [...]. A novelist has to be faithful to what he sees, and few see as well as Naipaul; yet one may wonder whether, in some final reckoning, a serious writer can simply allow the wretchedness of his depicted scene to become the limit of his vision.[18]

A Bend in the River, for all of Naipaul's brilliance, cannot hide his bleak vision. Perhaps Indar's expression of frustration to Salim may serve as both prologue and epilogue to the novel: "My rage wasn't only with the Africans. It was also with our community and our civilization, which gave us energy but in every other way left us at the mercy of others. How do you rage against a thing like that?" (142).

Notes and References

1. A. Sivanandan, "The Enigma of the Colonised," *Race and Class* 32.1 (1990): 33.
2. Edward Said, "Intellectuals in the Post-Colonial World," *Salmagundi* 70/71 (Spring/Summer 1991): 44-64 (53).
3. Hasan Suroor, "Naipaul's rants of self-promotion," *The Hindu* 2 Sept. 2001: 2.
4. Sara Suleri, *The Rhetoric of English India* (Chicago: U of Chicago P, 1992) 154-55.
5. Dennis Walder, "V.S. Naipaul and the Postcolonial Order," *Recasting the World: Writing after Colonialism*, ed. Jonathan White (Baltimore: Johns Hopkins UP, 1993) 82-119, 83.
6. In Derek Walcott, *Collected Poems, 1948-84* (New York: Farrar, Straus & Giroux, 1986).
7. Michael Gorra, *After Empire: Scott, Naipaul, Rushdie*. Chicago: U of Chicago P, 1997) 101.
8. For a discussion of Salih's reinscription of *Heart of Darkness*, see my article, "Reinscribing Conrad: Tayeb Salih's *Season of Migration to the North*," *International Fiction Review* 23 (1996): 7-15.
9. Frantz Fanon, *Black Skin, White Masks*, trans. Charles Lam Markmann (New York: Grove Press, 1967) 18.
10. V.S. Naipaul, *A Bend in the River* (New York: Knopf, 1979) 15-20. Hereafter, references to Naipaul's novel are parenthetically cited in the text.
11. Suleri 157.
12. Fawzia Mustafa, *V.S. Naipaul* (Cambridge: Cambridge UP, 1995) 143.
13. John Rothfork, "V.S. Naipaul and the Third World," *Research Studies* 49 (1981): 183-92 (191).
14. Gorra 99.
15. Mustafa 152.
16. I refer to the by now well-known attack on Conrad's *Heart of Darkness* by Chinua Achebe in "An Image of Africa," *Research in American Literatures* 9 (Spring 1978): 2.
17. Bill Ashcroft, Gareth Griffiths, Helen Tiffin, *The Empire Writes Back: Theory and Practice in Post-Colonial Literatures* (London: Routledge, 1989) 88.
18. "A Dark Vision," 13 May 1979. <www.nytimes.com/books/98/06/07/specials/naipaul-river.html>.

□

A Critique of Anita Desai's *In Custody*

Sadhana Agrawal

Anita Desai's novel *In Custody* (1984) marks a turning point in her career. Here for the first time Desai's preoccupation of writing about sensitive women "in an insensitive world" takes a back seat, and male characters occupy the centre stage. *In Custody* shows a significant broadening of the horizon of her views and ideas. The present paper attempts to deal with a strange theme through a stranger point of view, a male consciousness, which has not yielded the tense psychological drama of vitality and vibrancy, one of the distinctive features of Desai's earlier novels. *In Custody* stands alone and apart from the rest of the Desai canon. The novel presents an ineffective and fruitless but well-meaning young man whose problems are not just personal and private but public and social. The cause chosen for analysis is the plight of vanishing Urdu poetry. True to its statement, the novel describes the issues of language and poetry and, for the first time in Anita Desai's work, with momentary problems. Desai is surely treading an unfamiliar area with unsteady footfalls.

No critique of *In Custody* will be utterly relevant unless it is considered against the hitherto preoccupied fictional path of a Desai steeped in subtle feminine psychology charged with profound passion and an all-absorbing warmth of a rare kind. The prime concern of Anita Desai has ever been to understand closely the predicament of their female characters. She represents the welcome "creative release of the feminine sensibility" (Rao 50) which began to emerge perceptibly on the literary horizon after the Second World War. She has contributed psychic novels which she narrates as "purely subjective." She rightly analyses her psychological feelings:

> It has been my personal luck that my temperament and circumstances have combined to give me shelter, privacy and solitude required for

> the writing of such novels, thereby avoiding problems a more objective writer has to deal with since he depends upon observation rather than a private vision. (Desai, "The Indian Writer's Problems," 9)

Her writings right from *Cry, the Peacock* (1963) to *Clear Light of Day* (1980) expose inner realities and psychic echoes of her characters, as her forte is the quest of sensibility. Her heroines from Maya to Tara prove this point. She is "interested in peculiar and eccentric characters rather than everyday, average ones" (Jain 10). She presents the plight of the introspective hypersensitive woman in her earlier novels. As N. Ramchandran Nair remarks: "*In Custody* is a poor exception. Deven's crisis in *In Custody* lacks in purpose and intensity. Neither his passion for the decadent Urdu poetry nor his concern for the ageing noble poet Nur is sufficient to provoke such agony and ecstasy in Deven. Certainly the word, deed, and world in *In Custody* is at variance and at a low ebb in comparison with the wonted Desai world of dense feminine psyche, ethos and tension" (Nair 78).

In all her novels before *In Custody*, Anita Desai takes a keen interest in delineating a feminine world. We affirm in them a psychological upheaval of immense breadth and intense depth, especially with a feminine psyche planted at the very centre, and they attain a great significance in this perspective. Shanta Krishnaswamy remarks: "Her novels constitute together the documentation, though fiction, of radical female resistance against a patriarchally defined concept of normality. She finds the links between female duality, myth and psychosis intriguing; each heroine is seen as searching for, finding and absorbing or annihilating the double who represent the socially impermissible aspects of her feminity" (Krishnaswamy 237). Further, "what she portrays is the deeply felt and suffered rebellion against the entire system of social relationships. There is a quest towards the concept 'real love'" (Krishnaswamy 238). Being a writer, Anita Desai herself asserts her aim in an interview with Yashodhara Dalmia:

> One's preoccupation can only be a perpetual search—for meaning, for value, for—dare I say it—truth. I think of the world as an iceberg —the one-tenth visible above the surface of the water is what we call reality; but the nine-tenths that are submerged make up the truth, and that is what one is trying to explore. Writing is an effort to discover and then to underline, and finally to convey the true significance of things. (*Times of India* 13)

She feels that her novels "deal with what Ortega y Gasset called the terror of facing, single-handed, the ferocious assault of existence" (*Times of India* 13).

A serious concern of Desai's in all her novels except *In Custody* aims at inescapable, recurrent feminine tragedy arising out of the extraordinary sensitivity of women and the inexplicable insensitivity of men in relation to the finer aspects of life. Maya and Gautam in *Cry, the Peacock*, Monisha and Jiban in *Voices in the City*, Sita and Raman in *Where Shall We Go This Summer*, Nanda Kaul and her Vice-Chancellor husband in *Fire on the Mountain*, and the striking, imaginative Bimla and her limpid inebriated suitor Dr Biswas in *Clear Light of Day*—their relationships evince the underlying unsuitability that breaks marriages in the changed social structure. As Jasbir Jain rightly points out, Desai's world of women is primarily "a world where the central harmony is aspired to but not arrived at, and the desire to love and live clashes—at times violently—with the desire to achieve harmony" (Jain 23). Desai's main concern for the life of the mind, especially of her feminine characters, "enables us to see the Indian woman adequately from the inside" (Krishnaswami 243). Nair argues: "Maya, Sita, Nanda Kaul, and Bimla are powerful representatives of the 'new woman,' liberating themselves from the clutches of man-made society. They invariably assert their 'self' though the drama is faithfully depicted chiefly in relation to the confines of the inward terrain. If a finer sensibility, sharper awareness, and keener vision of the world focusing on the frightening disparity between an imaginative woman and mundane women around her on the one hand and sensible women and convention-bound men on the other are vital elements of feminism, then Desai has succeeded in shaping women of a different sort in crisis with a will to prove their undeniable 'true existence' and legitimate liberation in a larger and deeper sense in almost all her works" (Nair 87).

Obviously, all Desai's earlier novels are characterised by a quality of introversion, for she has been interested in capturing the atmosphere of the mind and she writes about the inner world of thoughts and emotions of her characters rather than their external world. The general tone in all these novels is that of despair. The same tone of despair continues in *In Custody*. It is primarily about the functioning of the human psyche. Here, we find neither a sensitive and highly-strung woman protagonist nor any violent neurotic woman. Bringing out the change, Meenakshi Mukherjee states: "Change is towards a widening of human concerns and a willingness to integrate concrete historical and specific cultural dimensions in the creation of interior landscape (Mukherjee 5). Deven, the protagonist of the novel, around whom the story is woven, a Lecturer in Hindi in a private college, Lala Ram Lal College at Mirpore near New Delhi, is singularly different from Desai's former male characters. Earlier her male characters subserved her design of being mere anchors to the plumb-lines into the feminine. Deven had had no emotional battles to conquer or reckon with the imponderables of existence: "All through his childhood and youth he had known only one way to deal with life and that was to lie low and remain invisible" (Desai, *In Custody*, 20). In some way he resembles Prem, the Hindi lecturer in Ruth Prawer Jhabvala's *The Householder*. They are similar in their working conditions, in their lack of confidence and their inability shows how to arrange their private and public lives in order and dignity; however, they differ in their desires. While Prem's concerns are wholly cosmic, Deven's concerns are chiefly literary.

The novel reveals the story of the unsuspecting and worldly Deven Sharma, who is moved by an idea of creating the work of his life, but is unluckily frustrated by his own helplessness. As the novel opens, Murad, a school chum of Deven's and an editor of the Urdu magazine *Awaz* requests Deven to interview Nur Shahjehanbadi, a great Urdu poet, for a special number of his forthcoming issue, since Deven is interested in Urdu literature: "Deven's hand fluttered on his knee as he melted at the suggestion and felt a glow creep through him at the thought of writing something in the language which had been his first language. The glow was also caused by pride [...] at being asked to contribute a piece by the editor of what he took to be a leading Urdu journal" (16). We see a dramatic change in the novel. Deven and Murad know each other since their schooldays, and their basis of friendship is not natural because they differ in nature and status:

> [...] Murad had been the spoilt rich boy with money in his pocket for cinema shows and cigarettes and Deven the poor widow's son who could be bribed and brought to do anything for him [...]. (11)

The difference of status in their friendship is of symbolic significance. Having no fatherly boon, Deven belongs to a lower-middle-class family. Socio-economic factors colour his personality and mould his psyche. The rest of the story oscillates between Deven's success and failure, his enthusiasm and hesitation, until he finally lands in disaster. Different energies work to help and deter him, till in the end he stands at a crossroads, not knowing where to turn to. In the end he finds strength in his inner self and determines to face life as it comes to him.

The prime characteristics of Deven that attract our attention are his helplessness, humility, suffering and nobility. He is presented as a young man, psychologically tense and yearning to indulge in some literary endeavour. Unfortunately Desai has not given us sufficient material to witness Deven in the manner in which she expects us to view him. Having only a poor helpless mother, Deven naturally grows into a meek, uncertain person. He is not satiable with his life and just because of it he becomes a victim of unhappiness and inferiority complex. As a child, he had watched closely the bitter disappointment of his mother, and the apologetic smile of his father for his failure in measuring up to her expectations. Evidently these family and social factors generated in him a yielding and submissive tendency. Deven is one born to be teased. He finds neither respect nor consideration from his colleagues, students or neighbours. During his class period he does not look at his students but at the open door, and he has "for years been practising this trick of ignoring his class and speaking to himself, or someone outside, invisible" (12).

The strained relationship between Deven and his wife Sarla is suggestively presented. Sarla had been selected as a suitable match for him by his mother and aunt, because they had known her to be plain, penny-pinching and congenitally pessimistic. They little realized that Sarla had her own yearnings for "fan, phone and frigidaire" and "dreamt the magazine dream of marriage; herself, stepping out of a car with a plastic shopping bag full of groceries and filling them into the gleaming refrigerator, and then rushing to the telephone" to invite her friends and "her husband who was beaming at her from behind a flowered curtain" (68). Sarla had been as much disappointed in him as he had been in her. Like her he was a victim:

> Although each understood the secret truth about the other, it did not bring about any closeness of spirit, any comradeship, because they also sensed that two victims ought to avoid each other, not yoke together their joint disappointments. A victim does not look to help from another victim, he looks for a redeemer. At least Deven had his poetry, she had nothing, and so there was an added accusation and bitterness in her look. (68)

Apparently Deven's protest against her disappointment seems to be the outcome of his hurt male ego. He is over-aggressive in his behaviour at home, though outside it he is meek and humble. Deven feels so deserted by his fate that he censures himself for his insufficiency to make any excellence in life: "[...] all he could measure up to was this—this shabby house, its dirty corners, its wretchedness and lovelessness" (67). Unable to cope with his circumstances, he leaves Mirpore for Delhi in search of fame and freedom: "The world of drama and revolving lights and feasts and furies" (67) was his dream, something like Nur's world. In a world of fantasy he does not notice the fact that Delhi itself is a "Walled City" (187), hoping it would provide him with opportunities of fulfilling his desire. In this regard Kunj Bala Goel remarks: "While Mirpore represents reality, Delhi becomes symbolical of fantasy" (Goel 96).

Though Deven acts under his passion for Urdu poetry and a reputed Urdu poet, Nur, Desai has not clarified the situation that makes him forgetful of the presence of his wife Sarla, and little son at home; almost in a world strange, unfamiliar and overawing setup. Deven is so captivated by the personality of the poet Nur that he is unable to come out of his shadow: "The fidelity and power with which Desai projected the dense mind of Maya, Sita, Nanda Kaul, Raka, or Bimla is not visible in the conception or execution of Deven and other characters in *In Custody*. Lake of intimacy and mastery over the material chosen for treatment cannot escape the attention of even a casual reader" (Nair 88). Deven, who has been leading an ordinary worldly life, is unexpectedly pushed out of this ordinariness, inspired by Nur's lines such as "Life is no more than a funeral procession winding towards the grave,/ Its small joys the flowers of funeral wreaths" (26), and is given the chance of a lifetime by being asked to interview Nur.

When Deven arrives at Nur's house, he finds there a mundane, not a divine atmosphere. The world in front of him is one of crowded homes, of greedy poets, of the backlanes and brothel houses in Chandni Chowk. We are made to see everything through the eyes of Deven, who is quite sentimental in his response to Urdu poetry and the poet, Nur. There is Nur the poet and Nur the senile, greedy, lustful man. The technique employed in this novel is primarily to tell the narrative, not to show. As Deven comes to know Nur, he is divided between the two Nurs, attracted by one and repelled by the other. In spite of all humiliation, Deven reaches the poet in all devotion:

> In the midst of all the shadows, the poet's figure was in startling contrast, being entirely dressed in white. His white beard was splayed across his chest and his long white fingers clasped across it. He did not move and appeared to be a marble form. His body had the density, the compactness of stone. It was large and heavy not on account of obesity or weight, but on account of age and experience. The emptying out and wasting of age had not yet begun its process. He was still at a moment of completion, quite whole. (40-41)

Overtly his image of Nur is hallowed by a dignity and glory which in actuality the poet lacks: "He had pictured him living either surrounded by elderly sages and dignified litterateurs or else entirely alone in divine isolation" (51). Contrary to this, he meets a senile and enfeebled old man presiding over a court of clowns and debauchees. Further, the real position of Nur excites pity and laughter alike. Here Desai intends to reveal the gap between the expected and the actual. In this sense her earlier novels like *Fire on the Mountain* and *Clear Light of Day* are artistically woven together, but *In Custody* lacks this: "Difference in theme, treatment or technique need not necessarily mean decadence. But with regard to *In Custody*, one is forced to echo such a critical credo" (Nair 89).

When Deven comes to see Nur, the poet asks his purpose. Deven tells the Urdu poet about the intention of his visit, that is to interview him for an Urdu magazine. At this Nur starts interrogating him, and criticising him for teaching Hindi in college. The poet foolishly argues that Hindi is being given top priority only to uproot the Urdu language, and that Deven is a party to this. At this Deven tells him that the reality of life is quite different from the dream of it. Although he loves Urdu poetry, he cannot earn a living from teaching it. After listening to such arguments from Deven, Nur gets very angry. The language controversy and the conflict between Urdu and Hindi are major themes in the novel.

To Deven, Nur is a significant poet not because he makes things immediate but because he removes them to a position where they become bearable: "That was what Nur's verse did—placed frightening and inexplicable experiences like time and death at a point where they could be seen and studied, in safety" (54). While Deven's aesthetic sensibility moves in the right direction, his confidence in translating it into a written document slowly dwindles, for Nur's health, the riff-raff that gathers round him every evening, and the incessant friction between his wives are the insurmountable obstacles any admirer of his has to face. He often sees himself struggling to reach some destination.

Deven's difficulty arises because he has no self-confidence, and he needs a prop to goad him and to support him. Luckily a liberal grant from the college authorities arrives for him. Deven arranges to record Nur's views on poetry and a few poems which he may recite from memory. But the whole thing fails to ignite because the tape-recorder does not work properly and the assistant sent by Murad does not know how to operate the recorder. Deven's quest ends up in contretemps. He feels betrayed:

> He could lead the rest of his life in this near unconscious state. He hoped his former life of non-events, non-happenings, would be resumed, empty and hopeless, safe and endurable. That was the only life he was made for, although life was not perhaps the right turn. He needed one that was more grey, more neutral, more shadowy. He shifted through alternatives like torn pieces of grey paper, letting them fall to the floor of his mind with a whisper and bury him in sleep. (183-84)

What he does not realize is that everyone is out to take advantage of him. Throughout the narrative Deven feels like a trapped animal emerging from a cultural matrix and a social milieu. The following passage very well illustrates the truth:

> Turning his mind decisively away from these dangerous shoals, he paced up and down in his bare feet, his pyjamas and the vest full of holes, scratching at mosquito bites, smoking an occasional cigarette, refusing to entertain poetry and thinking in strict prose that he must look like a caged animal in a zoo to any creature that might be looking down at earth from another planet. And that was all he was—a trapped animal. In his youth, he had had the illusion of having free will, not knowing he was in a trap. Marriage, a family and a job had placed him in this cage, now there was no way out of it. The unexpected friendship with Nur had given him the illusion that the door of the trap had opened and he could escape after all into a wider world that lay outside but a closer familiarity with the poet had shown him that what he thought of as "the wider world" was an illusion too—it was only a kind of zoo in which he could hope to find freedom, he would only blunder into another cage inhabited by some other trapped animal. Being an illustrious poet had drawn people to the zoo to come and stare at him but Nur had not escaped from his cage for all that—he was as trapped as Deven was even if his cage was more prominent

and attracted some attention. Still, it was just a cage in a row of cages. Cage, Cage. Trap, trap. (131)

This passage brings to a central focus the private and the public themes, with its recurring emphasis on "trap" and "cage." Marriage, family and even his friendship with Nur, appear like a cage in the public world of Urdu poetry and intellectual fame. Even after the failure of the entire project Deven is under social pressure. His students who help him to restore a semblance of coherence in the tapes demand first division marks. Nur writes to him asking for a medical allowance and an endowment for his child from the college authorities. Murad wants him to complete his article on Nur. Here we see two implications of the title. The first, as justified by the text, is that Deven is the true disciple of Nur and he would take "Nur's poetry into safe custody, and not realized that if he was to be custodian of Nur's genius, then Nur would become his custodian and place him in custodian too. This alliance could be considered an unendurable burden—or else a shining honour. Both demanded an equal strength" (203). However, the other implication of the title is one complication after the other, in which Deven himself suffers.

The central vision of the title is that in taking somebody into custody, one has also to surrender oneself to the other's custody. Both the novel's epigraph (from Wordsworth):

[...] they should take, who have the power
And they should keep who can

and its conclusion suggest the need to recognise that every true kinship is essentially a two-way commitment, an act of continued responsibility for the other. This way, it is between true friends, between husband and wife, between artist and art, between art and critic, between a person and his country, city, monuments. Deven rejuvenates his vision with the recognition that his friendship with Nur is not a trap but liberation. He has received "the gift of Nur's poetry and that meant he was custodian of Nur's very soul and spirit. It was a great distinction. He could not deny or abandon that under any pressure" (204). In the first instance, it is Deven who deserts the poet, while in the second, it is the poet, Nur who deserts Deven. In the last chapter of the novel, the resolution occurs—when it dawns upon Deven that having taken something from each other, neither could desert the other. In giving him custody of his work, Nur had earned the right to become Deven's custodian. Hence Nur could make demands on Deven—not only during his lifetime but also after his death, for his widows and his sons—and Deven would have to fulfil those demands of Nur's. Deven's agony and ecstasy are well exposed here: "He had hoped to stretch the night endlessly by walking on and on. Day would bring with it the board meeting, an enquiry, an interrogation exposure and blame" (202).

After sleepless nights he finally reaches the stage where he can see the perfection of art and imperfection of human nature. It is the fact that art is not separable from life. To him, reality and illusion all stand clearly illuminated. It suggests the two different attitudes towards art. For Nur's wife Imtiaz Begum, art is a means of earning money and livelihood, whereas to Nur and Deven art means total, selfless dedication. Usha Bande remarks: "he comprehends the secret of the transtemporal nature of art and literature [...]. An aesthetic experience enables a perceiver to reach beyond the conditions of his existence" (Bande 161). With this regard Jasbir Jain also remarks: "art could be responded to, understood, absorbed, identified with, but mystery it would still remain" (Jain 111).

When Deven's attempt to tape Nur's poem and voice fails, the support given to him is withdrawn and everyone abandons the project. As Viney Kirpal points out, "this realization is indicative of his growth as a human being" (Kirpal 127). Deven realizes that he has to find his own strength and not depend on others: "Oddly enough, the certainty he could expect no more help from Murad had a calming effect upon him. Perhaps when everyone had cut him off and he was absolutely alone, he would begin to find himself and his own strength" (189-90). Deven is able to find his own possibilities of standing by himself. His power is within, not without. His self-analysis at the final moment of danger is not unexpected, nor is it impossible, although it appears sudden: "Deven suffers from what Maslow terms 'Jonah Complex' meaning a tendency to run away from one's best talent [...] or mission in life [...]. Art is an instrument of liberation; it cannot be expected to offer solutions to problems as science can. Deven's quest ends in value discovery. Understanding of our failure enables us to see glory in all" (Bande 161).

Deven is presented as a timid and ineffectual but growth-oriented person who shows boldness and clarity of vision. Though throughout the novel he is presented as a weak figure, tossed by self-effacing drives, all his weakness is submerged at the crucial moment of self-scrutiny. His awakening typifies coherence and completeness. He really achieves some sort of firmness and independence through his physical and mental travails. He incorporates a more dynamic and integrated approach. Desai's characters are deeply sensitive to the grandeur as well as the sordidness of life. Desai is an artist, so she sees the sorriness underlying the grandest things and the grandeur underlying the sorriest things. Her preoccupation is how one gets along, not with others but with oneself. At first, Deven is trapped in his self-created mess, but finally he reaches a wholeness of self despite his challenging experience. He achieves spontaneity when he marches away from a self-created trap to the joyous affirmation of life after taking the solemn decision to be the custodian of Nur's poetry:

> He turned back. He walked up the path. Soon the sun would be up and blazing. The day would begin, with its calamities. They would flash out of the sky and cut him down like swords. He would run to meet them. He ran, stopping only to pull a branch of thorns from under his foot. (204)

This indicates Deven's preparation to annihilate all the troubles and problems which may be in the way of obtaining Nur's poems.

Thus, *In Custody* demonstrates the range of Anita Desai's superb gift. Desai's art becomes more and more mature, as can be seen in the clear, unambiguous images of this novel, which are precise in their visual quality without any trace of "excessive celebration" (Iyengar 465). It is more individual, less generalised and conventional than her earlier fiction. It is to be noted that in *Cry, the Peacock, Voices in the City, Where Shall We Go This Summer?, Clear Light of Day* and *Fire on the Mountain* the male characters are insignificant and serve only the peripheral needs of the story. Anita Desai has explored only the inner world of the feminine where the men are in the dock. If she has expressively come to occupy herself with the masculine, she has unmistakably isolated the feminine. *In Custody* frustrates because of this tilting of the measures. Artistically the work is a great achievement.

Works Cited

Bande, Usha. *The Novels of Anita Desai.* New Delhi: Prestige Books, 1988.

Dalmia, Yashodhara. "An Interview with Anita Desai." *The Times of India* 29 Aug. 1979: 13.

Desai, Anita. *In Custody*. London: Heinemann, 1984.

——. "The Indian Writer's Problems." *Indian Women Novelists*. Set 1. Vol. 2. Ed. R.K. Dhawan. New Delhi: Prestige Books, 1991.

Goel, Kunj Bala. *Language and Theme in Anita Desai's Fiction*. Jaipur: Classic Publishing House, 1989.

Iyengar, K.R.S. *Indian Writing in English*. 1962. New Delhi: Sterling Publishers, 1988.

Jain, Jasbir. "Anita Desai." *Indian English Novelists: Anthology of Critical Essays*. Ed. Madhusudan Prasad. New Delhi: Sterling, 1982.

——. *Stairs to the Attic: The Novels of Anita Desai*. Jaipur: Printwell, 1987.

Kirpal, Viney. "An Image of India—A Study of Anita Desai's *In Custody*." *Ariel* 19.4 (Oct. 1986): 127-38.

Krishnaswami, Shanta. "Anita Desai: The Sexist Nature of Sanity." *The Women in Indian Fiction in English*. New Delhi: Asia, 1984.

Mukherjee, Meenakshi. "A Broader View: A Review of *In Custody*." *Express Magazine* 7 Oct. 1984: 5.

Nair, N. Ramchandran. "In Custody: The Road Not Taken." *Indian Women Novelists*. Set 1. Vol. 4. Ed. R.K. Dhawan. New Delhi: Prestige Books, 1991.

Rao, A.V. Krishna. *The Indo-Anglian Novel and the Changing Tradition*. Mysore, 1972.

□

"Women's Voices" in Selected Short Stories of Shashi Deshpande

Murali Manohar

Indian women writers in English have been expressing their voices through the media of their writings, be they in short stories, novels and poems. It is easier for them to represent their views through the characters they create in the short stories. However, they do not always necessarily represent their views through the characters: sometimes it may happen that they cannot control the characters as they write.

Among the Indian women writers in English who are writing short stories, we may name Anita Desai, Shashi Deshpande and Anjana Appachana. In this paper I would like to argue, on the basis of a close reading, how women in Shashi Deshpande's short stories give importance to their voices without expressing any concern for the society, while raising their voices as their minds direct them.

After reading some of Deshpande's short stories, I find that women want to raise questions regarding: marriage without the wife's consent and the husband trying to have a complete right over her body; the wife not being prepared for sex as soon as the marriage takes place (in the story "The Intrusion"); whether to deliver a child should be with the consent of the woman (in "Death of a Child"); whether the decision to work at home or outside should be hers rather than her husband's, in-law's, friends' or society's (in "A Wall is Safer"); the issue of second marriage (in "The Cruelty Game"); and the issue of divorce and guilt (in "And Then [...]?").

The narrator of "The Intrusion" has been recently married against her will but complying with her parents' appeal. On her honeymoon, she recollects how her marriage has been fixed:

> "We are looking for a girl, simple but sophisticated," his mother had said. "My son is working in a foreign company. His wife must be able to entertain and mix with foreigners." She had made the word foreigners sound like 'martians.' Simple and sophisticated—was I that, I wondered? It had seemed I was, for my mother had joyfully told me that they had agreed to our proposal. No one had asked me if I had agreed; it had been taken for granted. I had taken it for granted myself, when suddenly, a few days before wedding, I had gone to my father, stricken my doubts. "Why?" he had asked me again, again and again. And, "What will you do then?" In a panic I had asked myself, but none to the question "What's wrong with him?" I had nothing to say, either, when my father said quietly, "I have two more daughters to be married."[1]

In the above passage it is clear that the boy's side's concerns are more important than the girl's side. They have already started "looking for a girl" who should be "simple but sophisticated." The bridegroom's job is highlighted as "working in a foreign company." The future "wife" should therefore be "able to entertain," as though girls were meant only for "entertaining," and "mix" with her husband's colleagues. The parents of the narrator have immediately "agreed" to the proposal without asking any opinion of her. Thus, the narrator says: "No one had asked me if I had agreed" and moreover "it has been taken for granted" that she will have no reason to refuse to marry the foreign company's employee. She too "had taken for granted" the marriage proposal. However, "a few days before the wedding" she goes to her "father" to clarify certain doubts about her marriage. The narrator has expressed, through her gestures, "doubts" about her marriage with the man. Thus her father anxiously asks her "What will you do then?" She herself does not have any answer to her father's question "what is wrong with him?" in marrying him. Moreover, her father reminds the narrator that she has "two" other sisters who "have to be married" after her marriage. Of course it is the problem of her father. Perhaps the narrator is unhappy about no-one asking her opinion and taking her consent. Otherwise she has no problem in marrying that man. However, her unhappiness continues in her honeymoon: she gives trouble to her husband, and raises her silenced voice when her husband wants to celebrate his honeymoon:

> His embrace was too sudden, too rough, and I wanted to scream, to cry out. But somehow I knew that this was just between the two of

us. I turned my face away from him, trying to escape, so that the kiss he intended for my lips landed in the air. He let me go abruptly. There was a foolish, angry look on his face. His glasses had fallen down in the struggle. Mutely I picked them up and gave them to him. He was silent while he wiped them and put them to him. He was silent while he wiped them and put them on. When he finally spoke, his voice was shrill, almost with a note of hysteria in it. "What's this? Why are you behaving like this?"

"Like what?" I tried to keep my own tone level, innocent. "Avoiding me. Don't think I haven't noticed it. Ever since we came here you've [...] been [...] avoiding me," he ended lamely.

"No I have not, I'm not [...]." It was the reflex denial of a child. "Do you think I enjoy feeling that I'm forcing myself on you? What's the problem? Why are you acting so strange?" [...]. I stood silent. Angry, hurt, crestfallen, he waited for my answer. "We [...] we scarcely know each other," I stammered at last. He seemed flabbergasted. "Know each other? What has that to do with it? Aren't we married now? And how will we start getting to know each other if you put on such a touch me—nottish air?" (39-40)

In the above passage the narrator is raising her voice indirectly, through her physical gestures initially, and later on verbally. Her contention is that she has married him, no doubt, but wants some time for them to "know each other." She feels uncomfortable suddenly at her husband trying to embrace his wife as though he has got every right over her body as he has legally and traditionally married her. The first gesture of her voice is through her turning "away" her "face from him"; the second, when he wants to kiss her. At the same time she too is not clear what she wants to do on her honeymoon. The husband gets "angry" and questions her "behaviour" in trying to "avoid" him. She has to be thankful for taking her out of their place in order to have privacy and celebrate their newly married life. At the same time she needs to express her opinion on her relationship with her husband. Her problem is that she wants to become close to her husband by "knowing each other." Thus she says: "We scarcely know each other," whereas her husband thinks since they are "married" they can go ahead with sex. She wants to take some more time to feel free with her husband. What I feel here is that she should have made it clear what is there in her mind, and how she wants to proceed in their honeymoon. However, it is very rare that wives ask for time from their husbands. In a way the narrator is breaking the stereotyped and traditional image of woman in this story.

In the story "Death of a Child," the woman has become pregnant for the third time. The husband does not have any problem in his wife becoming pregnant. Every time the man makes his wife pregnant he is proud of his manliness, especially so with her first-time pregnancy. However, the question here is whether the woman/wife is willing to continue to conceive and deliver the child or not? In this story it is she who is raising her "voice" to wash away her stomach, as in this conversation:

> He sees my face and goes on. "Don't get into a state. It's not as bad as all that."
> "Not so bad!" I echo his words despairingly. Not so bad? Hysteria rises in my throat at the thought of going through it all again.
> "I don't want it, I can't," I burst out. Now that I've said the words, I'm calmer.
> "But he seems amazed." "Why?" he asks [...].
> "But if it has happened," he says at last, "why not accept it?" [...].
> "No, I say sharply. I can't. I won't. Life is complicated enough [...]." (44)

The husband has no problem and tries to argue in favour of continuing to have the third child. He says: "it's not as bad as all that." As I have said earlier the husband's manliness boosts him. He will never say no to it. Thus, the husband is keen on having the third child. However, the woman is not willing to keep the third child. One reason could be that the difference between the second child and the third pregnancy is one year and a half. But this possibility is ruled out, as the woman does not want to go through it: she feels "hysteria rises in my throat at the thought of going through" the pregnancy and delivering the child "all again." Thus she raises her voice very strongly and expresses: "I don't want it, I can't." The first part of the sentence suggests that she does not want to deliver the child; the second part, that she is not capable of bearing a child for the third time. It is only the woman can say whether she can retain the third pregnancy for nine months and deliver the child, going through all that hell and coming out of it. However, the husband is still trying to convince his wife by saying that "if it has happened," "why not accept it" as though it is he who is going to undergo the pain of bearing the child. Nevertheless, we may stress the woman's firm "voice" to her husband:

"No [...] I can't, I won't. Life is complicated enough [...]." When the woman says life is complicated, she is leaving it ambiguous. One can interpret her view here as that she is questioning carrying the child for nine months, undergoing the pain of delivery, the number of children increasing in her family, running the house with three children when the government is stipulating one or two children per family in order to curtail the population explosion, to mention only a few factors.

As soon as the narrator has decided to terminate her pregnancy, she goes to a woman doctor and meets her. We may note coolly the narrator says:

> "You are pregnant," she tells me baldly.
> "I know," I say, feeling a little quickening in my pulse and heart. The words arouse something in me "I don't want it," I quickly blurt it out [...].
> "Think it over" [...].
> "What about your husband?" she asks, as if reading my thoughts. I shrug carelessly, as if there is no doubt about the matter at all [...].
> "You're lucky," I hear the doctor saying. "It's quite straightforward. You've come early. And now the law is in your side." (46-47)

The doctor declares the narrator pregnant. Earlier it was not confirmed for the narrator but she was sure of her pregnancy. However, it is now certified by the doctor. We may note the confidence of the narrator saying "I know." She raises her voice even with the doctor that she does want to continue: "I don't want it, I blurt it out." Perhaps the doctor was puzzled to see such an expectant mother having come prepared to terminate the pregnancy. However, it is the duty of a doctor to explain matters to the patient. Therefore, the doctor says: "Think it over." The next question the doctor asks is whether her husband is willing to terminate the pregnancy. After the doctor is assured that her husband has no problem, she tests the stage of pregnancy and declares that the woman is "lucky" that she has come at a very "early" stage and it is very easy to terminate her pregnancy. The termination is going to be "straightforward" and there will not be any complications. Moreover, it is not against the "law" as the pregnancy stage is very "early": legally, she is not committing any crime.

In a way what the narrator is doing is also not a mistake. She is following the small family norm, and no one can find fault with her as the pregnancy is not advanced. In fact one has to appreciate her act but it would not have been possible had she been not strong in her opinion with her husband.

In the story "A Wall is Safer," Hema is professionally a lawyer but wants to lead her life as a housewife. Her husband Vasant is working in an Agricultural Research Station, but has been advised to take up an alternative job in Bombay. He has decided to go for it whereas Hema is not willing to go with him and work as a schoolteacher. Sushma is a friend of Vasant and Hema, coming over "to stay for an evening and a night" (116). Perhaps Hema does not want to take up any job. Her husband as jobholder has to be away from his family. Sushma and Vasant try to convince her to take up some job. But she is not willing to do. The argument goes on:

> Now, after listening to Sushma, Vasant suddenly turns to me and says, "Look Hema, why don't you get involved with this thing of Sushma's? You can go once a week, maybe [...]."
> You don't have to feel guilty, I want to say to Vasant. It's my doing, this coming here. Nobody pushed me into it.
> "Sorry Vasant, it won't work," Sushma says.
> "Why not?"
> "Ask Hema" [...].
> "Oh, I'm all right as I am. After all, I'm good housewife now." (119)

Hema is very firm in her decision that she does not want to take up any kind of job, including work like Sushma's. Sushma is a social worker. She works for the women to make them aware of their legal rights. In fact Hema is a lawyer and she knows the legal rights. Social worker is different from a lawyer. However, Hema defends her being the homemaker. She expresses her "voice" to her husband and to her friend Sushma. It is her own decision and she does not need to be advised. Hema says that she is "all right" as she is. Moreover, she defends herself as having "been a good housewife."

Sushma has been wondering about Hema's decision. She could not resist asking her friend Hema thus:

> At night, after the children and Vasant have gone to bed, Sushma puts me through a cross-examination. Am I happy here? What do I do with myself?
> Can I go on this way?

> "I'm busy," I tell her. "I have enough to do. I cook, I clean, I wash, I iron, I read, I listen to music, help kids with their lessons, I visit [...]." (120)

It is strange in a world where women are trying to get away from being the homemaker: here is someone with a very strong opinion about being a homemaker and being happy. Moreover, she has a legal career but does not want to practise law. She rather prefers to be a housewife. Sushma wants to know whether Hema is "happy" like that. How is she going to spend all the day at home? Can Hema go on with this kind of life? Hema answers that she is "busy." She has "enough to do": she "cooks" food, "cleans" the house, "washes" all the family members' clothes, "irons" the same clothes, "reads" books, "listens to music" and helps her kids with their "lessons." In other words she seems to be concentrating on her "kids" studies and wants to give full care to her children. Perhaps she has the feeling that a job can be done at any time but looking after the children seems to be the priority for her.

The fourth woman, Pramila, is raising her voice in the story "The Cruelty Game," in which she aspires to a second marriage after the death of her first husband, Kumar. Pramila has a daughter named Sharu. She is intending to marry for the second time and to take as husband none other than her late husband's friend, Jagdish. Kumar's parents are a traditional family: his mother and father are represented as Grandmother and Grandfather. When Pramila is celebrating her daughter Sharu's birthday, the mother-in-law observes her daughter-in-law applying kumkum to her forehead. She immediately reacts thus:

> And then Grandmother came in [...].
> "My son—you killed him—enjoying yourself [...]."
> It was only when I followed Grandmother's pointing finger that I realized she was referring to Pramila Auntie's kumkum, a small dot, as small as the one my mother started off with every morning, sitting at the mirror, her fingers moving round and round, until the small dot became a perfect large circle. (128)

Grandmother blames Pramila for the death of Kumar. It is not clear how Kumar died in the story. The traditional women feel that it is the result of the daughter-in-law's entry into the family that the son dies in an unfortunate way. Here in the same way "Grandmother" is blaming Pramila and alleging that she is applying "kumkum" on her forehead as a widow. The act of applying kumkum and celebrating the birthday of her daughter itself suggests that she is a rebel and does things as she pleases. Furthermore, she has decided to marry her late husband's friend.

Sharu, the daughter of Pramila, comes to know her mother's plan of getting married again. Sharu's friends inform her about her mother's plan. She has also been told that nobody is going to talk to her mother if she marries again. The effect of second marriage is greatest on the children of the first marriage. Here it is the case of Sharu. It is revealed in the following passage:

> "Sharu's mother is getting married."
> Sharu reacted as if she had been slapped. "My mother! Getting married! But she's married. To my father."
> "Ha! She's getting married again and going away and nobody from this house is going to talk to her again, nobody is even going to see her face, no, not even yours if you go away with her [...]."
> "It's not true, it's not true." Sharu's face was an ugly, blotchy red.
> "Of course it's true. Everyone knows."
> "You're a liar [...]."
> "Come on, let's get away from here. Don't talk to her, anyone." (129)

We may observe the reaction of Sharu and her relatives. Moreover, Sharu has felt as though some one has "slapped" her. She still thinks that her mother is "married" to her father. Then her cousins inform her that her mother is "going to marry again and going away from the house." In addition to that, if the marriage takes place, "nobody" is "going to" talk with her again. Nobody is "even going to see her" mother's "face." Furthermore, Sharu too will have to face the same punishment as her mother. We may note the "face" of Sharu in the above description: "ugly" and "blotchy red." All of Sharu's cousins "get away from" her after giving a warning to her. Unfortunately Pramila does not inform Sharu that she is going to marry Jagdish's uncle. Sharu is getting all the information through her cousins but not from her mother. Also to be noted is how Sharu comes to know about their journey:

> "We're going to Bombay today. By the night train. And Grandfather has given me a present. And we're going first class [...]."
> "First class?" That was Gopal. "Who gave you the money? Your new father?"
> "New father?"
> "Hasn't any one told you? Everybody knows your mother is marrying Kumar Uncle's friend Jagdish." (130)

Sharu innocently declares that she is leaving for "Bombay by the night train." She also informs Gopal that her grandfather has given her a "present." She proudly declares that she is going in a "first class" compartment. The immediate question she fails to answer is that her "new father" has paid for the first class fare, not her mother or Grandfather. Gopal also informs her that her "mother" is getting married to Jagdish, who had been her father's friend.

Above all what Pramila is trying to prove is that she is not going to be a widow throughout her life. She has a lot of her life to live. She does not directly say so in the story, but the implication is that she is not going to be ruined by this traditional notion of widowhood. She does believe in widow remarriage. Thus she is raising her "voice" very loudly against the Indian traditional notion of widowhood.

The last woman in the stories considered, is Shaku in the story "And Then [...]?" Shaku has no regrets in leaving/divorcing her husband, who has been working in Kanpur whereas she lives in Bangalore. The narrator recognises Shaku thus:

> "You're Shaku."
> "That's right. I've put on so much weight, I was sure you wouldn't recognize me." The face breaks into a smile. "Just last week I visited your house in Bangalore, but it was locked."
> "What were you doing in Bangalore? I thought your husband lived in Kanpur?"
> "Still does. I've left him."
> I don't know what to say. After a moment I falter out an "I'm sorry."
> "I'm not. Not sorry I left him, I mean. I'm sorry I married him, though. He was, still is, I guess, a skunk. A mean skunk. Just my tough luck to have married him. Oh well," she sighs and shrugs. "And to think that I believed in the fairy-tale nonsense of 'and they lived happily ever after.'" (153-54)

Shaku introduces herself when the narrator does not recognize immediately. Then she speaks of her recent attempt to visit her in Bangalore. The narrator asks Shaku what she has been doing in Bangalore. The narrator remembers her husband living in Kanpur. Shaku tells her that her "husband" is still in Kanpur but she has "left" her "husband." The narrator does not know how to react to her taking divorce so easily. She says she is "sorry." However, Shaku tells the narrator that she does not feel "sorry" for leaving her husband. She regrets having married that "mean skunk." She considers her marriage as "tough luck." She even believed in the fairy-tale once the marriage is over everything will be all right, but in her case it proved to be wrong "that they lived happily ever after." Shaku does not hesitate in raising her voice and leaving her husband if he behaves like a "skunk." She never feels "sorry" for her divorce.

In conclusion, in these stories by Deshpande it is clear that women cannot be taken for granted, be it in getting married and trying to have rights over their bodies; be it in terminating the third pregnancy, indicating that the woman is the authentic person to decide whether she should continue with her pregnancy or not; be it in a professional lawyer sticking to the idea of being a housewife in order to look after her children and justify her motherhood; be it in widow remarriage breaking the barrier of traditional widowhood; or be it a married woman leaving her husband for his "skunk"-like behaviour. All the above discussed "women" characters in these short stories have raised their "voices" in their respective manner.

Note

1. Shashi Deshpande, *The Intrusion and Other Stories* (New Delhi: Penguin, 1993) 37. All subsequent references are to this edition.

□

"In Our Translated World": Transcultural Communication in Amitav Ghosh's *The Hungry Tide*

Christopher Rollason

I

The Hungry Tide (2004)[1] is the fifth novel and sixth substantial book by Amitav Ghosh.[2] Born in Calcutta/Kolkata in 1956 and now resident in New York, Ghosh is by now established as one of the best-regarded of the "post-Rushdie" generation of expatriate Indians writing in English. If his first three novels revealed a writer experimenting with a diversity of forms and genres (magic realism and picaresque in *The Circle of Reason* (1986), impressionistic family history in *The Shadow Lines* (1988), and, in *The Calcutta Chromosome* (1996, a mélange of detection and science fiction), *The Glass Palace* (2000) marked an embrace of mainstream realism of an almost nineteenth-century type, manifested in the genre of the historical novel. Ghosh's fiction has thus far exhibited a remarkable geographical spread, taking in, for *The Circle of Reason*, India, the Gulf region and Algeria; for *The Shadow Lines*, India, Bangladesh and the UK; for *The Calcutta Chromosome*, India and the US; and for *The Glass Palace*, Burma, India and Malaya.[3] Generically, *The Hungry Tide* continues in the realist mode of *The Glass Palace*, this time with a contemporary setting plus historical flashbacks; geographically, its scope is more limited than that of Ghosh's other novels, as it homes in on the human and natural ecosystems of a small and highly particular area of India, though also taking account of the wider world through characters hailing from Delhi and the US.

Ghosh's narrative, rather than encompassing vast swathes of South and South-East Asia, here prefers, then, to focus a magnifying lens on what might be called a micro-culture within the region[4]—namely, the Sundarbans or "tide country," the islets of the Ganges delta that lie south of Kolkata and just east of the West Bengal/Bangladesh frontier. The *Economist* reviewer took the view that "it is its sense of place that dominates the novel,"[5] and Ghosh himself might seem almost to vindicate such a view in his remark of 1998: "A novel [...] must always be set somewhere: it must have its setting, and within the evolution of the narrative this setting must, classically, play a part almost as important as those of the characters themselves."[6] That "almost" needs to be noted, however, and indeed *The Hungry Tide* highlights not only place but, crucially, dynamically evolving human relationships, in a context that includes—as in his other writings—the dimensions of work (he stated in 2002 that "even the most mundane forms of labour can embody an entire metaphysic"[7]), crosscultural barriers and communication, and the relationship between past and present. History is, indeed, a recurring theme in Ghosh's writing, as acutely noted by the critic Brinda Bose (2001), who states: "Ghosh's fiction takes upon itself the responsibility of re-assessing its troubled antecedents, using history as a tool by which we can begin to make sense of—or at least come to terms with—our troubling present."[8]

The story centres on two visitors to the Sundarban community, Kanai Dutt and Piyali Roy (Piya), and their interaction with that community and with each other. Kanai, a Delhi businessman in his forties, is a semi-outsider, paying a rare visit to his aunt Nilima, an NGO activist who runs a hospital on one of the islands; Piya, an Indo-American scientist from Seattle in her twenties, irrupts into the Sundarban world as—despite her Bengali origins—less a diasporic Indian than an outsider pure and simple, "the American." Kanai is there to pick up and read a journal left him by his late uncle Nirmal, an idealistic, Marxist intellectual in the Bengali tradition, whose contents will oblige him to delve deep into his family history; Piya's journey to the tide country is part of her ongoing research on dolphins. Piya knows no Bengali ("'you know no Bangla?' [...] 'I was so little when I left India that I never had a chance to learn'"—12). Her ignorance of her own language heritage induces her to take Kanai on board as interpreter between her and Fokir, the illiterate fisherman and protégé of Kanai's aunt who serves as her guide. Ghosh's novel takes as its task the exploration of a vast field of human communication, testing both its possibilities and its limits as the characters seek to cross multiple barriers—the barriers of language, religion and social class, those between human beings and nature, between traditional and cosmopolitan India, between urban and rural, between India and the wider world. The tension between global and local is articulated through the characters, with, for most of the novel, globalisation embodied by the Americanised Piya with her hi-tech GPS device, local identity symbolised by Fokir, and Kanai, the Delhi-resident, part-globalised modern entrepreneur, shifting uncertainly somewhere in between.

II

A central metaphor for the notion of communication in a hybrid world is provided by the theme of translation. Postcolonial or transcultural literature in general, and Indian Writing in English in particular, have frequently been viewed by critics via the concept of the already-translated text. This position is explicated by the translation scholar Dora Sales Salvador (2004): "Las narrativas transculturales son ejemplos peculiares de autotraducción derivados del bilingüismo de sus autores. Son textos *originales* que en sí ya llevan la carga de la traducción, *ya* constituyen una traducción [...], motivan un replanteamiento de las nociones elementales del proceso traductor." ("Transcultural narratives are highly particular instances of self-translation arising from their authors' bilingual status. They are *original* texts which already bear the burden of translation, are already a translation [...], thus giving rise to a new questioning of the basic notions of the translation process.")[9] Certainly, *The Hungry Tide* offers concrete evidence for such a textual model, as Kanai is shown across the novel cumulatively reading extracts from his uncle Nirmal's Sundarban journal: the extracts are "reproduced" in full and *in English,* but the reader is asked to imagine Kanai reading them *in Bengali.* An imputed transcultural shift is thus written into the very fabric of Ghosh's text. Meanwhile and across the entire text, Ghosh's narrative, in what might be called, at least for the non-Bengali reader, a deliberate "foreignising" strategy, incorporates a large number of Bengali terms, mostly italicised on first occurrence and in some (but not all) cases glossed. The reader is thus left in no doubt as to the cultural provenance of the text, even despite the overarching role of English as its matricial language.

Significantly, Kanai himself is a translator/interpreter by profession: he knows six languages (his native Bengali plus Hindi, Urdu, Arabic, English and French—199),[10] runs a translation and interpretation agency, and offers to act as interpreter for Piya, who only knows English and has no means of communication with the local Bengali speakers whose knowledge and lore are vital for her research. Nirmal's written records are presented to the reader *translated* (from Bengali into English); Kanai *interprets*—mediates orally—between Piya and Fokir. The need for translation arises from the phenomenon of multilingualism in an interrelated world. Multilingualism has always been a part of the Indian context, Ghosh himself is multilingual, and his earlier novels contain episodes reflecting a keen awareness of the complexities and difficulties of language interaction, both among Indians and between Indians and the wider world.[11] Kanai interprets for Piya for a portion of her expedition, but a certain point he concludes she does not in fact need his services, apparently supposing she can communicate intuitively with her guide Fokir: "'I think you'll be able to manage perfectly well without a translator'" (333). Piya has already shown an attitude to Fokir that supposes the two can communicate intuitively across the language and cultural divide that separates them: "'And all that while, you couldn't understand a word he was saying, could you?'" 'No' [...] 'but you know what? There was so much in common between us it didn't matter'" (268). What is involved here is an essentialist world-view, based on unexamined notions of a common humanity, that may seen as either enticingly utopian or dangerously naïve. At one point, Piya asks Kanai to explain the content of a traditional song that Fokir is chanting, asking him "'Can you translate?'" and Kanai replies: "'[...] this is beyond my power [...] the metre is too complicated. I can't do it'" (309). Later, he writes Piya what is intended as a farewell letter in which he focuses on the impossibility of (adequate) translation/interpretation: "'You asked me what Fokir was singing and I said I couldn't translate it: it was too difficult. And that was no more than the truth, for in those words there was a history that is not just his own but also of this place, the tide country'" (354). Rather than considering translation unnecessary, Kanai seems here to despair of it as impossible, because cultural barriers are too wide. Yet, paradoxically, in the moment of appearing to give up, he appends an approximate translation—rendered in verse presented as prose, in an act of generic hesitation that seems both to reflect and overcome Kanai's translator's doubts—of the Bengali folk poem that Piya had heard Fokir sing.[12] Indeed, Kanai even ends his letter reclaiming the translator's place in the scheme of things, curiously echoing the polemical ideas of the translation theorist Lawrence Venuti, in first affirming the stock notion of the "good translator's" invisibility and then turning things round to demand his own visibility after all: "Such flaws as there are in my translation I do not regret, for perhaps they will prevent me from fading into sight as a good translator should: for once, I shall be glad if my imperfections render me visible" (354). Against Piya's essentialist willingness to dispense with translation, then, Kanai stands as conscious of both its limitations and its necessity.[13]

Technically, and certainly within professional contexts such as university schools of translation/interpretation or international organisations, translation refers *only* to the written word and interpretation *only* to the spoken word. The UN, the European Union and similar bodies employ *translators* and *interpreters* via separate recruitment procedures, in separate career paths with no horizontal mobility between them. However, it is rare for the lay person to grasp, let alone practise, this semantic distinction. Certainly, Amitav Ghosh does not, despite the interest that, as we have seen, he shows across his novels in the world of work and the technical details of occupations. The text of *The Hungry Tide* repeatedly employs "translate/translator" ("'Do you know what your expedition lacks?' [...]. 'A translator!'"—231; "'Can you translate?'"—309) to refer to the practice and practitioners of what is technically interpretation,[14] the conceptual confusion is, be it added, shared in equal measure by Ghosh's reviewers.[15] It is, though, also true that Kanai, working in the private sector and in contradistinction to the usual public-sector practice, does himself practise both activities: "'I'm a translator you see, and an interpreter as well, by profession'" (10). The very lexical hesitation between the terms "translator" and "interpreter," even if unjustifiable in strict technical and semantic terms, throws into relief the potentially ambivalent role of translation/interpretation—is the activity a transposition of meanings between cultural systems (translation), or is it, by its very nature, a rewriting and recoding of others' messages (interpretation)? Both translation and interpretation may theoretically be considered as forms of linguistic transfer, but it remains important not to occlude the dialectic of similarity and difference between the two activities.

Kanai's role as translator/interpreter is also significant in the sense that his work straddles the divide between the written (translation) and the oral (interpretation). This is of interest in the light of the wider interplay, or counterpoint, that operates across the text between written and oral modes. Kanai comes to terms with his past through a written text, his uncle's journal; Piya's scientific work relies on written reports and data sheets; Fokir is illiterate, and his illiteracy is a long-standing cause of tension between him and his upwardly mobile and literate wife, the nurse Moyna. As is frequent in Indian writing, in a country where an ancient heritage of written literature coexists with a rich oral tradition, Ghosh's novel, written text though it is, also invokes the popular storytelling tradition—with the inevitable references to the *Thousand and One Nights* (Nirmal in his journal compares himself to 'some misplaced, misgendered Scheherazade [...] trying to stave off the night with a fleeting pen'—148). The 'Nights' are, of course, a text which, though written, is based on older oral materials and which is structured around the act of storytelling, as, to save her life, the celebrated princess Scheherazade spins out tale after tale, many of them of Indian origin.[16] For the illiterate popular strata, the oral narrative tradition is crucial: thus, Nirmal's journal has a episode in which he converts material from a book he is reading into oral form to make it accessible to his villager companion Horen ("'Saar, what is that you're reading? Are there any stories in it? Why not tell me too [...]'"—145). The novel's translation theme thus embraces not only conversion between languages (Bengali and English), but conversion between written and oral modes of the same language (Bengali). In addition, the tell-tale verb "Listen," signal of the storyteller, occurs, indeed, in Nirmal's journal—not only in the above episode with Horen ("'All right, then [...] Listen,'") but also in a true story told by a fellow Bengali woman to Fokir's mother Kusum ("'Listen, sister, we'll tell you: this is the story'"—164).[17]

The translation factor in the text is further complicated by a curious intertextual element, namely the recurrent quotations in Nirmal's journal from a work of Western literature originally written in not English but German—the *Duino Elegies*, the celebrated sequence of nine poems from 1923 by the Austrian Rainer Maria Rilke.[18] The extracts from Rilke appear in a "real" English translation, but are imputedly quoted by Nirmal, and read by Kanai, in (for the Indian reader) the more domesticated form of a Bengali version.[19] It is, furthermore, from one of Rilke's texts (the First Elegy) that Ghosh's own text quotes (within the journal) the crucial lines: "we're not comfortably at home/in our translated world," later to paraphrase the same lines as if from Kanai's viewpoint: "being so little at ease in your translated world" (206, 328).[20] It is if, in the complex and multiple social universe bequeathed by colonialism and traversed by globalisation, even so basic a phenomenon as human communication has, more often than not, to be handled at one remove, indirectly, through a process of mediation that may also prove a distortion. Nonetheless, to translate is, necessarily, to communicate, however imperfectly, across human-made barriers.

III

The Hungry Tide is, like *The Glass Palace* before it, impeccably researched, and appears as an example of the novel as both history and ethnography. Ghosh's ethnographic qualifications (he has a doctorate in anthropology from Oxford University) are well-enough known and have been amply demonstrated in the pages of *In An Antique Land*; here, he delineates a series of cultural features of the tide country's micro-community—of its human ecosystem, placed in both complementary and conflictive relation to the natural ecosystem which it is Piya's task to explore. History, meanwhile, intervenes in the particular areas of utopia and class conflict.

The alternation between Kanai's here-and-now experiences and his reading of his uncle's journal brings past and present into a symbiotic encounter. The Bengali location allows Ghosh the immediate possibility of drawing on the particular utopian tradition of a part of the subcontinent where, over a good two centuries, Western rationalist influences have coalesced with an older vein of Indian syncretism to produce a unique strain of social thought, as expressed in the movement known as the Bengali Renaissance and notably manifested in the work of Rabindranath Tagore and his school and, later, university at Shantiniketan. This tradition is strongly present in Ghosh's earlier writing—in *The Circle of Reason*, with its rationalist village school and cult of Pasteur, and in the fusion of western scientific endeavour with native esoteric thought in *The Calcutta Chromosome*. Here in *The Hungry Tide*, it reappears in various forms, both exogenous and endogenous: in the utopian community founded in the Sundarbans at the beginning of the twentieth century by the visionary Scot Sir Daniel Hamilton ("Here there would be no Brahmins or Untouchables, no Bengalis and no Oriyas. Everybody would have to live and work together."—51); in Nilima's hospital and school, which despite her insistence on the need to temporise with government nonetheless offer the local community the hope of a better world; and in Nirmal's eminently Bengali brand of Marxism (after all, West Bengal, along with Kerala, has long been exceptional among Indian states in the continued institutional presence of the local communist party). It resurfaces, too, in Piya's doomed belief that she can somehow communicate seamlessly across cultural barriers with the illiterate Fokir.

The idea of utopia, as conceived by the visionary Hamilton and hankered after by Nirmal, always runs the risk of eliding the concrete historical realities of class. The vexed issue of social class barriers appears in Ghosh's novel twice over, across two generations—in the refugees' revolt of which Kusum is a part, and in the friendship (if that is the word) that develops across class lines between Fokir, her illiterate son, and the cosmopolitan outsider Piya. The failed popular revolt is, not surprisingly, a recurrent topos in postcolonial/transcultural/third-world writing: examples in Latin American literature include the salt rebellion of the indigenous women in José María Arguedas' *Los Ríos profundos* (1958) and the banana workers' strike in Gabriel García Márquez's *Cien años de soledad* (1967),[21] while in Indian literature Raja Rao's *Kanthapura* (1938), with its Gandhian women villagers' insurrection, provides a classic exploration of the theme. In *The Hungry Tide*, Kanai reconstructs, via his uncle's journal, the revolt of a group of resettled refugees from the then East Pakistan, their creation of a short-lived community in the Sundarbans with visible utopian-rationalist features, and the bloody retaliation of the authorities. Kusum, Fokir's mother, is part of that revolt, and dies in the course of its repression.

The refugees' plight is in the first place the product of Partition, and therefore ultimately of British colonialism and its divide-and-rule strategies (Ghosh's novel thus connects with the dominant theme of his earlier *The Shadow Lines*). The refugee community is forcibly resettled by the Indian government in Madhya Pradesh state, hundreds of kilometres from Bengal, but in 1978 makes the collective decision to return "home"—if not to East Pakistan/Bangladesh, at least to West Bengal and the Sundarbans. Its members bed down on one of the islands—that on which Nilima's hospital stands—and begin to create the bases of an organised micro-society, and both Nirmal and Kusum find themselves drawn into the refugees' struggle. Nirmal, in his journal, finds a strong utopian strand in their endeavour, in this attempt by the dispossessed to possess something of their own: "[...] there had been many additions, many improvements. Saltpans had been created, tubewells had been planned, water had been dammed for the rearing of fish [...]. It was an astonishing spectacle—as though an entire civilisation had sprouted suddenly in the mind" (191). However, the utopia cannot and does not last: it is brutally repressed by the government forces (which recruit gangster elements for the purpose), and in its aftermath Kusum is killed, while Nirmal, whose journal ends at the moment of the repression, having got mixed up in the events loses his sanity and dies soon after.

If Nirmal as a Marxist believed in a rapprochement across class barriers that could bring him and Kusum together on some level, a generation later Piya repeats this pattern with Kusum's son Fokir. As we have seen, Piya, it seems not feeling at home in a translated world and seeking one where translation is not necessary, naively believes she can do without Bengali/English interpretation in her interaction with Fokir. This attitude is at one with her imported, greenish view of the world: on witnessing an invading tiger set on fire by villagers, she is horrified and gets on a moral-absolutist high horse, rejecting such an act out of hand. At that point Piya, shocked at Fokir's approval of the killing of the tiger, admits to Kanai: "'Fact is, you were right and I was wrong [...] about there being nothing in common between—?' 'You and Fokir'—'Yes [...]; You were right. I was just being stupid'" (297). At such a moment, Piya temporarily distances herself from her desire for a translation-free world. However, she soon reverts to type and accompanies Fokir, without Kanai there to interpret, on a fresh expedition which will soon be subsumed into all the rigours of a tide-country storm. And here indeed she and Fokir get as close as they ever will: the storm takes Fokir as he clasps Piya's body with his protective arms. He, the illiterate villager, perishes; she, the privileged outsider, lives to tell the tale: "She tried to break free from his grasp, tried to pull him around so that for once, she could be the one who was sheltering him. But his body was unyielding, and she could not break free from it, especially now that it had the wind's weight behind it. Their bodies were so close, so finally merged that she would feel the impact of everything hitting him, she could sense the blows raining down on his back. She could feel the bones of his cheeks as if they had been superimposed upon her own: it was as if the storm had given them what life could not, it had fused them together and made them one" (390).

On one level, this denouement seems to call in question the utopian imperative and interrogate the possibility of transcending cultural barriers. If Fokir dies that Piya may live, if the storm makes them one only to disgorge Piya as sole survivor, then surely the privileged are still in their position. Nonetheless, if we now look at the novel's presentation of the Sundarbans' human ecosystem, a fresh utopian dynamic may be distinguished, in a conciliatory form of popular religious syncretism. This impulse manifests itself in the curious tale of Bon Bibi.

The cult of Bon Bibi, peculiar to the community in which Kanai finds himself, has been handed down through the generations, through the oral tradition of story and song: the tale, "told by Abdur-Rahim" (354), appears to have been written down at one point, and at one point is staged as a theatre play, "The Glory of Bon Bibi" (101), but its transmission remains essentially oral. It may fairly be seen as representative of a certain strand of Hindu-Muslim syncretism[22] that runs through the byways, and sometimes even the highways, of Indian history. The tide people are *a priori* Hindu, and have ended up in India rather than East Pakistan/Bangladesh, but that does not prevent them taking on substantial elements from the adjacent world of Islam. According to the story, two twins, Bon Bibi and her brother Shah Jongoli, were born in the holy city of Medina to a Sufi faqir. They are marked out for a special destiny: "When the twins came of age, the archangel [Gabriel] brought them word that they had been chosen for a divine mission: they were to travel from Arabia to the "country of eighteen tides"—*atthero bhatir desh*—in order to make it fit for human habitation. Thus charged, Bon Bibi and Shah Jongoli set off for the mangrove forests of Bengal dressed in the simple robes of Sufi mendicants" (103). Bon Bibi becomes the tutelary deity of the islands. Kusum sees the dolphins as her messengers (234); and Piya is amazed to find Fokir and his son praying at a shrine dedicated to her: "Piya recognised a refrain that occurred over and over again—it contained a word that sounded like 'Allah.' She had not thought to speculate about Fokir's religion, but it occurred to her now that he might be Muslim. But no sooner had she thought this, than it struck her that a Muslim was hardly likely to pray to an image like this one. What Fokir was performing looked very much like her mother's Hindu *pujas*—and yet the words seemed to suggest otherwise" (152). The strange coexistence of the name of Allah with puja-type gestures points to a transcultural fusion of elements from both Hinduism and Islam, at the opposite pole from the Hindu-Muslim confrontations that have too often disfigured the post-Raj subcontinent.[23]

Syncretist phenomena such as this may be viewed as part and parcel of the islands' human ecosystem (the ethnologist in Ghosh also notes that the observance of widowhood in the Sundarbans differs from the usual Hindu norm: "here, on the margins of the Hindu world, widows were not condemned to lifelong bereavement: they were free to remarry if they could"—81). That human ecosystem is, of course, inserted problematically into a wider natural ecosystem—or eco-polysystem. The migratory dolphins have their own logic, while that of the tigers and crocodiles, if part of a greater natural whole, is not in any immediate sense compatible with that of the human community those animals prey on: to that, Kanai can vouch when he escapes as if miraculously from a tiger's clutches. No less unkind is the logic of the horrendous storm that kills Fokir and almost sweeps away Piya too. Piya, true to type, tends to sentimentalise the animal world and its imagined beneficent relation to humanity, asking herself when a group of dolphins seem to be consciously sharing a catch of fish with their human acquaintances: "Did there exist any more remarkable instance of symbiosis between human beings and a population of wild animals?" (169) but is later sharply taken to task by the tiger-burning episode and the awkward questions it raises. Across the novel as a whole, and despite the attractive notion of idealising cetacean communities, the general sense is that the basic humanity/nature relationship in the Sundarbans remains highly problematic (death and destruction, from storms or tigers, can face the villagers at any moment) and is not susceptible to facile ideological simplifications.

IV

Neither human nor natural ecosystem in Ghosh's novel appears easy to place or interpret. Here, though, the reader may recall that a novel is not only a narrated tale but a construct within a wider literary system, and at this point the notion of intertextuality may come to our aid. *The Glass Palace* already exhibited a significant intertextual element, recalling and rewriting images and themes from Rudyard Kipling and George Orwell, and this novel too finds Ghosh the writer taking on certain of his distinguished precursors. To take the Bon Bibi, Hindu-Muslim element first, it is possible to hypothesise a curious dialogic encounter, implicit in the text, between Amitav Ghosh and one of his most celebrated "Indo-Anglian" peers, Salman Rushdie.[24] There are, in fact, a number of interesting convergences between *The Hungry Tide* and Rushdie's work. Rushdie has himself briefly featured the tide country in his own fiction, in a chapter of *Midnight's Children* (1981), indeed entitled "In the Sundarbans," in which his narrator Saleem, in the wake of the Bangladesh war, finds himself lost in a dark, sinister and rather Kiplingesque jungle world, "through incomprehensibly labyrinthine salt-water channels overtowered by the cathedral-arching trees"[25] (Ghosh, one may speculate, may in part be motivated by the desire to make comprehensible what Rushdie treats as "incomprehensible"); in *The Ground Beneath Her Feet* (1999) Rushdie too quotes Rilke (the *Sonnets to Orpheus*), in the epigraph and intermittently across the text; and in *Shame* (1983), the narrator, who may approximately be identified with Rushdie himself, anticipates Ghosh's notion, via Rilke, of a "translated world" by referring to himself, formed by the life-experiences of more than one culture, as a "translated man."[26] The most significant case of intertextuality with Rushdie, however, relates to no less a text than that writer's famously controversial novel of 1988, *The Satanic Verses*.[27]

Bon Bibi and her brother are born in Medina, "one of the holiest places in Islam" (103), and, indeed, one of the two holy cities in what is now Saudi Arabia; Rushdie's novel locates its two controversial chapters in a place named Jahilia, a thinly disguised version of the other holy city, Mecca. Ghosh's twins are fathered "through the intervention of the archangel Gabriel," a figure who later instructs them to go to India and who also appears in Rushdie's ironic rewriting of the dictation of the Koran to the Prophet, in the demented dreams of his filmstar namesake Gibreel Farishta ("Gibreel, hovering-watching from his highest camera angle"[28]). The twins' crossing from Arabia to India, too, parallels in reverse the "crossing of the Arabian Sea" delusion from the Ayesha episode, another of Gibreel's dreams in *The Satanic Verses*. It needs to be stressed, however, that where Rushdie's text, intentionally not, ended up stoking the fires of religious controversy, Ghosh's rewriting of themes from *The Satanic Verses* works in the direction of syncretism and, therefore, intercommunal understanding: it is as if Ghosh, via his mentor Rushdie, had been through the confrontational, hardline secularist attitude to religion, and come out on the other side with the objective of finding common areas between the subcontinent's two largest faiths—a dynamic of rapprochement that is movingly symbolised in the image of Fokir and his son worshipping Bon Bibi in a ceremony that is, at one and the same time, both Sufi and Hindu.

On the vexed plane of the humanity/nature relationship, Ghosh's intertextual practice appears to play a similar role. We are certainly dealing with an important theme in the novel, for Ghosh himself has declared in a 2004 interview: "I wanted to write a book that is grounded in nature."[29] Here, *The Hungry Tide* matches itself against not an Indian text but one from Piya's adopted America—Herman Melville's famous maritime epic of 1851, *Moby-Dick*. When Piya pronounces the term "cetologist" before Kanai, in explanation of her work ("'I'm a cetologist. That means [...]' [...] 'You don't need to explain. It means you study marine mammals'"—11), the reader familiar with the Anglo-American literary canon will immediately think of Melville's whale of a novel, which not only holds vast amounts of marine-mammal lore in its belly, but actually entitles its thirty-second chapter "Cetology." The analogy is confirmed later in Ghosh's text, when Kanai declares to Piya, "'I thought you were going to lead me to my Moby Dick'" (304). However, where Melville's novel pits man against whale, Piya's research, focusing not on whales but dolphins, aims not to kill cetaceans but to understand them, and, as we have seen, has a strong—if at times naïve—utopian element. If Ahab is driven by the will to power ("'Oh, his unappeasable brow drives on towards one, whose duty tells him he cannot depart'"[30]) Piya seems to embody the will to knowledge (as Kanai puts it: "'You go through a lot for these creatures'"—226)[31] : her desire is, metaphorically at least, to dive into the depths of the dolphin world and return with scientific treasures, in a quest which she would certainly see as non-exploitative towards the natural environment. It is as if Ghosh were reversing Melville by seeking in his text the essence of a non-confrontational, cooperative relationship between humanity and nature. In the Sundarban world, such a relationship can—the crouching tiger reminds the reader—be sketched only in embryo. Nonetheless, it may still be argued that through Piya Ghosh is edging his readership away from Melville's heroic-confrontational mode, centred on the nineteenth-century Western notion of the mastery of nature, towards a different kind of human insertion into the natural world—where, as Walter Benjamin put it in 1926, what matters is "not the mastery of nature but of the relation between nature and man."[32] The intertextuality of *The Hungry Tide*, in ambivalent dialogue with both Melville and Rushdie, seems to be pointing away from heroic-male literary models, be it for crosscultural or for culture/nature relations, and towards less polarised and more dialogic frames of being.

V

For all the above conciliatory trends in its writing, Ghosh's narrative nonetheless, as we know, climaxes harshly in the dark and tragic death of Fokir in the storm. With such a denouement, it may, somehow, fairly be asked whether Kanai was not right, and whether Piya's notion of a seamless communication beyond words with Fokir was not, at bottom, an impossible reverie born of a naively idealist world-view. Their relationship in fact goes as far as it could and no further: the moving image of the dying Fokir with his body protectively surrounding Piya's, yet calling out for his wife and child in his last moments, serves to establish the outer limits of their communication. On the one hand, Ghosh eschews all sensationalism: as a visual image, the Fokir-Piya pair, apparently transcending the barriers of class and literacy, might remind some readers of another male-female dyad, Velutha and Ammu in Arundhati Roy's best-selling novel set in Kerala, *The God of Small Things* (1997) and their doomed, cross-caste love affair, but Roy's unlikely pair perpetrate a transgression which Ghosh's narrative carefully falls short of.[33] Piya does not take her relationship with Fokir beyond the culturally permissible limits. On the other hand, though, those same limits serve to point up the difficulty of communication too. The monolingual Piya, knowing neither Bengali nor Hindi, appears, despite her Indian origins, as typifying the monoglot attitudes of the Anglo-Saxon world in general and the US in particular. Those who only know English are doomed not to understand other cultures, unless they draw on the services of a translator-interpreter and cultural mediator like Kanai—services which, however flawed and imperfect, prove indeed to be necessary, in the very context of the globalisation that brings the likes of Piya to locations like the Sundarbans.

Despite this, the novel's conclusion, though open-ended, paradoxically seems to find Ghosh—and, in all probability, the reader—moving tentatively towards an admission of the possibility, after all, of communication across cultural barriers, at least within certain limits and subject to a rational effort of will. At the end, both Piya and Kanai voluntarily undertake a reconstruction (and reinterpretation) of their experiences in the Sundarbans: each has lost the textual evidence (the sea claimed both Kanai's uncle's journal and Piya's cetological data-sheets), but each is willing to piece the text back together from memory. Beyond this, both actually, and surprisingly, return to the Sundarbans: Kanai shifts his residence from Delhi to Kolkata to be near the tide country and visit often, thus moving at least halfway, towards a neo-Gandhian renunciation of cosmopolitan and metropolitan India in favour of the more demotic claims of what some call the "real India" (in a evolution that might recall the nativist conversion of the English Teacher in R.K. Narayan's novel of that name of 1945). Piya goes further, electing to base herself and her research in the Sundarbans themselves and to learn Bengali, giving a surprising preference to the local over the global, to her Indian roots over her globalised-American identity. A madeover, Bengali-speaking Piya could indeed have greater possibilities of communicating cross-culturally with the likes of Fokir than the "American" whom the reader has accompanied across the book. Meanwhile, whether the future will hold any convergence of a more affective nature between Piya and Kanai is left open, but clearly their paths will cross once more.

It is as if the diverse strands of Ghosh's narrative have finally come together. In his earlier work, Amitav Ghosh employed the metaphor of weaving—the spinning of yarns, in more than one sense—as symbol for the connective role of writing and of human communication in general. In *The Circle of Reason*, weaving—the activity of the main character, Alu—appears as an emblem of connection, even being linked to the development of computers, and the text offers the pregnant aphorism: "Weaving is hope because it has no country, no continent,"[34] while the pages of *In An Antique Land* contain the image of the weaver as storyteller: "Later, when I got to know [the weaver] Zaghloul better, I discovered that besides being very fond of stories, he had a manner of telling them that was marvellously faithful to the metaphorical resonances of his chosen craft."[35] However, in both texts the weaving image seemed more a matter of unrealised potential: in *The Circle of Reason* Alu's creative gift finally leads him nowhere, while the Indo-Egyptian encounter of *In An Antique Land* runs up against cultural differences that at times appear unbridgeable. By contrast, the narrative of *The Hungry Tide* is made up of interwoven strands—Kanai's narrative and Piya's, the present lived by the characters and the past of Nirmal's journal—that variously alternate, converge, diverge and reconverge. As the novel comes to an end, the utopian possibility opens up of a coming-together of all the book's narrative and conceptual strands: global and local, urban and rural, linguistic and scientific, anglophone and Bengali-speaking—even, it may be, male and female. The hungry tide has claimed its sacrificial victim in Fokir, but Piya plans a memorial to him and even begins to speak of the Sundarbans as "home" (399). The utopian goal of mutual understanding, implicit in this novel's recurrent theme of translation, begins to appear as something actually possible. As both Piya and Kanai seem to morph into a new kind of cosmopolitan who can actually feel at home in a place like the tide country, the reader finds this latest of Amitav Ghosh's fictions opening up new and unexpected perspectives: the postcolonial text, product and reflection of a translated world, nonetheless proclaims the need and the desire, for us as global citizens, to communicate in new forms—to think transculturally, and to build new bridges across that world.

Notes

1. All quotations and page numbers refer to the edition of *The Hungry Tide* published by Harper Collins in 2004.

2. Ghosh's non-fiction includes *In An Antique Land* (1992), which combines ethnographic reflections on Egypt with the reconstruction of a historical episode linking Egypt with India; *Dancing in Cambodia, At Large in Burma* (1998), a travel book; and *The Imam and the Indian* (2002), a volume of essays. The generic status of *In An Antique Land* has given rise to critical disagreement. Salman Rushdie, in his preface to *The Vintage Book of Indian Writing 1947-1997* (1997), describes Ghosh's book as a "non-fiction study," further hazarding the view that his "greatest strength [may] turn out to be that of an essayist of this sort" (xxii). Tuomas Huttunen, in "Connections beyond Partitions: Amitav Ghosh's *In An Antique Land*" (2003), treats *In An Antique Land* as a novel, as too does Brinda Bose, in "Footnoting History: The Diasporic Imagination of Amitav Ghosh" (2002). However, such readings are, to say the least, contentious, especially as large portions of that book also appear in a different form in the essay collection *The Imam and the Indian*. John Thieme ("The Discoverer Discovered: Amitav Ghosh's *The Calcutta Chromosome*," 2001) is on firmer ground when he stresses, in general terms, Ghosh's "blurring of the boundaries between anthropology and fiction" (178-79).
3. A similar geographical breadth characterises Ghosh's non-fiction. *In An Antique Land* shifts between Egypt and India; the title of *Dancing in Cambodia, At Large in Burma* is self-explanatory; and *The Imam and the Indian*, apart from the alternate versions of parts of *In An Antique Land* mentioned above, also contains pieces dealing with Sri Lanka and Tibet.
4. Some intertextual continuity with the novelist's earlier work is nonetheless supplied by references to Calcutta/Kolkata (Ghosh's text, in a suitably hybridated compromise, uses both "old" English and "new" Bengali names), Burma and Cambodia. It may be added that *The Hungry Tide* continues in the line of Ghosh's earlier work (notably *The Shadow Lines* and *The Glass Palace*) by drawing on his family history. Kanai's uncle Nirmal is partly based on an actual uncle of the author's—Ghosh states in his "Author's Note": "My uncle, the late Shri Chandra Ghosh, was for more than a decade the headmaster of the Rural Reconstruction Institute founded by Sir Daniel Hamilton in Gosaba" (401).
5. *Economist Review* 73.
6. Ghosh, "The March of the Novel through History: the Testimony of my Grandfather's Bookcase," 1998, rpt. in *The Imam and the Indian* (2002: 294).
7. This quotation is from Ghosh's "Acknowledgements" to *The Imam and the Indian* (2002: x), where he refers to his own writerly "interest in patterns of work" and stresses the presence of that theme in *The Circle of Reason* and *The Glass Palace*. Indeed, in the former Ghosh homes in on the details of weaving and gardening, while the latter brings to the fore such diverse activities as timbering, oil production and photography.

8. Bose, "Footnoting History," 235. For readings of Ghosh's earlier work through the notion of coming to terms with (colonial/postcolonial/subaltern) history, see, for *The Shadow Lines*, Kevin Jonas Lenfest, "Reflections from the Cave: Negotiating Identity in *The Shadow Lines*" (2003), and N. Nagaraju, "Entity and Nationality in the Fictional Narratives of Amitav Ghosh" (2004); for *The Glass Palace*, Shanthini Pillai, "The Gaze of a Diasporic, the Voice of a Subaltern: Amitav Ghosh's Articulation of the Indian Immigrant Labour Experience in *The Glass Palace*" (2002), and T. Vinoda, "Reflections on the Crystal Palace: *The Glass Palace* as a Postcolonialist Text" (2002).
9. Dora Sales Salvador, "Literaturas transculturales y ética de la traducción" (2004), 70.
10. Kanai's language skills correspond closely to Ghosh's own. Indeed, he tells Piya, "an opportunity turned up [for him] to learn Arabic in Tunisia" (199)—as was actually the case for his creator.
11. In *The Circle of Reason*, a policeman from Delhi posted to Kerala finds the Malayalam language all but unlearnable: "'You chaps in your home states are lucky. You don't know what it's like for us [...] I've got myself a teacher and I've tried to learn the bloody lingo, but it's impossible.'" (162-63); while in another episode, a Hindi-speaking woman has to ask for help with a Bengali text (Tagore's drama *Chitrangada*) from a native speaker of that language: "'I have a Hindi translation of the original done by my father, but there are a couple of places where I can't read his handwriting. He copied the original down with the translation, but the trouble is I can't read Bengali [...]. So, if you could just help a little'" (394). In *The Glass Palace*, the multiple examples of the complexities of language interaction include the Burma-resident Indian Rajkumar, who speaks "fluent but heavily accented Burmese" (3), and the Burmese princesses exiled in Ratnagiri (in today's Maharashtra), who "learned to speak Marathi and Hindustani as fluently as any of the townsfolk" (77).
12. Krishna Dutta, the UK-based writer and author of an acclaimed book on Kolkata, says in her *Independent* review of *The Hungry Tide* ("At sea in the waters of Bengal," 2004) that this passage is "an English pastiche of the Bengali metre *dwipadi poyar*: a rhymed couplet of about 12 lines with a caesura."
13. Translation is, besides, present as an element in Ghosh's other work, in the specific context of the Bengali/English dyad. Ghosh has written: "It happens that although I write in English, my native language is Bengali" ("The Fundamentalist Challenge," 1995; rpt. in *The Imam and the Indian*, 2002: 278), and *The Imam and the Indian* includes both mention of the translations of his work into Bengali ("Acknowledgments," 12) and his own translation of 1995, from Bengali into English, of Rabindranath Tagore's short story "The Hunger of Stones." In this connection, it is far from tangential to note

that, according to Ramya Ramamurthy ("'I think in images,'" 2004), Ghosh "has announced that he may translate *The Hungry Tide* into Bengali."

14. Ghosh, it has to be said, displays a similar lexical looseness in his essay "Dancing in Cambodia" (1998): "The friend who I had persuaded to come along with me to translate [...]" (7); "King Sisowah spoke no French, and it was Minister Thiounn who served as his interpreter" (23).

15. Of the reviews listed below under "Works Cited," two (Alfred Hickling in *The Guardian* and Khushwant Singh in the *Deccan Herald*) refer to Kanai as an interpreter ("found[er of] a successful interpretation agency"; "runs a firm of language interpreters") and three (Mitju C. Banerji in *The Observer*, Partha Chatterjee in *The Hindu* and Indrajit Hazra in *The Hindustan Times*) describe him as a translator ("from a translating job in New Delhi," "runs a successful translation bureau in New Delhi," "(heads) a professional translating company," but none gets it right or makes it clear that he actually does both!

16. Ghosh's textual invocation of the *Thousand and One Nights* runs in a tradition of Indo-Anglian cultural reference that includes Salman Rushdie, Vikram Chandra and, indeed, Tagore. Rushdie's *Haroun and the Sea of Stories* (1990), with its names Haroun and Rashid—the latter its storyteller hero—refers back self-evidently to the *Nights*, while in his *The Moor's Last Sigh* (1995), Moraes Zogoiby ends up telling stories to save his life, "made a Scheherezade" (421); Chandra rehandles the "writing ape" theme from one of the "Nights" in a central image of his *Red Earth and Pouring Rain* (1995); while in Tagore's "The Hunger of Stones" (1895), the story translated by Ghosh, the protagonist declares: "It seemed to me that a night from the Thousand and One Nights had transported itself here from the realm of fiction" (*The Imam and the Indian* 332).

17. The verb "Listen," similarly, plays a key role in the strongly orally-influenced fictions of Vikram Chandra, *Red Earth and Pouring Rain* (1995) and *Love and Longing in Bombay* (1997).

18. Ghosh also mentions Rilke in "Dancing in Cambodia." Here, the context is Rilke's relationship with no less a European artistic icon than Auguste Rodin, whose personal secretary he was in 1905-1906: the poet is cited as praising, in a letter of 1907, the artist's sketches of Cambodian dancers: "For me, these sketches were amongst the most profound of revelations" ("Dancing in Cambodia," 42). The intertextual link between essay and novel indicates that the presence of Rilke in the Bengali consciousness is not historically innocent: the Rodin sketches evoked by the poet derive from the official visit of the King of Cambodia, then a French protectorate, to Marseille in 1906, and would not have existed had it not been for French colonialism in Indochina. Rilke, though not French, was thus an indirect participant in France's colonial enterprise.

19. Ghosh explains in his "Author's Note" that his Rilke quotations are from the English translation of 1975 by A. Poulin Jr., while the Bengali translation imputedly used by Nirmal is that by Buddhadeva Basu, from the 1960s (402-03).
20. Curiously, where the translation used by Ghosh has "in our translated world," another rendering of the First Elegy, that by J.B. Leishman (in the Penguin *Selected Poems* of Rilke, 1964), reads "this interpreted world." The German original has "in der gedeuteten Welt," and "gedeuteten" means "interpreted" rather than "translated" ("deuten" = "to interpret"). These discrepancies point up, yet again, the complexities of the conceptual slippage between translation and interpretation.
21. Partha Chatterjee, in her review in The Hindu (2004), suggests García Márquez's novel as a major influence on *The Hungry Tide* (cf. also Amit Chaudhuri's comments in note 24 below). Also to be noted is the circumstance that Arguedas, like Ghosh, was at home in the worlds of both anthropology and fiction.
22. One may here compare a historical example from a completely different part of India: William Dalrymple narrates in *White Mughals* (2003) how the Muharram celebrations in Hyderabad in 1801 were "transformed into a sort of syncretic Indo-Islamic saturnalia which had almost as much in common with Hindu river festivals such as the Kumb Mela as it did with the purely Islamic Muharram" (293).
23. Indeed, the novelist and critic Khushwant Singh (who, as author of the celebrated novel of 1956, *Train to Pakistan*, is, to say the least, informed on such issues), speaks in his review of *The Hungry Tide* of "scheduled caste Hindus subscribing to a faith which is a happy blend of Islam and tribal Hinduism" ("Legendary writer," 2004).
24. For Rushdie on Ghosh, see note 2 above; for Ghosh on Rushdie, see note 27 below. Amit Chaudhuri, in *The Picador Book of Modern Indian Literature* 2001, sees Ghosh's *The Circle of Reason* as "a response to his readings of [García] Márquez and Rushdie," and *The Shadow Lines* as still under the latter's influence (538).
25. Rushdie, *Midnight's Children* (1981), 360.
26. Rushdie, *Shame* (1984), 29.
27. In his 1990 essay "The Diaspora in Indian Culture," reprinted in *The Imam and the Indian* (2002), Ghosh refers to Rushdie as among the "fine[st] writers writing in the English language today," and openly attacks the Indian government's "reprehensible and senseless" ban on *The Satanic Verses* (*The Imam and the Indian* 243).
28. Rushdie, *The Satanic Verses* (1988), 123.

29. Quoted in Ramya Ramamurthy, "'I think in images'" (*Mid Day*, 2004).
30. Melville, *Moby-Dick* (1851), 621.
31. The will to knowledge is also a major theme in *The Calcutta Chromosome*, with the quest to penetrate the enigma of malaria, but in that novel the overall context is altogether more ambivalent.
32. Walter Benjamin, "One-Way Street" (1926), 104.
33. With regard to the possible intertextual relation between Roy's and Ghosh's novels, it may be noted that Piya's surname happens to be Roy, and that Ghosh locates an episode of *The Circle of Reason* in Kerala.
34. Ghosh, *The Circle of Reason* 58.
35. Ghosh, *In An Antique Land* 137.

Works Cited

"Ebbs and Floods on the Ganges." Rev. of *The Hungry Tide*, by Amitav Ghosh. *The Economist*, 17-23 July 2004: 73. http://www.economist.com/books/displayStory.cfm?story_id=2921266.

Arguedas, José María. *Los Ríos profundos*. 1958. Madrid: Alianza, 1981.

Banerji, Mitu C. "Tales from the Indian Riverbank." Rev. of *The Hungry Tide*, by Amitav Ghosh. *The Observer*, 20 June 2004. <http://books.guardian.co.uk/reviews/generalfiction/0,6121,1242913,00.html>.

Benjamin, Walter. "One-Way Street." 1926. *One-Way Street and Other Writings*. Trans. Edmund Jephcott and Kingsley Shorter. London: NLB, 1979. 45-104.

Bose, Brinda. "Footnoting History: The Diasporic Imagination of Amitav Ghosh." *In Diaspora: Theories, Histories, Texts*. Ed. Makarand Paranjape. New Delhi: Indialog Publications, 2002. 235-45 (235).

Chandra, Vikram. *Red Earth and Pouring Rain*. 1995. London: Faber and Faber, 1996.

——. *Love and Longing in Bombay*. London: Faber and Faber, 1997.

Chatterjee, Partha. "Inadequacy of Craft." Rev. of *The Hungry Tide* by Amitav Ghosh. *The Hindu* 4 July 2004. <http://www.hindu.com/lr/2004/07/04/stories/2004070400300100.htm>.

Chaudhuri, Amit, ed. *The Picador Book of Modern Indian Literature*. London: Picador, 2001.

Dalrymple, William. *White Mughals: Love and Betrayal in Eighteenth-Century India*. London: Harper Collins (Flamingo), 2003.

Dutta, Krishna. "At Sea in the Waters of Bengal." Rev. of *The Hungry Tide*, by Amitav Ghosh. *The Independent* 11 June 2004. <http://enjoyment.independent.co.uk/books/reviews/story.jsp?story=530162>.

García Márquez, Gabriel. *Cien años de soledad.* Barcelona: Plaza & Janés, 1975.

Ghosh, Amitav. *The Circle of Reason.* 1986. London: Granta Books, 1998.

——. *The Shadow Lines.* 1988. New Delhi: Ravi Dayal, 2001.

——. *In An Antique Land.* 1992. New York: Vintage, 1994.

——. *The Calcutta Chromosome.* 1996. London: Picador, 1997.

——. *Dancing in Cambodia, At Large in Burma.* New Delhi: Ravi Dayal, 1998.

——. *The Glass Palace.* London: Harper Collins, 2000.

——. *The Imam and the Indian: Prose Pieces.* New Delhi: Ravi Dayal, 2002.

——. *The Hungry Tide.* London: Harper Collins, 2004.

Hazra, Indrajit. "The Tides and Eddies of Human Nature." Rev. of *The Hungry Tide. Hindustan Times*, 20 June 2004. <http://www.hindustantimes.com/news/5922_838012,0015002200000093.htm>.

Hickling, Alfred. "Islands in the stream." Rev. of *The Hungry Tidei*, by Amitav Ghosh. *The Guardian* 19 June 2004. http://books.guardian.co.uk/reviews/generalfiction/0,6121,1242913,00.html.

Huttunen, Tuomas. "Connections Beyond Partitions: Amitav Ghosh's *In An Antique Land.*" *The Atlantic Literary Review*, 4.3 (July-Sept. 2003): 87-107.

Lenfest, Kevin Jonas. "Reflections from the Cave: Negotiating Identity in *The Shadow Lines*" (2003). *The Atlantic Literary Review* 4.1-2 (April-June 2003): 109-20.

Melville, Herman. *Moby-Dick or, The Whale.* 1851. Harmondsworth: Penguin, 1992.

Nagaraju, N. "Entity and Nationality in the Fictional Narratives of Amitav Ghosh." *IJOWLAC* (*Indian Journal of World Literature and Culture*) 1.1 (Jan.-June 2004): 64-67.

Narayan, R.K. *The English Teacher.* 1945. London: Vintage, 2001.

Pillai, Shanthini. "The Gaze of a Diasporic, the Voice of a Subaltern: Amitav Ghosh's Articulation of the Indian Immigrant Labour Experience in *The Glass Palace.*" *The Atlantic Literary Review* 3.4 (Oct.-Dec. 2002): 128-44.

Ramamurthy, Ramya. "'I Think in Images.'" Interview with Amitav Ghosh. *Mid Day* 4 Aug. 2004. <http://ww1.mid-day.com/entertainment/news/2004/august/89207.htm>.

Rao, Raja. *Kanthapura.* 1938. New Delhi: Orient Paperbacks, 2001.

Rilke, Rainer Maria. *Selected Poems 1905-1926.* Trans. J.B. Leishman. Harmondsworth: Penguin, 1964.

Roy, Arundhati. *The God of Small Things.* London: Flamingo, 1997.

Rushdie, Salman. *Midnight's Children.* 1981. London: Picador, 1982.

——. *Shame*. London: Jonathan Cape, 1983.

——. *The Satanic Verses*. London: Viking, 1988.

——. *Haroun and the Sea of Stories*. 1990. London: Granta Books, 1991.

——. *The Moor's Last Sigh*. London: Jonathan Cape, 1995.

——. "Preface" to Salman Rushdie and Elizabeth West, eds. *The Vintage Book of Indian Writing 1947-1997*. London: Vintage, 1997. ix-xxiii.

——. *The Ground Beneath Her Feet*. London: Jonathan Cape, 1999.

Sales Salvador, Dora. "Literaturas transculturales y ética de la traducción: Cuando narrar es traducirse." *Ética y política de la traducción en la época contemporánea*. Ed. Assumpta Camps. Barcelona: PPU, 2004. 61-84.

Singh, Khushwant. *Train to Pakistan*. 1956. *Memories of Madness: Stories of 1947*. New Delhi: Penguin, 2002. 3-172.

——. "Legendary Writer." Rev. of *The Hungry Tidei*, by Amitav Ghosh. *Deccan Herald* 14 Aug. 2004. <http://www.deccanherald.com/deccanherald/aug142004/edst.asp>.

Tagore, Rabindranath. "The Hunger of Stones." 1895. *The Imam and the Indian: Prose Pieces*. Trans. Amitav Ghosh. New Delhi: Ravi Dayal, 2002. 326-39.

Thieme, John. "The Discoverer Discovered: Amitav Ghosh's *The Calcutta Chromosome*." *Studies in Indian Writing in English*. Vol. 2. Ed. Rajeshwar Mittapalli and Pier Paolo Piciucco. New Delhi: Atlantic Publishers, 2001. 170-83.

Vinoda, T. "Reflections on the Crystal Palace: *The Glass Palace* as a Postcolonialist Text." *Kakatiya Journal of English Studies* 22 (2002): 77-95.

□

Hybrid Identities: History, Ethnicity and Gender in Female Fiction of the Indian Diaspora

Subhendu Mund

Emigration/immigration is not a new phenomenon: nor is diaspora writing. India has had its share of emigration/immigration since the colonial era, and diasporic writing—novels, short stories, travelogues, and essays—has not been new to Indian writing in English. In fact, *The Travels of Dean Mahomet* (1795),[1] believed to be the earliest available narrative in Indian English, was written when the author Dean Mahomet/ Mahomed (1759-1851) lived in Ireland and England as an émigré. The writings of Raja Rammohun Roy (1772-1833) during his famous England visit are much too well-known to be elaborated on. In the nineteenth century a number of Indians visited England and other European countries, and most of them wrote on their experience of the West. Toru Dutt's (1856-77) *Bianca: Or the Young Spanish Maiden* (1878, reissued in 2001),[2] inspired by the young author's experience in England and France, was set in England with non-Indian characters, English, Spanish, and Italian, the last two categories being diasporic. Through Bianca and her father Mr García, who were Spanish immigrants, and their characteristic resistance to hybridation, Dutt tried to narrate how émigrés were easy victims of otherisation in the conservative Victorian society. Interestingly, the novel *Le Journal de Mademoiselle D'Arvers*, also by Dutt, was written in French, with French characters and locale.[3]

On the other hand, a number of immigrants, especially from Europe, who came to India made use of their Indian experience to write fiction. After the First World War a number of Indians went to the West for various reasons, and many of them settled down there. Some of them, like Dhan Gopal Mukerji (1890-1936) (*Caste and Outcast*, 1923), V.V. Chintamani (*Vedantam: Or The Clash of Traditions,* 1938), Dosoobhai

Framji Karaka (*Out of Dust*, 1941, *Just Flesh*: 1941, *Oh! You English!*, 1942, and *I Go West*, 1942), G.V. Desani (*All About H. Hatterr*, 1948) and B. Rajan (*Too Long in the West*, 1961) may be called the forerunners of the diaspora writing in Indian English. The works of these writers went considerably beyond the commonplace East-West conflict stereotype to explore the multidimensional anxieties of émigré life.

Of late there has been a huge shift in perspectives and perceptions among the émigré elite insofar as individual/national/cultural identities are concerned. Large-scale immigration in recent years has led to unprecedented anxieties of adjustment and a hypersensitive aspect like individual identity has come into conflict with the demands of the immigrant's adopted homeland. Such conflicts are not exclusive to immigrants of Indian origin: they apply to settlers from other countries/cultures as well.

For various reasons, the present diaspora tends to alienate the immigrants from their roots in spite of themselves, compelling them to live between two worlds: the imaginary and the real, the past and the present and the virtual and the material. Things were perhaps not exactly so in the past. Notwithstanding the diasporic conflict, the sentimental attachment that one had to one's homeland was perhaps not 'imaginary': it kept renewing itself by frequent physical and emotional contacts with the native land. In *Imaginary Homelands*, Salman Rushdie tries to address the issue in a manner which could be representative of the immigrant's "profound uncertainties":

> It may be that writers in my position, exiles or emigrants or expatriates, are haunted by some sense of loss, some urge to reclaim, to look back, even at the risk of being mutated into pillars of salt. But if we do look back, we must also do so in the knowledge—which gives rise to profound uncertainties—that our physical alienation from India almost inevitably means that we will not be capable of reclaiming precisely the thing that was lost; that we will, in short, create fictions, not actual cities or villages; but invisible ones, imaginary homelands, Indias of the mind. (Rushdie 10)

It is a strange paradox that the members of the present diaspora seems to be consciously distancing themselves from their place of origin. Bharati Mukherjee, like Rushdie, postulates that Indianness is merely a "metaphor" for "semi-assimilated Indians" who have "no real desire for permanent return." In her introduction to the short story collection *Darkness,* she writes:

I have joined imaginative forces with an anonymous driven underclass of semi-assimilated Indians with sentimental attachment to a distant homeland, but no real desire for permanent return [...]. Instead of seeing my Indianness as a fragile identity to be preserved against obliteration (or worse a "visible" disfigurement to be hidden) I see it now as a set of fluid identities to be celebrated. Indianness is now a metaphor, a particular way of comprehending the world. (Mukherjee 3)

Nevertheless, terms like "homeland" and "home" have acquired new definitions in the postmodern context. Lately, influential theories on the concept of nation have altered the intellectual perceptions, and transnationalism seems to have replaced nationalism. The idea of *nation* has considerably lost its relevance and concepts like *patriotism* and *nationalism* have suddenly become old-fashioned. Under the new aura, the new diaspora is noticeably relieved of the limiting anxieties of *patriotism* and *nationalism*. It has naturally created the necessary space and possibility for "fluid identities."

Diasporic life has its own tensions, and it motivates writers to fictionalise their subjective and collective experiences, generally in the form of autobiographical fiction. Expatriate living is invariably associated with very complex cultural collision as well as problems of adjustment on the part of the émigré population. Women are perhaps the worse victims, as, in the patriarchal perceptions, they metaphorise stereotyped role expectations. Every community looks upon them for the preservation and continuation of ethnicity. Even women themselves seem to subscribe to such a construct and fall easy preys to multiple patriarchies. The constituency of diasporic women invariably has a former colony for their "home," and despite their experiences of gender discrimination in the cultures of their "homelands," they cannot do away with the traditions. Thus, even in their new locations and in the face of deculturation/ acculturation, they act as agents in the process of cultural production.

Such a complex position induces diasporic women to write their lives. Their literature is generally charged with intense anxiety of dislocation and adaptation. In their endeavour of self-expression, they make fictions out of their lives and as a result, their novels become autobiographical. This convergence of fiction and autobiography has given rise to a hybridised form, highly visible among South Asian diasporic women writers. Through their narrations they unconsciously strive to destabilise the conventional expectations by creating alternative histories and narratives of identity.

In this context, it may be mentioned that feminist theorists in the 1980s and the 1990s sought to theorise specific national identities, hybridity and distinct ethnic histories: Afro-American, Asian-American, Native, Canadian, and so on. Moreover, during the 1980s, substantial theoretical engagement of postcolonial studies with women's status as multiply-colonised in many parts of the world had its influence on perceptions. Recent feminist studies relate subjectivity to the material and economic conditions of women's lives, and alternative notions of subjectivity are being explored. According to Isabel Duran, these are not based on:

> [...] the humanist idea of a unique and universal self, but in very complex collective identities which feature autobiographical subjects as existing at particular and changing intersections of race, nationality, religion, education, profession, class, language, gender, sexuality, a specific historical moment, and a host of material conditions. The new geography of identity insists that we think about women writers in relation to a fluid matrix instead of an outworn binary opposition of male/female or masculine/feminine. (Duran, "Autobiography" [Online article])

Seen from this fresh viewpoint, we can relocate the diasporic woman writers at a very complex position, "a fluid matrix," and this explains why they have to preserve as well as reconstruct identities. In her *SPAN* article of 1993, Anne Brewster appropriately observes how Bharati Mukherjee, one of the foremost American-Indian writers, "constructs a personal mythology of immigration and 'assimilation' in numerous autobiographical and quasi-autobiographical writings." The following excerpt from Kavita Sharma's review of Ginu Kamani's *Junglee Girl* succinctly sums up the problem:

> Diasporic experiences are always gendered although they tend to be presented as neutral. Emigration to a new country requires readjustment in traditional roles in the domestic sphere. It makes new demands in which gender relations have to be renegotiated. On the one hand, women who earn an independent income even if it is in an exploitative and racist society, experience greater independence and control over their lives than they had earlier in traditional patriarchal societies like India. On the other hand, they are simultaneously required to maintain homeland kinship networks and religious and cultural traditions in order

> to transmit them to their children. This tends to reinforce patriarchy and makes the domestic sphere both a refuge from the material and spiritual insecurities of exile and a trap in which the conflicting demands of family, work, and old and new patriarchies have to be dealt with. The situation is painful but preferable to the option of return to the homeland especially on terms dictated by men. Diaspora women are caught between patriarchies, ambiguous pasts and futures. (Sharma, "Othering the Other" [Online article])

What is remarkable in the present diaspora life and writing is the emphasis on hybridation while coping with the demands of multiple patriarchies. On one hand, the new generation of immigrant writers, especially the women novelists seek to leave behind the hackneyed East-West encounter theme to entertain a more sensitive and realistic perception of the problematic, and on the other they try to fictionalise the multiple cultural tensions of diasporic life resulting in multiple identities.

Recent theories of 'Identity'[4] state that we have different kinds of identity/ies—national, social, cultural/racial, class, familial, gender, sexual, etc—and all these identities are formed beyond our control, at least partly. Further, this explains why some contemporary theories say that we have multiple identities and that our identity is 'split.' The present-day diasporic life calls for multiple identities, and out of these interrelated identities, the individual forms his/her personal identity. Interestingly, this assumed identity is overtly asserted and aggressively defended by the individual.

Taking a cue from these theories, we can easily appreciate the urge of the present day immigrant writers to "articulate and/or defend" their new identity. The following pronouncement of Bharati Mukherjee in her article "American Dreamer" (1997) may be seen:

> I am an American, not an Asian-American. My rejection of hyphenation has been called race treachery, but it is really a demand that America deliver the promises of its dream to all its citizens equally [...]. I am a naturalized U.S. citizen and I take my American citizenship very seriously. I am not an economic refugee, nor am I a seeker of political asylum. I am a voluntary immigrant. I became a citizen by choice, not by simple accident of birth.

In her articles and interviews, Mukherjee keeps asserting her new *American* identity: "I am an American, not an Asian-American." She writes in "American Dreamer" that she rejects any "hyphenation" of her identity, but then she gives herself a hyphenated identity when she declares: "I'm a Hindu-American" (qtd. in 'Bharati Mukherjee's cultural journey': Anita Amirrezvani, *Mercury News*). Further, in a televised interview with Bill Moyers, she is reported to have said: "I feel very American [...]. I knew the moment I landed as a student in 1961 [...] that this is where I belonged. It was an instant kind of love" (qtd. in Rustomji-Kerns). It may be recalled here that most of our diasporic women writers now live in the US. Even some of those who were living elsewhere have of late been migrating to America. America has always attracted immigration as the Promised/Promising land, and this has made it a migrant nation. America not only accommodates the largest number of immigrants of Indian origin, it also apparently assures the individuals/groups the desired space in their social and private life. It is assumed by settlers that there is no colonised-coloniser tension for immigrants of the Indian origin in the US, and every individual could have his/her freedom of living. Perhaps that is why there are instances of hybridity occurring in the reverse direction. Comparing Canada and America as host countries to immigrants, Bharati Mukherjee writes in "American Dreamer":

> For all its rhetoric about a cultural "mosaic," Canada refuses to renovate its national self-image to include its changing complexion. It is a New World country with Old World concepts of a fixed, exclusivist national identity.

It seems that postcolonial discourses largely dwell on only one side of the issue: that dominant cultures cannibalise the non-dominant ones, whether in the colonial or the neocolonial context. The other side is, the non-dominant cultures of the minority groups equally tend to hybridise the dominant ones. Salman Rushdie's observation in this context is worth mentioning:

> To migrate is to experience deep changes and wrenches in the soul, but the migrant is not simply transformed by his act, *he also transforms the new world*. Migrants might well become mutants, but it is out of such hybridization that newness can emerge. (BBC "Conversation" Series. Emphasis mine)

In an interview with the *Massachusetts Review*, Mukherjee states: "the immigrants in my stories go through extreme transformations in America and at the same time they alter the country's appearance and psychological make-up." Rushdie also holds an identical opinion: "the migrant is not simply transformed by his act, he also transforms the new world" (BBC "Conversation" Series).

As suggested earlier, it is the women who become the shock absorbers in any new social/cultural situation. That women have to bear the onus of negotiating the immigrant psyche is unmistakably seen in the diasporic writing. Male writers, especially novelists, are as such less in number, and whenever they try to fictionalise the émigré experience it is usually superficial. While novelists like B. Rajan, Saros Cowasjee, John B. Alphonso-Karkala or Timeri Murari have more or less confined their representation to the one-dimensional East-West conflict theme, Rushdie's fiction scarcely shows any concern with the issue. For example, Anurag Mathur's *Inscrutable Americans* (1991) is a very readable novel, no doubt, but it offers only a linear presentation of the experience. It does not reflect the complexities involved in the process of cultural assimilation/ hybridation of the émigré. It is therefore the fiction of the women writers—Anita Desai, Santha Rama Rau, Sara Banerji, Meira Chand, Bharati Mukherjee, Meena Alexander, Anjana Appachana, Reginald and Jamila Massey, Chitra Banerjee Divakaruni, Ginu Kamani, Shauna Baldwin Singh, Jhumpa Lahiri, Kiran Desai, Anita Rau Badami, Radhika Jha, Nalini Warior and the like—which shows greater sensitiveness to the immigrant's identity crisis. As women, they are more responsive to the process of hybridation. They are not only very articulate about their positions, they also seek to fictionalise their tensions through their own prototypical characters.

As the diaspora women are caught between patriarchies—often opposing—they seem to develop confused identities. Their pre-migration Indian background extends even to the distant land as an ominous shadow. Even the women émigrés, who are economically independent, who are supposed to enjoy greater freedom than their Indian and even American counterparts, are expected to be responsible for familial and social relationships, as well as for preservation of religious and cultural traditions. They are expected to rear the children, and inculcate the traditional "values" in them. These anticipations bring in multiple patriarchies and in order to cope with the challenges, women unconsciously grow multiple identities, even confused personalities. Consequently, the works of most of these novelists focus on the cultural adjustment of the immigrants—as individuals as well as ethnic groups/communities. There are several instances in their fiction which show how women protagonists try to cope with the problem of identity crisis by acquiring multiple disguises/identities. In Bharati Mukherjee's *Jasmine* (1989), the protagonist has to go through several phases of identity construction: Jyoti, Jasmine and Jane. Similarly in Chitra Banerjee Divakaruni's *The Mistress of Spices* (1997) the protagonist lives a life of multiple identities: Nayan Tara, Bhagyavati, Tilottama and Maya. Critics find Mukherjee's women protagonists to be her own prototypes, metaphorising the creator's gradual progression from one identity to another, sometimes from the "other" to the "centre." Taramoni Chatterjee Cartwright (*The Tiger's Daughter*, 1971), Jasmine (1989), Dimple Dasgupta (*Wife*, 1975), and Padma and Tara Chatterjee in the later novels (*Desirable Daughters, The Tree Bride*) are multiple portraitures of the same persona undergoing changes in succeeding phases of hybridation. They are also suggestive of the multiple identities of the diasporic women.

This draws our attention to an interesting aspect of diasporic women's writing: the autobiographical nature of their fiction. It seems that women writers are more inclined to fictionalise their own private as well as public experiences, fears, anxieties, hopes and frustrations. Moreover, the émigré experience becomes all the more complicated because it is not exclusive to the adopted land; it keeps embarrassing the protagonist even in her own home and "homeland." She is treated as an "outsider" even in her parental home. For instance, in Bharati Mukherjee's *The Tiger's Daughter* (1971), the conservative mother Arati does not like Tara's entering into the kitchen, "the sacred room" of Hindus, because after her marriage to an American Christian, she is "no longer a real Brahmin" (50). Tara finds her relatives and friends also hostile to her "foreigner" status; the men she meets look upon her as a sexual object.

Two of Mukherjee's recent novels, *Desirable Daughters* and *Tree Bride*, of which the second is a sequel to the first, not only continue the stories and characters of her early novels, but also document the progressive saga of acquiring multiple identities. In *Desirable Daughters,* the transformation is presented through two sisters—Tara and Padma—of opposing attributes. While Tara tries to discard most signs of Indianness and chooses to live as an American, Padma is "more Indian than an Indian." Tara is a divorced single mother, teaching in a kindergarten. She lives with a biker, and exhibits her sexuality as a mark of liberation. Padma, on the other hand, safeguards her cultural past, and even displays her Indian identity by wearing only saris, eating Indian food, and socialising only with Indians. Interestingly, Tara's adolescent son Rabi is at ease with both worlds, which is perhaps a pointer towards our hypothesis that somehow men can cope with the anxieties of immigration better than women.

Women writers of Indian origin have no doubt dealt with the issue of identity in their works quite effectively, particularly the complex process of hybridation in the women protagonists. Many of the writers themselves, as individuals, flaunt their new American identity in interviews, essays and seminars. They wish to be identified as "unhyphenated Americans." But all said and done, is it possible for an individual to discard the past altogether and adopt a new identity? Can one consciously hybridise oneself to one's new environment and acquire a new identity or identities? Can one discard one's past, one's history? While acknowledging "Mukherjee's ease with discovering her identity as a mainstream American," Roshni Rustomji-Kerns wonders about such a "stance," writing, in *The Heath Anthology of American Literature*:

> One wonders, however, if one can really discard a part of one's personal/political history even in the process of transformation, especially since the past displays a tenacious, trickster-like ability to appear at the oddest times and in the most astonishing disguises. The insistence on being known as an American, without acknowledging one's Asian heritage, may grate on those who see the term "American" as denoting the *Euro*-American socio-politically dominant group only. For those of us who feel that it is absolutely necessary to continue emphasizing our essentially non-European American identities until we are truly acknowledged as Americans with our own distinctive American presence, Mukherjee's stance may seem simplistic (Rustomji-Kerns, Online article).

Malashri Lal remembers that during her visit to India in 1989, Mukherjee avoided all questions on her "Indianness." She informs:

> Yet the audience saw her [Bharati Mukherjee] sari-clad, dark-eyed, dark-haired, retaining an obvious Bengali-brahmin name, and heard her use Indian material in the extracts she read from her fiction. Mukherjee has, deliberately, problematized her identity, perhaps over-reacting to the likelihood of being enclosed in a coterie culture geographically and ideologically separate from her chosen home and citizenship. (Lal 150)

This brings me to Inderpal Grewal's comment on a review of *Jasmine* published in the *Baltimore Sun.* The review said that *Jasmine* is the story of "the transformation of an Indian village girl, whose grandmother wants to marry her off at 11, into an American woman who finally thinks for herself" (qtd. in Sharma, Online article). According to Grewal this "constructs South Asian women as oppressed and exploited in contrast to the free and independent American woman" (qtd. in Sharma). This also suggests anticipatively that the process of transformation becomes complete only when the immigrant woman of South Asian/Indian origin becomes "American" by casting away her inherent identity. It may also be assumed that Mukherjee and the other diasporic women novelists demonstrate the completion of the process of transformation/liberation by professing their new American identity and writing "American" novels.

It may be interesting to mention here that Bharati Mukherjee's *Leave It to Me* (1997) has been touted by the publishers as an "American novel!" The blurb leaves no doubt in the reader about this new avatar: "[...] vulgar and clever, menacing and hilarious, sexy and violent, the language that struts Bharati Mukherjee's narrative embodies the intoxicating qualities of America itself." The novel takes non-Indians as characters, and mentions India only in a passing manner. The theme, content and worldview of the novel in general give the unfailing impression of being non-Indian/American.

Ginu Kamani's stories exhibit an identical situation. In *Junglee Girl,* characters like the narrator in "Cipher" or Anju in "This Anju" are "liberated by America," whereas Indian characters in India are seen as "neurotic victims of their suppressed sexuality that leads them to unnatural behaviour bordering on the perverse." Even Jhumpa Lahiri's *Interpreter of Maladies* aims at being a corrective to America's melting-pot cultural politics. It has been said of her immigrant characters that they "live neither here nor there—neither fully comfortable in their skins nor steeped in fear and nostalgia" (Hajari, "The Promising Land," Online article) and that they "are not traumatized refugees but are negotiating a path in a country (America) that seems to provide opportunities" (Aull, "*Interpreter of Maladies* by Jhumpa Lahiri," Online article). However, Chitra Banerjee Divakaruni's *Sister of My Heart* (1995), *The Mistress of Spices* (1997), and *Arranged Marriage* (1997) do not completely negate the past—though her characters, uncomfortable as they are, apparently idealise American life as an upgrading Western canon.

The impact of America's dominant culture can also be seen on a very senior and mature novelist like Anita Desai, who declares that she has no desire to classify herself as an Indian writer. She admits that on her annual visits to India (to see her husband and eldest son), she feels more and more a stranger. "One likes to imagine that things have stood still, but so much happens. I have become an observer, and not a participant" (Hoggard, "A better painter than novelist," Online article).

Does this imply that individual identities are finally to be devoured by the dominant culture? It seems so. Hybridation is a natural process, and re-accommodation of values is certainly desirable for healthy and normal growth in the immigrant's individual/collective life undergoing transformation. But we have the impression that there is a willing and conscious discard of one's roots, one's history and one's culture among the highbrow, thinking individuals, in their attempt to assimilate themselves to the new (dominant) culture. Thus, in the process of hybridation/transformation, identities apparently become either confused or erased.

Notes

1. Toru Dutt's novel *Bianca: Or The Young Spanish Maiden* was first published in the *Bengal Magazine* 6 (Jan.-Apr. 1878). The scholarly reissue of this novel has been edited by Subhendu Mund and published in 2001 (New Delhi, Bhubaneswar: Prachi Prakashan).
2. *The Travels of Dean Mahomet, a Native of Patna in Bengal, Through Several parts of India, While in Service of the Honourable The East India Company Written by Himself, in a Series of Letters to a Friend,* included in Michael H. Fisher's *The First Indian Author in English: Dean Mahomed (1759–1851) in India, Ireland, and England* (New Delhi: Oxford UP, 1996), is generally accepted as the first Indian narrative work in English.
3. See *The Diary of Mademoiselle D'Arvers,* N. Kamala's English translation ofToru Dutt's French-language novel *Le Journal de Mademoiselle D'Arvers* (New Delhi: Penguin, 2005).
4. See for details: *World Literature in English*, available at: www.eng.fju.edu.tw/worldlit/diaspora/identity.htm.

Works Cited

Amirrezvani, Anita. "Bharati Mukherjee's cultural journey." *Mercury News*. Available at: www.mercurynews.com/mld/mercurynews/entertainment/9489566.htm. Posted on 08/25/2004.

Aull, Felice. "*Interpreter of Maladies*, by Jhumpa Lahiri." *Literature Annotations*. 57th ed. April 2005. Available at: <http://endeavor.med.nyu.edu/lit-med/lit-med-db/webdocs/webdescrips/lahiri1563-des-.html. Date of entry: 05 Nov. 1999. Last modified on 04 Nov. 2000>.

Brewster, Anne. "A Critique of Bharati Mukherjee's Neo-nationalism." *SPAN Journal of the South Pacific Association for Commonwealth Literature and Language Studies* 34-35 (1993): Diasporas. Ed. Vijay Mishra. HTML created: 3 Jan. 1997 URL: Available at: <http://kali.murdoch.edu.au/~continuum/litserv/SPAN/34/Brewster.html>.

Chopra, Sonia. "Interview with Bharati Mukherjee." Bookreporter.com. Available at: <www.bookreporter.com/authors/au-mukherjee-bharati.asp>.

Duran, Isabel. Autobiography (2000 BCE). *The Literary Encyclopedia.* First published 2003. Available at <www.LitEncyc.com>.

Gobel, Walter. "Bharati Mukherjee: Expatriation, Americanity and Literary Form." *Fusion of Cultures?* Ed. Peter O. Stummer and Christopher Balme. Amsterdam: Rodopi, 1996.

Hajari, Nisid. "The Promising Land: Indian-American Jhumpa Lahiri's heralded debut only partly lives up to its advance hype." Rev. of *Interpreter of Maladies*, by Jhumpa Lahiri, 15 Apr. 2001. Available at: <http://www.time.com/time/asia/magazine/99/0913/books.html>.

Hoggard, Liz. "A better painter than novelist." Rev. of *The Zig Zag Way*, by Anita Desai. *The Observer*, 29 Aug. 2004. Available at: <http://observer.guardian.co.uk/review/story/0,6903,1292869,00.html>.

Jain, Jasbir. "Foreignness of Spirit: The World of Bharati Mukherjee's Novel." *Journal of Indian Writing in English* 13:2 (1985).

Kamani, Ginu. *Junglee Girl.* New Delhi: Penguin, 1995.

Lal, Malashri. *The Law of the Threshold.* Simla: IIAS, 1995.

Mukherjee, Bharati. *The Tiger's Daughter.* 1971. New Delhi: Penguin, 1990.

——. Introduction. *Darkness.* 1980. New Delhi: Penguin, 1990.

——. *Leave It to Me.* London: Chatto & Windus, 1997.

——. *Desirable Daughters.* New York: Hyperion, 2002.

——. "American Dreamer." *Mother Jones* (Jan.-Feb. 1997). Available at: "American Dreamer." <www.motherjones.com/commentary/columns/1997/01/mukherjee.html>.

Rushdie, Salman. *Imaginary Homelands: Essays and Criticism, 1981-1991.* London: Granta, 1991.

Rustomji-Kerns, Roshni. *The Heath Anthology of American Literature.* General Editor Paul Lauter. Fourth ed. <college.hmco.com/english/lauter/heath/4e/students/author_pages/contemporary/mukherjee_bh.html>.

Sharma, Kavita. "Othering the Other: Ginu Kaman's *Junglee Girl.*" *IndiaStar Review of Books.* Available at: <www.indiastar.com/kavita.htm>.

□

Jayanta Mahapatra's *Bare Face*: The Sad Voice of the Earth

Chhayakanta Sarangi

Jayanta Mahapatra is a distinguished Indian poet who has by now produced a significant body of poetry in English. He also writes in Oriya, and by now has, indeed, become a very prominent Oriya poet. As far as his work in English is concerned, we may say that his poetic career of the last three decades, beginning with the publication of *Close the Sky, Ten by Ten* (1971), is a quest to find himself in relation to his country's present as well as past. In volumes like *A Whiteness of Bone* (1992) and *Shadow Space* (1997), the political turmoil of the country, poverty, violence, moral degradation and perversion of Gandhian values in post-Independence India engage his poetic scrutiny. Though he finds to his utter dismay that poetry has neither brought any change in the society nor alleviated human suffering, he does not stop writing poems. His latest volume, *Bare Face,* divided into two parts, came out in 2000.

Part I of *Bare Face* includes 26 poems, and Part II, titled "Requiem," is a long poem of 24 pages divided into 20 sections. Commenting on Mahapatra in this volume, a critic observes: "His imagination is triggered, sustained and spelt by his awesome ability to be literally intuitive and exact to an emotional depth worthy of the finest poetry written" (*Gentleman* review, 101). What is more remarkable in this volume is the poet's social commitment as an unacknowledged legislator of the world. As such he is not an alienated individual, but an insider in the society. One unmistakably hears the voice of a poet who, to quote S. Dasgupta, "is aggrieved, outraged and disenchanted as he experiences the mindless bigotry and hypocrisy of the country of his birth" (Dasgupta 2). *Bare Face* articulates "the sad voice of the earth" (20) as heard by Jayanta Mahapatra.

This volume brings out Mahapatra's concerns over the post-Independence India of fifty years. Here we find him as a poet relentlessly exposing the death of a dream and the collapse of a vision. "One Clear Night" presents freedom as a puppet that "sways to the pulls of unseen masters." People feel "betrayed," though more than fifty years have passed since Independence. The poet finds all day to be "night inside" and lives in a world of self-deception: "And I can find myself lying about my life" (17). In "Freedom" he refers to those people "who never had even a little rice/ for their one daily meal these fifty years." The poet doesn't find freedom any where in the country. The only freedom he gets is "the freedom of the body when it's alone" (17).

The long poem "The Return" presents the poet's attempt to be a good citizen in an environment with the red glow of "bureaucrats' eyes," "walls of maniacal government buildings," "passing of the Minister's Mercedes," "promises of leaders unfulfilled" and "the motives of our darker selves": "The script of the forgotten emperor" has been "stiffened in the cold of the government's night" (21-23). The poet directly addresses the Rock, the altar of his ancestors to:

teach those who rule my impoverished land today
to stand in your valley of the tortures of the dead
and feel the shudder that runs down your granite back,
not revel on the churnings of funeral oceans:
but remember those unwritten names
before the falling of the Wall,
and before the stares of reality
terrify the childlike blue waters of the Daya. (22)

The poet is disappointed at failure of political leaders to take his native land ahead. He cries for his motherland, but is left "with futile tears":

as I watch the land of my birth
run roughly like a clock
that was always thirty minutes slow
no matter how often it was adjusted. (22)

He says the same thing in "Postcard from Home":

My country,
moving from plan to plan,
from government to government,
unable to make up its mind
to light a lamp or do anything sensible. (48)

Like other volumes, *Bare Face,* too, reveals Mahapatra's concern for women. In "Traveller" he refers to a girl "dying in her mother's arms," "the woman with her knees drawn to her chest," and "the scream of the girl/ who is dying in her mother's arms" (16). "In a Time of Winter Rain" shows how "in the writings on ancient rock, young women/ bound and gagged, etch the grey walls/ with their dead brown bellies, their joyless eyes" (18). In "The Return" he speaks of "the blisters of women coolies tarring the wide hot streets near Raj Bhavan" (23). "Not in Defence of the Poem" exposes the poverty, oppression and ill luck of a girl married to an old man. It refers to an old man,

who in exchange
for an overdue mortgage,
lives in the hope of having
the sweetest, long suffering daughter
of a threatened family (25).

This volume shows Mahapatra's search for a saviour in this dehumanizing social, political and cultural decadence. Perhaps, to the poet, the only possibility of redemption is the resurrection of Mahatma Gandhi, who could dispel the encircling gloom. But the irony is that in the post-Independence India Mahatma Gandhi has become the forgotten icon of truth. In gagged, etch the grey walls/ with their dead brown bellies, their joyless eyes" (18). In "Concerning August 1998" he questions rhetorically:

Wasn't the one voice who spoke of truth
A greater force than this fleet of legislators and scholars? (20)

In "Sometimes" once again he says:

Even the headless torso of Gandhi
in the city square can speak.
Like truth, unsaid most of the time
yet almost said. (29)

It is evident from his statements on many occasions that he had expected poetry to bring about a change in the society. In his search for identity as a poet he experiences his failure as a poet in this respect. His questioning the efficacy of poetry in this regard had started in "Last Night the Poem (Life Signs)." In *A Whiteness of Bone* and *Shadow Space* he becomes more eloquent about it. The latest volume, *Bare Face*, brings out his utter frustration as a poet who could not do anything to rid the society of its ills and evils. Many of the poems in this volume reveal

Mahapatra's sense of despair. In "The Return" he says: "poems too fail to sooth my grief." In "Not in Defence of the Poem" he analyses the role he has played as a poet and finds the poem:

as one who stands
with her arms folded,
as if holding herself for control,
although she were cursing me,
like I had cheated her,
word by word, through the years.
Yet the ironic thing about the poem
is that it easily says farewell,
shuts itself up in silence. (24-25)

In "For Days Together" Mahapatra remembers how "nameless manuscripts on palm leaves in a dead language of aborigines" do not belong anywhere any more and have become "fragments of consolation," "the undigested calcium of ages" (36-37). He describes the effect of his own poetry in the same way:

For all its intellectual appearance, this poem
of mine is sealed in a layer of glass,
forbidding, unearthly,
like the hesitant flowering scarlet
of palas every January [...] (37)

Referring to poetry in "Progress," written after an Australian missionary and his two young sons were burnt alive in Orissa on the night of 22 January 1999, Mahapatra says: "It suffers from a frantic darkness." His poem with "its hands folded, eyes shut" looks down at "those three charred corpses/ of a father and his two young sons." But it can do nothing but "merely wonder/ if it had not been a cruel, unjustifiable need" (50). Mahapatra is, above all, a humanist. In a conversation with Norman Simms he has said: "I don't think I am a religious person in the way most Indians are [...]. My concept of religion would be not to hurt others, or try not to do so" (quoted in Prasad 292). In "For Days Together" he expects his poetry to speak for human values. Therefore he was hurt "when a father and his two children were burnt alive/ Just because they had another faith." His poetry has not been able to stop "the contagion of religious revenge":

The poem's fate hangs like an old calendar
on a nail on my conscience's wall.

Blankness stumbles on its bones.
Trying to rid itself of its dates (38)

Mahapatra loses his hopes in the regenerating power of poetry. In "The Lines of My Poem" he finds his poem "stumbling over the hunger of another starving child" and says, "perhaps the lines of my poem/ will be lame for a long time" and "dragged along the wide streets of New Delhi" (43). The poem becomes "the cocoon of (my) broken heart" and wounds the poet. Mahapatra says:

Today a line of this poem
has lost the use of its healthy legs,
trapped like a sparrow
which has strayed inside,
beating its wings against
the bars of the world's conscience. (44)

Once again, in 'The Tame Ending' he deals with the same theme and says:

The poem is like a lost child wailing
near a lamp post, uncomforted by the coin
thrust into its fist by a passer-by. (39)

Mahapatra always tries to present the naked truth on this earth, but apprehends: "Maybe truth will kill it if it touches the earth" (39). Despite his apprehension, he does not cease writing, because "what poetry cannot do is to acknowledge it is mute" (39).

Part II of *Bare Face* is entitled "Requiem" and is divided into 20 sections. It is an emotional tribute to Mahatma Gandhi. It is like a dirge resurrecting moments of Indian history from the Salt Satyagraha of 1930 till Gandhi's death. Mahapatra had earlier declared that he was going to write a long poem on Gandhiji, and it came true with the publication of *Bare Face*. That he was fascinated by the personality of Gandhi was conspicuous as early as 1971 when a poem entitled "Gandhi" appeared in *Close the Sky, Ten by Ten*. There are references to the perversion of Gandhian values in many a poem of other volumes, too. This long poem "Requiem" is dedicated to Mahatma Gandhi, who passed away on 30 January leaving "the diabolical air of history." In the light of an assessment of a great personality one can evaluate his own self, and this is what Mahapatra does in "Requiem," when he reflects upon this great personality and says: "In this past I am always alive" (64).

Mahapatra recollects how "the shadow of India/ weighed him down" (58) and how Gandhiji, "quietly stooped and picked up/ a handful of salt" that lighted "the gentle English countryside far away." The earth saw "the blood of a country's heroes/ seeping into the haunted amber sands" (59). There was no fight, no struggle and no violence from their side. The marchers of the Salt Satyagraha simply walked forward till they were struck down. Today it appears "as if the events were never real" (60). If Gandhiji, the apostle of non-violence had been alive today, he could not have stood the sight of the violence and bloodshed that are rampant in post-Independence India. Hence the poet says:

Perhaps he had seen death
as the most honorable way to ask forgiveness of the world,
perhaps the frozen life of the freedom he wished for
was beyond his own conception of mortality
or, had he only set a trap for his own death? (65)

Mahapatra is so influenced by Gandhiji's life and philosophy that he celebrates him as an embodiment of human values. In Gandhiji he finds that:

the segments of uranium,
of Hindu and Muslim thought,
began to rush together,
seeking the union
that made humanity to flicker
like a firefly against the night. (67)

According to the poet, Gandhiji's *ahimsa* assumes "the clear, self-sustaining light of suns: a redefinition of beauty" (67). Mahapatra feels that now he lives "without a past/ with an uncertain future" (68). In his quest of self he tries to reach for Mahatma Gandhi:

I reach for you through many gestures
may be a karma yogi
like a Parvati whose penance to be united with Siva
lies trapped by the strange shape in her own mind [...] (68)

Mahapatra recollects Gandhiji's death with his two final words "He Ram," and finds in them "the briefest of silences,/ a touch of the silence of immensity" (64). Addressing Gandhi directly, he says "Even the iron that pierced your frail chest/ had a human voice" (76). But this voice is heard no more in post-Independence India. Today it:

floats over the breath of discarded ideals,
the breath of dead flowers day after day at Raj Ghat;
it becomes the breath
that the children of Kalahandi breathe in their dreams
in their interminable starvation sleep. (78)

The poet compares Mahatma Gandhi to Buddha, the apostle of non-violence in ancient India, who left aside "the gaudy universe/ of colours, scents and sensuous densities" and "closed the distance between himself and God" (71). Like Buddha, Gandhiji was seen "moving slowly against the current/ with inexorable patience" (71). Living in an age when Gandhian ideology is disrespected, the poet says, "defending you today hurts my tired eyes," because "what I try to defend/ falls to darkness" (76). Therefore, Mahapatra does not want to carve Gandhiji in stone to perpetuate him. He ironically says:

So we can carve
some darkness
into the icy forehead of India
and some imperfection
into her perfect creation. (70)

The poet acknowledges his responsibility for the total loss of human values in the society. Mahapatra always identifies himself with the society, be it well or ill. He does not free himself from guilt when the apostle of nonviolence was killed by violence:

I know I have never
pulled the trigger of any gun.
But does that make me less of a conspirator?
in me
long forgotten scars rise up
to become fresh wounds,
In me
your body opens slowly
as if you have been bound tight all your life,
as if flesh could see
what the mind believes is true. (77)

On the whole, the poem is marked by an unredeemed tone of resignation. The poet feels a deep sense of isolation and agony in this land of discarded ideals. The poem ends on a note of lament with a direct address to the Father of the Nation:

> What you have left behind are
> faded pictures on bare office walls. A day
> every year as a national holiday. (79)

Mahapatra's search for his own identity leads him to search for a saviour, and *Bare Face* expresses this search in what the poet calls "bad heart." Mahapatra has said:

> Poetry makes me write poems with a bad heart. I don't know what that exactly means, but it is the heart that makes one turn secretly into someone—a leader or loser perhaps—pushing one to choose values, attitudes, and to do the not-so-obvious; this heart, as it keeps on trying to hide the wounded walls of its house, and at the same time asking itself for a meaning to our lives. (Mahapatra, quoted in *Haritham* 7)

In this ailing society Mahapatra finds Gandhian ideology as a way of redemption. His "bad heart" is his wish to see "a just and fair society."

Works Cited

Dasgupta, Sanjukta. "Search for a Saviour." *The Sunday Statesman* 19 Aug. 2001: 2.

Mahapatra, Jayanta. *Bare Face*, Kottayam: D.C. Books, 2000.

Mahapatra, Jayanta. "Piercing the Rocks, Silence to Poetry." *Haritham* 8 (1996): 7.

Prasad, Madhusudan, ed. *The Poetry of Jayanta Mahapatra: A Critical Study*. New Delhi: Sterling Publishers, 1986: 292.

Rev. of *Bare Face*, *Gentleman* (April 2001), 101.

□

The Autobiographic Impulse: Themes and Conventions in Malaysian Biography and Autobiography

S.N.R. Kazmi

The genre of autobiography has drawn much attention from critics and scholars over the last few decades, with scholars antedating the term itself beyond Robert Southey's 1809 use of it to the late eighteenth-century English working-class poet Ann Yearsley and critics delineating as many as fifty-two "genres of life narrative" ranging, alphabetically, from "apology" to "witnessing." In addition, a line is now drawn between autobiography proper, in which the author looks within, and memoir, in which he or she looks at other people.[1]

The writing of lives in English is a recent phenomenon in Malaysia and Singapore. The Japanese occupation of South-East Asia combined with some experience of using English served as an impetus to writing memoirs. The earliest of these records of the war years, Chin Kee Onn's *Malaya Upside Down*, published in January 1946 and reissued only three months later, promised memories of the Japanese occupation, but throughout the book the first person is only used once and then too in the generic form: "It was cheaper to import the rice [before the war] than to plant it ourselves" (56). Chin gives merely "a record of the times—a commentary on the history of the period" (xi). In an inspired moment he prophesies: "The day is not far off when Malaya will knock at the door and seek admission into the family of industrialised countries" (173). Otherwise he is far from personal in his book.

Another early attempt at a war memoir in Malaya or Singapore was Gurchan Singh's *Singa: Lion of Malaya: Being the Memoirs of Gurchan Singh* (London: Quality Press, 1949; reprinted, Kuala Lumpur: Printcraft, n.d.), in which focus is kept sharply on the author. In fact, this little book opens with a mention of the author's birth in May 1914 and his early years, leading to his joining the police and his rise through the ranks. Then came the war and the Japanese occupation, against which Gurchan Singh carried on his underground campaign involving hair's-breadth escapes, assumed identities and encounters with the dreaded Kempetei (Military Police). The book offers a very consistent account of the author's actions and throughout gives attention to what he did and saw until the end of the war and the return of British rule to Malaya. His post-war years are not even touched on.

Yet another early memoir is Sybil Kathigasu's *No Dram of Mercy* (London: Neville Spearman, 1954), the harrowing account of a nurse's ill-treatment by the Japanese military police intended to extract the names of her accomplices in sending medicines and food to the "hill-people," the Chinese who were resisting the Occupation from their bases in the jungle near Ipoh in Perak. At one point Mrs Kathigasu's five-year old daughter Dawn was hung from a tree under which a fire was lighted, but both mother and daughter resisted this pressure to betray relatives and friends. At the end of the war the nurse and her doctor husband were left alive, but Mrs Kathigasu died after two years of medical treatment in London for injuries inflicted on her by a Kempetei sergeant in course of interrogation. Here again the account of the war years gains in being kept to the writer's own actions and first-hand experiences, especially her care of the anti-Japanese people in their sickness, and her frequent misgivings about the rightness of her care of the resistance members as far as her household were concerned.

The longer narratives which followed were usually given a run-in about early days, sometimes beginning with the authors' "origins" in China or Sri Lanka, and laced with curious customs and manners of the home village. Often the follow-up from 1945 was rushed, even hushed. One 260-page account, completed in 1961, compresses "The Post War Years" into an 18-page chapter.[2] Another puts the war years as part of childhood's half-understood anxiety.[3] The anxiety lingers in other cases, along with the anger.[4]

Most of the lives were written by those who spoke languages other than English, but they had followed professional and/or academic courses in England. One of them, the author of three autobiographies, "learned his English by ear [...]. After completing the [first] book in Chinese, he narrated it in English to Austin Coates [...] who helped him with the translation as they went along."[5]

The autobiographies employ some of the procedures of fiction: for example, conversations which took place ten to forty years earlier than the date of composition are given *verbatim*. The device usually works well when the author has an ear for the idiom of the time, but the slightest *faux pas* can undermine the claim of authenticity. In Tan Kok Seng's three books conversations are frequently supplied but, even when the participants are young Chinese coolies and greengrocers, the English is both faultless and adult.[6] We are dealing here with an extraordinary technical difficulty in the use of English dialogue in memoirs set in non-English-speaking countries, and the willing suspension of linguistic disbelief is necessary.

One writer hovers uncertainly between autobiography/biography and fiction. In his *Southward Lies the Fortress: The Siege of Singapore* (Singapore: Educational Publications Bureau, 1971), Lim Thean Soo attempts "a historical account of the siege of Singapore in novel form and not a novel with a historical background."[7] Of course, he adds that, in spite of the possible "intrusions" of his personality, the "I" in this book is not himself but "a composite of Volunteers" who defended the island in 1941-42. In his *Destination Singapore* (Singapore: Pan Pacific, 1976) he gives up altogether his claim of historicity and offers his narrative as "essentially a piece of fiction" based on coffee-shop rumours in February 1942 about the loss of certain British naval plans.[8] Since these two books not only mix fiction with fact but subordinate fact to fiction, they cannot be seen to be attempting "the history of the lives of individual men" or "the story of one's life written by himself."[9] In consequence they are not given further consideration below.

Even biography (and autobiography) proper may take a variety of forms, especially in response to the aims of the writer. It can take the form of a straightforward presentation of facts and scenes from someone's life, as in Yeap Joo Kim's life of her maternal grandfather, a Penang Chinese businessman of the old school. The entire span of the subject's career may be covered and the focus hardly allowed to stray for long; in fact, the subject can even be presented in a single role, as a paterfamilias in the case of Khoo Sian Ewe. A biography can also have a mixed, hazy or shifting focus, as in E.J.H. Corner's *The Marquis: A Tale of Syonan-to* (Singapore: Heinemann Asia, 1981) and S.H. Tan's *Now You Know* (Kuala Lumpur: Penerbit Jaya, 1978). Corner's book is an unresolved tangle of war memoir, biography (of the last Marquis of Tokugawa) and "apology" (for continuing his own scientific and preservation work during the Japanese occupation). Similarly, Tan supplies "biography" in the third person in his preliminary pages and memoir or "apology" in a first-person narrative of his rise and fall on the *Straits Times* group of newspapers. From Chapter 2 onwards he lapses into anecdotes, often seemingly imagined ones. The ordinary business of writing a life is not kept as the *raison d'être*.[10]

Sometimes the memoirs show a clarity of outline as self-portraits even though events of the war years loom large in them. Mamoru Shinozaki's *Syonan—My Story* (Singapore: Asia Pacific Press, 1975), for example, does not attempt a full-scale autobiography, but this balanced account of what one Japanese official did and felt during the occupation has value as a self-portrait, for the reader does not lose sight of the doer in the doings. The form of memoirs can be seriously affected by their mode of publication too. The four volumes of Tunku Abdul Rahman's reminiscences are collections of his Monday columns in the then Penang-based newspaper *The Star*.[11] They are printed in the order in which they appeared originally and not in the sequence in which the events remembered had occurred. A frequent subject in these books are the events leading to Malaya's independence and the Tunku's prime ministership. Here the public man tends to provide wise comments after the act but on occasion the private man comes through, especially in the sections dealing with his Prince Hal days.

The memoirists reflect the region's race-consciousness. Thus, van Cuylenburg, born in Singapore in 1895 of a Dutch Burgher father from Ceylon and a Sarawak Eurasian mother, still talks of the time "when we declared war on Germany on 3 September" (*Singapore: Through Sunshine and Shadow*, 54) and of the mutiny of Indian troops in February 1915 in which hundreds died "in pitched battles with our combined forces" (49). He goes on to record that "many of our Indian troops" were strangled to death by the Japanese invasion forces, and to refer to his neighbour as "a Chinese friend of ours, who lived next to us" (112). Again, Janet Lim says about her rescuers: "When I opened my eyes a kind Malay put his hand on my forehead." At the first-aid station at Senajang near Sumatra she was examined by "a Chinese doctor" who shook his head and moved on.

In her *Sold for Silver* (London: Collins, 1958), Janet Lim begins with her childhood days in China (she was born in Hong Kong in 1923). She recalls without comment or self-commiseration what she saw, heard and, above all, felt, as she grew up in China or worked as a slave girl in Singapore. A child's natural tone hands over quietly to the "grown-up" world's overtones. She records the story of her life as a *mui tsai* or slave girl during 1932-34 and her rescue by the Lady Assistant Protector of Chinese in Singapore, and the story of her indecision between her father's Christianity and her mother's Buddhism until she was given refuge in a Church of England boarding school in Singapore.

Not content to narrate events in a rather eventful life, Janet Lim looks within to serve her avowed aim of writing "An Autobiography." She recalls: "Even after I had been a nurse for about eight months I was still unsettled, as in the hospital there was no home-like atmosphere. I visited the school almost weekly—it was the only home I knew [...]" (94). Such personal touches move the memoir towards autobiography proper. However, Janet Lim's narrative of the war years is action-packed—nursing casualties in a camp hospital, evacuated in a small boat, supporting herself on two floating corpses and later on a raft for a whole day and night, resisting persuasion, torture and threat of death by water from the Japanese Kempetei to dwindle from a nurse to an admiral's "comfort girl." It is to Janet Lim's credit that she does not completely subordinate self-life to mere history.

A contrast to Janet Lim's autobiography is presented by Mamoru Shinozaki in *Syonan—My Story: The Japanese Occupation of Singapore*, dedicated "to the war victims." The book is not the "story" of Shinozaki, but the story of what he did in "Syonan" (Singapore) before and during the Japanese Occupation. It opens *in medias res*, with the brief visit in September 1940 of two Japanese strategists to see the coastal areas of Singapore and Malaya. Shinozaki, a minor diplomat who took them round, was immediately after detained and sentenced to three and a half years on a charge of spying. The rest of the book is an account of his work during the Japanese rule over Singapore, especially in coming to the aid of a number of British officials and ordinary Chinese and in setting up the Endau and Bahau camps in Malaya for ill-nourished evacuees from Singapore.

However, Shinozaki does not merely report all the time: his book offers an occasional comment which brings it alive as a human document. For example, after recording the harsh details of his life in Changi Prison ("After a day's work, at 5 p.m., we would gather at the E block to get our ration of three small pieces of bread"), he adds: "I did not realize it at that time, but my stay in Changi Prison was providing me with valuable experience [...]. In prison I learnt a great deal about human relations. Nobody puts on airs or graces in prison. Everyone is forced to behave naturally" (19). Sweet indeed are the uses of adversity to Shinozaki who, as head of the Welfare Department, was to work hard to sweeten the adversity of Singapore Chinese under Japanese military rule: "Had Japan won the war, I believe I might have been charged with aiding the enemy, of being a traitor" (101).

That Shinozaki did not attempt to turn himself into a marble statue may be seen from John Bertram van Cuylenburg's *Singapore: Through Sunshine and Shadow* (1982). Calling him "that arch-spy of pre-Pacific war days," the writer admits that Shinozaki did his best to aid and rescue Singaporeans during Japanese rule. Van Cuylenburg calls his own book "a true personal narrative of Singapore," and in his shapeless first chapter draws attention not to himself but to "what Singapore was like at the beginning of the century" (3), but he slips in an occasional reminiscence of himself or his family ("My mother, I remember well, had an Irish terrier that used to run between the ricksha wheels when she went shopping!"). After the 52-page "Reminiscences" the book is largely filled with a coherent narrative of the war and the Japanese Occupation. The post-war period, between September 1945 and December 1961 (the date of the Preface), is compressed into the seventeen pages of the finale, which is both ponderous and cliché-ridden (259): "All good things must come to an end!" "colonialism [is] as dead as doornails."

Van Cuylenburg rarely looks within, shows a sense of humour or gives an example of largeness of sympathy. He can record gleefully of the treatment of Japanese prisoners of war after the return of British rule: "A pleasant surprise awaited us the next morning. A gift from the Gurkhas? Word went around that Japanese P.O.W.s had made their appearance in our village. There was a rush of settlers for this preview! Yes, a contingent of Japanese was there all right; they had been sent up from P.O.W. camp at the town of Bahau to do odd jobs for the settlers. It was now the turn of the Japanese to do something for each internee. This was only fair as we were all still *hors de combat* after our illnesses and privations" (249-50). After noting that the year 1945 "was to bring in its wake the most devastating events the world had ever known" he adds: "The two atom bombs that destroyed Hiroshima and Nagasaki saved us!" (228). It is perhaps just as well that we do not see more of the man behind the memoir.

In *The Marquis: A Tale of Syonan-to*, E.J.H. Corner refers to the same year in more humane terms: "The prospect for 1945 was disease, starvation, and putrefaction, which the atom-bomb forestalled. Syonan-to was becoming a starvation camp" (137-38). In fact, Corner's account of his war years in Singapore is exceptional in recording the work of conservation of scientific specimens and documents with the support of several Japanese civilian officials, including the last Marquis of Tokugawa who was President of the Raffles Museum and Botanical Gardens from 1942 to 1944. When Corner (afterwards Professor of Tropical Botany in Cambridge) and two other British scientists were interned for six days in January 1945, their Japanese colleagues Kwan Kariba and Yata Haneda took them from the camp to the former's house for a bath and for a banquet: "The internment grieved them more than us for whom it was a good test of our precautions" (142). Corner also notes that without humour he could not have survived the Occupation, but is far from facetious.[12]

We are neither promised nor offered a reappraisal of the author's own life. Of course, he does provide an "apology" for working for the Japanese military administration, but only intermittently does he give the reader a sense of interrelatedness of the episodes of his tale or of the maturing of his personality through them. Incidents are often related in isolation and irritating breaks are left unfilled. On page 154, for example, there is a comment on "This tale of Sir Shenton [Thomas]'s pencilled note" which has really not been told. In such a miscellany, not surprisingly, characters appear briefly and then disappear without leaving a trace. This means that awkward jerks are given to the reader's attention.

A continuous narrative is certainly to be found in Tan Sri Dato Mubin Sheppard's *Taman Budiman: Memoirs of an Unorthodox Civil Servant* (Kuala Lumpur: Heinemann, 1979), which covers half a century in the life of an Irishman who joined the then Malayan Civil Service in January 1928.[13] The book's ten chapters are assigned their own dates as well as descriptive titles, beginning with "Clifford Cadet 1928-1929," the story of M.C.ff. Sheppard's work in the then malaria-prone Temerloh district of Pahang. A reading of this opening chapter throws some anticipatory light on the rest of the book. We are first told that the district did not boast more than ten slow cars, and next that the High Commissioner's powerful Daimler one day pulled up with a loud screech in front of the villagers. We go on to learn about Sheppard's arrival in Malaya, his posting as a "Clifford Cadet" to Temerloh to master Malay, and his District Officer's reluctance to introduce him to Sir Hugh Clifford or other visiting officials. We get brief glimpses of a number of British and Malay dignitaries. However, we do not get more than a passing glimpse of the author himself; even vital facts about him are dropped casually, for example on page 13 we are told that his "twenty-third birthday fell on June 21 [1928]," on page 7 that he "had taken an honours degree in History at Cambridge" and on page 12 that his "father, a Dean in the Church of England, [was] deeply concerned at the near-pagan existence which [he] appeared to him to be leading in Temerloh." These are slim pickings from a chapter which is packed with telling details about other people. The story begins with the author's life as a civil servant without a backward look at his early days in Ireland and England.[14]

Of course, this niggle has been anticipated by the author in his preface: "[...] this is not an autobiography: it is an attempt to describe the life of a Malayan Civil Servant between 1928 and 1956, in conditions [...] which then provided opportunities for the exercise of initiative which are no longer available" (xi-xii). He eschews the bumpy road to autobiography and follows instead the smooth road to memoirs. As a result, his gaze turns inwards only on rare occasions. Usually he reminisces about people, places or episodes; sometimes he is full of wise saws about them; for example, when he remarks: "A civil servant is necessarily a bird of passage during his thirty years or more in Malaysia […]" (213). But on one or two occasions he tries to come to grips with a change in himself, as in his idea of religion in general and of Islam in particular. He traces his sense of "a conscious spiritual link with God" (215) to his experiences as a prisoner of the Japanese in Singapore and to his many Malay friends. However, he does not let us follow the state of mind in which he decided to stay behind in Malaya after Independence in 1957 and to take Malayan citizenship in 1958. We are only told that before he had completed three years in Malaya his "close identification with Malay interests had aroused comment, and [he] was described by many Europeans of both sexes as 'Malay mad'" (32-33). The most thrilling sections of the book tell the story of the war years, during which Sheppard became an officer in the Federated Malay States Volunteer Force and was chosen to lead a "Stay Behind" party in the East Coast area, with which he was familiar. His group was to operate a wireless transmitter and carry out guerrilla activities behind the Japanese lines. A packed-up transmitter, a bout of tropical typhus and the swift Japanese advance sent him south to Singapore, where he was still in the General Hospital when the Japanese landed.

In the rest of the book Sheppard recounts his life as a prisoner and later his return to civilian life, with the success of his "unorthodox" ways. An aside hints at the failure of his marriage, but generally the "civil servant" keeps the private man out of our view, to the detriment of the autobiography. The reader is not given a sense of the cumulative interrelatedness of the parts of the story or the gradual development of the personality.

If Mubin Sheppard's *Taman Budiman* is about his adult life, Dr. Mohamad Said's *Memoirs of a Menteri Besar* (Singapore: Heinemann, 1982) is about his "Early Days" (its sub-title). It does not purport to be just the first instalment of a longer account, and yet it stops with its author still in his teens with his sights set on King Edward VII College of Medicine in Singapore. As a result, it does not tell of "the battles, sieges, fortunes,/ That [he has] pass'd." The book's "onlie begetter," Tun Mohamed Suffian, had implored Dr. Said to write his autobiography: "So few Malays can write and those that can, should" (xii). Dr. Said had had some experience of writing: letters to newspapers, articles in *The Malayan Medical Journal* and in a Bahasa Malaysia journal, and translation work. He had also published, in a Kuala Lumpur newspaper, a series of ten articles on his old school, the residential Malay College, Kuala Kangsar. All the same he hesitated because he could not tell "the truth, the whole truth and nothing but the truth" about his own religious views and about certain people still living. He decided on a compromise, to confide to a "private diary" the round unvarnished tale about himself, about other people, and about events. By implication, this "private diary" is a continuation of Dr. Said's *Memoirs* meant to satisfy his autobiographical impulse.

The book is divided into three long chapters entitled "My Heredity and Environment," "The Koran Reader and the Primary Schoolboy" and "Kuala Kangsar." The third chapter, devoted to his school, fills just over half the book. Chapter One opens disingenuously: "I was born at Kampung Tengah, Linggi, on 31 October 1907 [...]." It goes on to describe the house in which Mohamad Said was born—the picture facing page 110 shows it to be a traditional Malay plank house on pillars or stilts. A note on his family tree leads to a six-page disquisition on the long-term effects of in-breeding. But the story of Mohamad Said gets back to an even keel, with recollections of his father (at one time a house-boy to a European planter but afterwards a forest guard) whom he feared rather than loved. He confesses that his father's early death "did not make

[him] feel any feeling of grief or sense of irreplaceable loss" (27), but he superimposes an adult's point of view in an earlier comment on the same lack of filial grief (14). Memoirs cannot but reveal more of the rememberer than of the people and events remembered, and the above comment reveals the good-humoured vein in which Dr. Said sees things.

In Chapter Two, he talks about how at the age of nine he celebrated in some style his reading of the whole Koran and went on to his avid reading of Malay romances or *hikayat* and verse narratives, which he quotes without translating. His recollection of kite-flying, a popular sport in Linggi in those days, ends on a sad note: "I was neither good at making kites nor at flying them" (49). Of course, he recalls too that he became so good at playing marbles that he rarely failed to hit an opponent's marble five yards away.

The long third chapter, about Mohamad Said's six years at the residential Malay College, gives an account of his teachers, friends and intellectual interests. While this section suffers from a lack of sharp focus on the subject of the memoirs, it does have two pages (149-50) on how Mohamad Said moved from his monograph on physical anthropology to scepticism. Later on he was to read *The Origin of Species* and other works on evolution, to conclude that "the truth was on the side of the astronomers and the anthropologists, and that the Biblical and Koranic versions of the origin of man [...] [were] to be regarded not as untrue, but as in some sense allegorical in intent" (150). At Malay College itself he was prepared by his headmaster, Mr Charles Bazell, not to reject offhand the scientists' views on the age of the earth and the coming of man. No wonder Mohamad Said records paying Mr Bazell visits long after he had left the Malay College in 1925 (and Mr Bazell in 1938), his last one being in 1974, when Mr Bazell had "just turned ninety, but was amazingly, or as he expressed it, absurdly fit" (178).

Mohamad Said's book reads well in its chatty, good-natured way. However, it bears the mark of its earlier version, the ten articles on his school commissioned by *The Straits Times* and *The Sunday Times* in 1973. The average page is split up into a number of paragraphs: page 207, an exceptionally chopped-up one, has as many as ten one-sentence paragraphs. What was a help to the newspaper reader is an obvious hindrance to the book's reader. Errors, too, abound: thus, on page 128, the poet Newbolt's name is given as "Sir Henry Newbold" and on page 167 the grammarian Nesfield's as "Nestfield;" on page 187 the colonial administrator Ernest Birch's name is given as "Earnest Birch." An inspired error occurs on page 189: "fragrant eau-de-Quinine." It is likely that some of these and other errors are the result of mishearing by an amanuensis.

Tan Sri S. Chelvasingam-MacIntyre's original intention in writing his memoirs was to produce not a book or a series of articles but, more modestly, "a family heirloom for the edification of future generations of [his] kith and kin."[15] Even the 300-page book, *Through Memory Lane* (Singapore: University Education Press, 1973), that he did publish has the character of an heirloom. Landmarks in the family's saga are pointed out, branches of the family indicated and highlights of the career of the author himself recorded. MacIntyre does not set out to know himself, or help the reader to know him. At no point in the long narrative does he look within seriously or wear his heart on his sleeve. The book is divided into four Parts with their own introductions. Part I offers "Glimpses of the Past," including the fortunes of his family as known to tradition. Extensive quotations are made from his father's diary and letters, especially in chapters 2 and 3, but no attempt is made to understand him as a man. After the regulation "early recollections" of Malaya and of his schooling in Kuala Lumpur and Kandy, the writer passes on to his training at Lincoln's Inn, where he enrolled in 1924. He records listening to and/or meeting people like Conan Doyle, Annie Besant, Jagdish Chandra Bose, Ramsay MacDonald and Bernard Shaw. He recalls visiting Cambridge, Salisbury and Brighton. Cycling to Amesbury one Sunday afternoon, he found all places of amusement closed, and when he asked to be directed to a cinema, he was told rather sharply that Amesbury was not London, and sent instead to the cathedral across the road. On a visit to Paris with two Ceylonese friends, he had a pleasant surprise when Thomas Cook's manager loaned him some money merely on the strength of his verbal assurance: "[...] he was convinced of my story because I had behaved in a way in which a student of my age was expected to behave in Paris and from my deportment and speech he was satisfied that my financial position was sound" (58). While reading in chambers he was taken to Old Bailey to watch a trial before Sir Henry Dickens, but passed the time "gazing with awe on the countenance of the judge because he happened to be the youngest son of the great Victorian novelist" (59).

MacIntyre began his professional career in 1927 as a legal assistant in Singapore and has much to say about the firms for which he worked and the cases which he defended, but his book makes only a passing reference in the chapter on "A Decade of Troubles" to his engagement and marriage to his cousin in 1933. He devotes the "Epilogue" (285) entirely to her and the grief he felt at her sudden death in 1971. In Part II (73-140) MacIntyre offers an anecdotal history of the Japanese occupation of Malaya and Singapore. In a perceptive introduction to this section he notes the psychological impact of the fall of Fortress Singapore: "[...] the rigours and travails of Japanese military rule induced a profound change in our thinking. The very idea of peoples and nations being pushed about by imperial powers to serve their interests and vanities seemed more immoral and obnoxious than ever before. This feeling accounts for the resurgence of the spirit of nationalism throughout the region [...]" (71).

The rest of the war section consists mainly of what MacIntyre did or saw during the Japanese invasion and the subsequent occupation. For a time the lawyer earned his livelihood as a taxi-driver, but in August 1942 he set up, in partnership with a doctor, the Diamond Cigarette Factory, which could turn out as many as 300 cigarettes per hour. He was also active in the Indian Independence League, for which he was worried he might be treated like Roger Casement when British rule was restored. In this section which does not show much introspection or even reflection, MacIntyre dismisses with a sneer two of the greatest acts of destruction in human history: "[...] there are those who were never in danger of being potential victims of Japanese fury who still throw up their hands in holy horror at the use of atom bombs against Japan" (127). At the end of the war he was taken to Delhi as a witness in the Indian National Army trials, but after 38 days in a "cage" in Kabul Lines meant for a prisoner of war was left to fend for himself. It was another two and a half months before he could be back in his home town of Batu Pahat in Johore.

The remaining half of the book continues, in a rather peripatetic fashion, with the postwar years in Malaya and in MacIntyre's own career. In Part IV we see him as a diplomat, serving for seven years as Malaya's (later Malaysia's) High Commissioner to India. In an unusually personal mood he records his early feelings about India: "The world of my childhood fantasy was filled with heroes and heroines, demon kings and apes, who had walked out of the pages of the Ramayana and Mahabaratha [sic]" (203). After a couple of pages in this strain he relapses into "Ramblings and Reminiscences of a Diplomat" (the title of Part IV), where the man is lost in the diplomat and the self-portrait in

"Glimpses of the Past" (the title of Part I). Taken as a whole *Through Memory Lane* must take its place as an heirloom, or perhaps as a vanity book; its claim on our attention must rest on the inspired typo in "a bridal path to virgin jungle" (16).

Tunku Abdul Rahman's four collections of memoirs have, of course, greater interest both as revelations of the self and as records of events. Their aims are modest: to chart the events which led to an independent Malaya and afterwards Malaysia, and to record the part played by the writer in them. They are based on the articles which appeared in the weekly column "As I See It" in *The Star*. In the first collection, *Looking Back: Monday Musings and Memories* (Kuala Lumpur: Pustaka Antara, 1977), the articles are called articles on the contents page and dated, but in the second, Viewpoints (Kuala Lumpur: Heinemann, 1978), they are, rather misleadingly, called chapters (the book has 39 of them) and their dates of original publication are withheld. In the third collection, *As a Matter of Fact* (Kuala Lumpur: Heinemann, 1981), the contributions are not identified as chapters or articles, but their dates are supplied. In the fourth collection, *Lest We Forget: Further Candid Reminiscences* (Kuala Lumpur and Singapore: Eastern Universities Press, 1983), the Tunku refers in his Foreword to his "forty-one short articles" and supplies their dates of first publication in an appendix.

The first volume, which is a gathering of articles published during 1974-76, explains in a brief preface that the articles were written "to bring home to our young people [...] the historical significance of events since World War II which led to our independence and nationhood." The first Prime Minister of Malaysia was stung into writing them because someone wrote a book on Malaysia's Independence without mentioning him. The preface (which reappears in the second collection with just the omission of the last two paragraphs) admits that the articles were not based on any diaries or memorandums, which actually helps to save them from turning into impersonal accounts of events. Of the 53 articles in this first volume only about four can be regarded as fragments of an autobiography, but the rest still bring in the Tunku as witness, participant or commentator. Even in these personal articles (nos. 9, 24, 29 and 37) the public events are very much there. Article 9, for example, is about the Tunku's assumption of office as Chief Minister of Malaya on 3 August 1955 after the country's first general elections. It opens with his recalling how he felt in his finest hour, when he came to know about his party's resounding success: "I sat back in a chair, quite at a loss for words, unable to express myself, or even think clearly, except to feel an overwhelming glow of gratitude to all who helped make this landslide victory possible. I kept repeating to myself, 'Allah be praised!' over and over again" (52). That the words are not a routine gesture is suggested by the Tunku's speech on his horse Think Big's winning the Melbourne Cup in 1975: "Thank God for this victory" (313). After giving the names of his first cabinet the Tunku passes on again to something at least partly personal: the leaky old house allotted to the new Chief Minister made him vow during a thunderstorm to win the country's freedom in two years, not four. In Article 24, entitled "Men who Helped to Shape the Nation, 1: My Friend Datuk Suleiman," the writer blends the private and the public worlds quite easily. He talks of Datuk Suleiman's widow, Datin Tom, seeking the Tunku's help in getting a Thai girl's father to consent to Suleiman's son marrying her. He goes on in this article to record Suleiman's quiet generosity, his sense of humour, his devotion to duty and his sudden death in Australia. But in the remaining third of this article the Tunku goes on to talk of a number of other people and "moments of rich humour."

In Article 37 again he mixes memory and history when he recalls how he intercepted his father the Sultan of Kedah when he was being taken to Penang after the first Japanese landings in Malaya in December 1941. It is curious that he had acted on a dream in which he heard his father calling "Putra, tolong aku, tolong aku" ("Prince, help me, help me"). Late in 1942 his father again appeared to the Tunku in his dream, saying "Putra, I am sick." The Tunku rushed to what turned out to be the Sultan's deathbed. Along with this personal story he supplies in this article some facts about the Japanese occupation of Kedah.

The rest of *Looking Back* is largely a series of reminiscences of an elder statesman, with some comment on current events. As a book, *Looking Back*, which jumps from topic to topic, makes awkward reading. Even individual articles do not maintain their focus for long, due partly to their having been dictated and partly to their having so many short paragraphs to suit their original mode of publication.

In *Viewpoints*, the same blend of personal reminiscences and political events is offered in thirty-nine undated articles. The opening "chapter" ("Remembrance of Things Past") is about the Tunku's days in Bangkok during World War I. He was dazzled by his elder brother's military uniform and aspired to a place in the Thai Military School, but Tunku

Yusof's sudden death in 1915 put an end to his hopes. In the same article he tells us how he had his brother's remains brought from Bangkok and reinterred in Kedah more than fifty years later. He comes to events nearer at hand: the burial of the first Malaysian leader in the Heroes' Mausoleum of the National Mosque and the rumours that the Tunku had built the mausoleum for himself. In Chapter 23 ("The Case for English and Malay") we find more a personal essay on the language issue in Malaysia than a memoir. In one article (Chapter 7) he sets out to answer the question "How do I feel to be seventy-five?" and manages to tell us not only that he feels happy to be "going strong" but also that he came out unscathed from his trials and tribulations. What is remarkable here is his candid reference to the little slights he suffered after September 1970 when he surrendered the Prime Ministership. Throughout this article he keeps his own life, if not his self, in sharp focus. As a whole, *Viewpoints* is better copy-edited, especially inasmuch as it has longer paragraphs.

As a Matter of Interest again ranges over events of the previous fifty years in which the Tunku was a witness or a participant. In articles 25 (3 September 1979) and 36 (17 December 1979) he returns to the Japanese Occupation and recalls his decision to stop his father from being taken to Penang. In articles 20 (10 September 1979) and 37 (24 December 1979) he comments on current events of the time, namely the leadership dispute in the Malaysian Chinese Association in September 1979 and Iran's demand for the return of the Shah. A more personal note is struck in article 22 (6 August 1979), which contains his musings on reaching the age of 77. In fact, this article turns out to be a potted autobiography in itself, beginning with the writer's early days: "There was no cinema to go to, no television so [sic] see and no radio to listen to. There was no electric light to brighten up the homes" (135). He recalls how his pranks with his Riley sports car brought on a Cambridge ban on undergraduate driving at certain hours of the day. He admits, too, that when he took up law at the Inner Temple "there was much too much temptation in London and with nobody to look after me I gave vent to my pleasures and ended up a cropper" (139). It was not until twenty-five years later that he passed his bar examination. Tunku Abdul Rahman's summing up of his life in London is brief: "I enjoyed life, but at the same time I was a responsible man and always conscious of my duty to others" (140). Not quite a confession, and yet far from what might seem to Tristram Shandy "a panegyric upon himself."

Tunku Abdul Rahman's fourth book, *Lest We Forget: Further Candid Reminiscences* collects articles contributed to *The Star* between 14 July 1980 and 1 June 1981. Most of these pieces actually take off from topics of the day, giving the impression that the elder statesman may be scraping the barrel of his memory. His aims, as explained in the Foreword, remain the same as before: "to place on record events of importance of which I have first-hand knowledge" and thus "to make sure that the true facts are not forgotten": hence the title. However, on account of their original mode of publication, the Tunku's recollections had to be baited with some event of the day. Their mode of composition too inevitably affected these articles. The Foreword explains that a secretary took them down in shorthand, typed them and read them out to the author whose sight was failing at the time. Some articles were typed more than once before they were sent to the press. For their issue in book-form these articles were "edited" by Tan Sri Mubin Sheppard, who, the author gleefully suggests, should take the blame for any errors.

As regards content, *Lest We Forget* has little to offer by way of autobiography. Even what it does offer is only slipped in by the way. In article 3, for example, the caption reads "Songs of the Holy Book" and the opening paragraphs indicate the occasion to be the International Koran Competition of 1980. The Tunku says how this annual event has made Malaysia known to other Muslim countries and recalls how it was launched during his prime ministership on the national level in 1960 and on the international in 1961. It hurt him when in 1970 the Chairman of the Organizing Committee said in his opening address, "Now we have a dynamic Prime Minister [...]."

It is with some relief that one turns to Yeap Joo Kim's *The Patriarch* (Singapore: MPH Distributors, 1975), the one biography of a private person to come from the Malaysia-Singapore area. No doubt it is based on family tradition and recollection rather than on solid archival material, for Miss Yeap gives an account of her own grandfather's life and times. She frequently quotes from the Penang newspaper *The Straits Echo* and from the letters she herself received from the subject of her book, which adds to the authenticity of her portrait of the Straits-born Chinese patrician. Traditional respect for family elders makes her refer to the Patriarch only as "KSE;" it is not until page 147, a mere twelve pages before the end, that Khoo Sian Ewe's name turns up, in a newspaper headline reporting the funeral of his wife. The author's own relationship to KSE is indicated in a roundabout way too.

The book is divided into four Parts spanning the four "ages" of the Patriarch's life. Part I, about his "Childhood and Adolescence," opens with a lengthy account of KSE's funeral in Penang, but takes us back to his "origins." KSE's grandfather, Khoo Cheng Lim, came to Malacca from Fukien, and, like many Chinese in the nineteenth century, paid the captain of his junk with three years' labour on a pepper plantation. KSE's father, based in Asahan in Sumatra, was a substantial businessman, who retired to Penang when KSE was ten years old. He sent KSE to an English school and had his pigtail docked, but otherwise he instilled in him a love of Chinese mores.

In his own turn KSE "ruled the house with an iron fist," visiting his country estate of Hazelwood every evening in his Daimler to ensure that the orchards were well guarded and the telephone was used only by himself. His official wife Sim would sometimes go with him from Sunbeam Hall in the city centre, but Jade, the mother of his fifteen children, always stayed at home and was called "Aunt" by her own children. It was Sim who had chosen Jade from the ranks of domestic slaves (*char bor kang*) to bear KSE's children: "She exercised tact and wisdom in allowing his indiscretions with the slave girls, and had the situation absolutely under her control." Of course, "there arose a few occasions when Tok, the popular Malay abortionist of the time, was summoned" (59).

KSE, who made his fortune in real estate, owned three seaside bungalows and an English-style house called (rather nostalgically) Great Wall on Penang Hill, the resort of Europeans. His receptions were held in regal style at Sunbeam Hall to mark a wedding, a birthday or a Chinese festival. By the 1920s he had become a leader of the Penang Chinese community, heading the Chinese Chamber of Commerce, the Chinese Town Hall, the Chinese Merchants' Club and the Rotary Club.

Then came the war. The family moved to Hazelwood, though KSE believed the Japanese could never break the Royal Navy's protective ring around Malaya. Penang was bombed on 11 December 1941; Sunbeam Hall was hit and burnt down. Worse was to follow: the Japanese imposed a "donation" of $1 million on KSE, and he had to part with some of his properties to raise the sum. He also suffered physical ill-treatment at the hands of the Kempetei.

As a biography, *The Patriarch* succeeds in presenting its subject with insight. Its focus is kept steadily on the great man, as seen through the eyes of one of his own grandchildren, and it avoids filial piety partly through its faintly ironic yet essentially sympathetic view of the paterfamilias. It does not waste much time on the origins of the family or the fortunes of its members. As a result, it achieves a fairly high degree of readability.

Taken as a whole, the biographical writings in English to stem so far from Malaysia and Singapore have followed the lines of those memoirs of life in foreign places that British district officers made into a genre. At times it is not quite clear for what audience these memoirs are intended, or what kinds of readers would be most likely to benefit from them. Of the many writers, not one reaches the point at which he can, with Keats, say: "on the shore/ Of the wide world I stand alone, and think/ Till love and fame to nothingness do sink."

Notes and References

1. See Sidonie Smith and Julia Watson, eds., *Reading Autobiography* (Minneapolis: U of Minnesota P, 2001) 1-4; 183-207; Linda Anderson, *Autobiography* (London: Routledge, 2001) 7.
2. See John Bertram van Cuylenburg, *Singapore: Through Sunshine and Shadow* (Singapore: Heinemann Asia, 1982).
3. See Tan Kok Seng, *Son of Singapore: The Autobiography of a Coolie* (Singapore: U Education P, 1972).
4. See van Cuylenburg, 240, 249-50, 259-60.
5. Tan Kok Seng, *Son of Singapore*, back cover. On their title-pages this and the two subsequent volumes, *Man of Malaysia* (Kuala Lumpur: Heinemann, 1974) and *Eye on the World* (Kuala Lumpur: Heinemann, 1975), carried the legend "Rendered into English by the author in collaboration with Austin Coates."
6. See Tan Kok Seng, *Son of Singapore* 35.
7. Lim Thean Soo, *Southward Lies the Fortress* 1.
8. Lim Thean Soo, *Destination Singapore* vii.
9. The quoted words are from the definitions of "biography" and "autobiography" to be found in the *OED*. Alberto Moravia once told Saul Bellow: "Every novel is some kind of higher autobiography" (quoted in Michiko Kakutani, "A Talk with Saul Bellow," *Dialogue* 4 [1982]: 60). On the other hand, William B. Dubin in Bernard Malamud's *Dubin's Lives* (1979) observes that "all biography is ultimately fiction" (20). See also George P. Landow's "Introduction" to George P. Landow, ed., *Approaches to Victorian Autobiography* (Athens, Ohio: Ohio UP, 1979) xv.

10. See i-iii and 1-23 for S.H. Tan's biography and autobiography. The rest of the book (23-98) is largely about other people, though with an occasional remark by the author in his own person.
11. Tunku Abdul Rahman, *Looking Back* (Kuala Lumpur: Pustaka Antara, 1977); *Viewpoints* (Kuala Lumpur: Heinemann, 1978); *As a Matter of Fact* (Kuala Lumpur: Heinemann, 1981); and *Lest We Forget* (Kuala Lumpur: Eastern UP, 1983).
12. See, for example, p. 154.
13. The ten chapters span the years 1928-1974, not 1928-1956, as the preface might lead one to suppose.
14. Paul Murray Kendall argues that twentieth-century autobiography avoids the Freudian depths of self by keeping close to the safe coasts of memoir: "Undertaking an autobiography, under the aegis of modern psychology, is like signing a contract with the Devil: there is much to be won and everything, especially honour, to be lost" (*The Art of Biography* [New York: W.W. Norton, 1965] 125).
15. "Author's Acknowledgement," *Through Memory Lane* ix.

□

Homecoming in Catherine Dunne's *The Walled Garden*

Elisa Armellino

In Catherine Dunne's novel *The Walled Garden* the event which leads Beth to go back to Ireland from London is the illness of her mother, Alice, who is dying in the family house in Dublin. Gradually, this homecoming takes the form of a complex immersion into the characters' past and produces a slow flowing back of memories linked with the familiar context. The characters have, therefore, the chance to reflect upon their lives and to acquire a better awareness of the present.

Yet the realisation of this goal comes only at the end of a long and hard process of recollection, which involves at the same time Alice and Beth. Alice, in fact, understands that she is going to forget the major part of her memories as a consequence of a stroke, so she decides to preserve them by writing a series of letters to her daughter. Beth, while attending to her mother, finds the letters and by reading them begins to remember the time of her childhood and adolescence.

United by a silent communication, the two women retrace all the steps of their tormented relationship and unravel their still unclear feelings towards each other. However, Alice's state of health and the unavoidable differences between her personal memories and those of her daughter on the same past events deny them the opportunity to share the truths found in their distinct meditations. Each has to achieve a comprehension of her own life separately, by following an individual and personal path.

This also leads both to experience a kind of final rebirth. Beth actually abandons her native town with a renovated image of herself and her future, and Alice, before dying, can fulfil her wish to keep the memories of her life alive by entrusting them to her daughter. The physical return of the emigrant in this novel represents, therefore, the starting point of a psychological return to family roots and a rediscovery of the characters' inner self. The difficult task of achieving a better understanding of one's identity is attained through the means of memory.

Memory itself is connected with some of the most important themes in the text: the fear of death, the ambition for immortality, the struggle for rebirth. In other words, in the story to remember means to live, and the whole process of return appears as a means to escape from death.

I. Beth's return

Beth's return to her native city, Dublin, is not motivated by a true desire to see her native places again. She is in fact almost compelled to go back to her family house in order to attend to her seriously ill mother. Furthermore, as a rebellious daughter she fears homecoming and explicitly admits her ambivalent feelings about it. Even the words chosen by the narrator to describe the character's journey back reveal the nervousness and anguish felt by her while going home.

As we can read in the very first passage of the novel:

> It was always like this, on the last leg of the journey. Everything conspired against her: the pale, yellowish light slanting irregularly across the airport motorway, the droplets of rain crowding on her windscreen, the menacing approach of speedy headlights in her rear-view mirror. (Dunne 1)

Instead of being reassuring and familiar, then, the native places appear threatening and gloomy. The negative description of the landscape reveals that the return is not considered as a chance or an opportunity but as a monotonous repetition of unpleasant gestures and events. The sense of "being at home" is completely absent from this first part of the narrative and the whole journey back is burdened with irritation and apprehension.

However, later on we understand that the idea of "home" is related by Beth neither to her country nor to her native city. The places she feels attached to are the personal and intimate ones connected with her family surroundings. From this point of view, her condition is similar to that described by Ernesto De Martino, who argues that the boundaries of the emigrant's world "are formed by his house and by the familiar ancestral territory" (De Martino 22). Therefore, the true homecoming, for Beth, only begins when she crosses the threshold of her private microcosm.

The mental territory she is going back to is that of her family memories. This explains why she feels reassured only when she finally sees the house in which her brother, James, is waiting for her and in which she has spent her childhood:

> She turned the car in the broad driveway and pointed it towards the house, the wheels spitting out gravel. The hazy sweep of headlights caught the wooden plaque on the right-hand side of the front door. *Woodvale*. Even the name started a tug somewhere towards the bottom of Beth's heart. It spoke of tranquillity and shelter, something which she felt this house had not offered her, not since she was a very small child. Somebody, no doubt James, had picked out the black lettering again, and the wood was shiny with new varnish. (Dunne 8)

Interestingly, the element which makes her feel at home is something new which belongs only to the present (the wooden plaque at the entrance door, probably made by James, her brother). This novelty immediately suggests that she should reflect on the past and leads her to remember that she had never received enough emotional support from her family. By acknowledging this, she also acknowledges the difference between her past condition and her present one (in which a quiet refuge can finally be found).

In other words, she begins that retrieval of memories which will be developed throughout the text. The peculiar feature of this process is that instead of being an unfruitful recollection of lost events, it is a productive reconstruction of them.

Thus, the difference between Beth's attitude towards being at home at the beginning of the novel and that developed later on is quite clear. While at first she was inclined to interpret her journey back as an obvious recurrence of identical actions, images and impressions, later on she begins to unravel her memories of the past in order to understand her condition in the present. This ability to relate the different stages of one's life and to recreate one's identity again and again, in relation to its ever-changing aspect, is defined by Kierkegaard as one of key importance in the whole process of human existence. This notion of "return," then, admits the possibility of renewal and change thanks to the very movement back to the past, which, far from being a mere repetition or sterile recollection, allows a real movement forward in the present.

Thus, to define her new self and to accept the reality in which she lives now, Beth has to take a leap back to the world of the past as it is contained in her mind. Since, as we have seen, the sense of belonging to a 'home' coincides for her with the family dimension, the only place where she can reunite the different threads of her personal story to find a new start in life is the house in which she was raised. However, this is not an easy task to fulfil, and her emotions appear initially paralysed:

> Beth felt herself gaze stupidly at her brother. There was nothing to say. She knew she should feel shocked, sad, anything. But there was nothing there. The earlier feeling she had had in the car, of being suspended, beyond reality, had not gone away. It was as though all her emotions had been hung up somewhere and were waiting quietly, like clothes hanging limply in a wardrobe, until Beth came back to fit them around her again. (Dunne 13)

Nevertheless, after considering the several changes produced by the passing of time on the objects of the "old Victorian house," the character perceives the impression of "being home":

> It was a big, sprawling old Victorian house, but every time Beth came back she was struck by how small it was compared to her childhood memories. Then the rooms had been vast, bright, honey-coloured deserts in summer; huge, bare, freezing plains in winter where a game of hide-and-seek could take all day. The broad, pock-marked floorboards had been varnished again, but the old rug was now badly worn in places; the fabric on the sagging armchairs was threadbare. She felt suddenly overwhelmed by a sense of being home. (Dunne 11)

As the word "overwhelmed" may suggest, however, the gained perception of being home is not wholly positive. The process of slow recognition of the places abandoned many years ago has to pass through hard trials. Among these, the most painful one is the discovery of Alice's present condition:

> Beth's first reaction was a start of surprise. *This* was not her mother! Had there been some grotesque mistake? Where was the cloud of robust energy, the unmistakable air of authority and *capability*? Although Beth had thought she'd understood the implications of her mother's sudden, massive stroke, she had not expected to find her so thoroughly absent from herself. (Dunne 16)

This is a crucial moment in the novel, since it marks the beginning of Beth's rehearsal of the memories linked with her mother's figure. The tormented relationship between the two women brings back painful events. As the narrator comments on Beth's memories: "She would rather have not remembered. They carried a debt which she didn't know if she was able to repay" (Dunne 18).

Gradually, the old contrasts with Alice begin to emerge through flashbacks produced by images of familiar objects. These acquire a metaphorical meaning and give access to the most concealed memories of the past. By leading to a series of mental associations, they also bring to life resentments and grievances. This is clear from the following passages, in which a "big apple tree" reveals the effects of the passing of time and a swing seems to represent the good relationship with the father and the difficult one with the mother:

> A gust of sudden wind threw a shaft of streetlight onto the big apple tree, now gnarled and ugly in its winter bareness. Beth could only ever remember it as full and leafy, part of endless childhood summers. With a bright-green jolt of memory, she saw the swing her father had made for them, the toy with the edge of danger that had kept the neighbourhood kids swarming all over them one July, begging for a go. She had wanted to charge them a penny, she remembered, instinctively understanding the value of novelty. Her mother had been adamant that she should do no such thing. It was the first of many battles they had had over that swing. (Dunne 27)

Among the objects considered, the "key" is the one which carries the most important symbolic meaning. If on the one hand it represents the difficulty of communication between Alice and her daughter, on the other one it stands for their chance to communicate.

While trying to find a lip-balm in the bedside locker, Beth actually remembers an episode of her childhood in which she was scolded by her mother for prying into her things. This is why, as the narrator explains, she now asks herself: "Was it ever since *that* day that her mother had begun to lock away everything that was precious to her?" (Dunne 32). This may already indicate Alice's fear of disclosing her heart and thoughts to her daughter. Furthermore, it explains Beth's reaction when she sees again the "brass key" she had used many years before:

> Suddenly, she felt a small shock of recognition. There it was, the brass key. Now that she saw it, she remembered it again, remembered the abrupt way her mother had used it that day long ago, placing it when she had finished into the pocket of her apron. (Dunne 34)

However, by repeating that gesture she can finally identify the way to begin a dialogue with Alice. By opening the locker, in fact, she finds the letters which her mother had written to her before falling ill. These letters become the means through which the memories of the two women can, in some way, interact. They also allow Beth to start that process of self-discovery which can be carried on only through personal memories, since, as Robert F. Sayre puts it: "There is no new image of the future without a corresponding new image of the individual, including the image of the past" (Sayre 19). This last image, slowly shaped in Beth's mind, is reconsidered and renovated thanks to the discovery of Alice's point of view on the same remembered facts. The invisible thread which links the bedridden old woman and her daughter is in fact created by the double perspective they offer on shared experiences.

The positive effect of learning about her mother's memories is well known to the character herself. As the narrator explains:

> Beth was deeply moved by her mother's letter, too deeply even for tears. The written words had filled her with a tangle of emotion and memory. She felt as though all her senses had been heightened, that she was seeing and feeling with a sharpness of perception she had never known before. (Dunne 61)

The awakening of emotions and feelings described is only the starting point of Beth's inner renewal. Slowly, in fact, she also becomes aware of her own desire to change and to begin a new path in life. But to do this, some kind of deep and intimate revolution is needed. The text, again, explicitly declares:

> Turning her life upside-down at this point had a special appeal for Beth. Being awake all of yesterday had, in some way, made her conscious of new possibilities, of a new way of living. It was as though Alice's fragility had shaken her roughly by the shoulders, shocking her into wakefulness, into the realization that she, Beth, would not live for ever either. (Dunne 70)

Reversal and subversion of one's known world are, therefore, intended as a necessary part of the character's struggle for rebirth. The verbs "shaken" and "shocking" in the passage above indicate that the act of separation from the usual self is perceived by Beth as a painful one. As Françoise Lionnet, referring to Nietzsche's ontology of self-healing, states: "The will to power (over oneself) is a process of self-overcoming, a stripping from the ego of its masks, a creative rebirth, albeit a sometimes cruel and violent one" (Lionnet 242).

Thus, involved in this hard process of self-revelation, Beth detaches herself from the outside world and also from the traditional notion of time:

> Her last conscious thought, before her eyes drifted closed at last, was how strange a thing the passing of time was. It no longer seemed to be a measurable presence—the hours had slipped away in what could have been an instant or a lifetime, and ordinary living seemed to be something that had happened to her a long time ago. Even the flight from London yesterday evening felt as though it had been undertaken by someone else, someone playing at her life. Here and now was the only reality; the rest of time and space existed in another dimension where other people lived and which she could no longer enter. (Dunne 71)

The first part of the passage seems to depict the character as living in a sort of limbo—in a non-place removed from ordinary life and ordinary measures of time. This is not an unusual condition in the emigrants' experience. Referring to the event of homecoming, Cesare Pitto points out:

> Meanwhile, the village or community reacts as a body that has lost an organ, adapting the missing part, and re-establishing a new balance that renders the migrant superfluous for its day-to-day life, placing him [the emigrant] in a kind of limbo, from which those who have gone, to exist elsewhere, can sometimes return like souls in premonition dreams. (Pitto 191)

However, in Beth's case the impression of being in a kind of suspended dimension is not due to the attitude of others. She herself creates an invisible frontier between her thoughts and the outer world. As for the slow disappearance of "the rest of time," this is a necessary element and a consequence of the character's process of re-creation and return. The perception that reality is only "here and now" is, in fact, the positive consequence of the journey back to her true self, and we may link this to Otto Weininger's interpretation of return. According to this philosopher, the present offers the only chance of contact between the past and the future and is the only dimension in which human beings can act on and modify reality. Memory to him represents, then, the opportunity to understand one's existence in continuity with one's past. At the basis of this notion lies, evidently, the sense of responsibility towards life which, together with the focus on the present time (as that in which the wholeness of personal experiences can be summarised and contained), is an important part of Beth's homecoming too.

In particular, by recollecting the episodes of her adolescence she can come to terms with the rebellious girl she was, and can understand that her real motivation for leaving Dublin was revenge against the strict upbringing imposed on her by her mother. After repeating a journey back to that time, she finally takes a decision: "She no longer wanted to escape, to flee mindlessly from something that made her unhappy" (Dunne 176). This helps her also to reflect upon her broken marriage. The last chapter, titled 'Holding on," ends with Beth's going away from home with her husband, after Alice's funeral.

II. Alice's homecoming

Although Alice never moves from her house in Dublin, she is the very first character in the novel to undergo a process of homecoming. Her story runs parallel to Beth's in the text, since the narrator constantly shifts the time of the narrative from the present to the past. In this way, the reader is allowed to know what happened before the old woman became bedridden, and to understand her deep motivations for writing the letters.

The kind of return she is involved with again represents a mental reconsideration of the past in order to solve inner conflicts and contrasts. However, her scope is wider and more complex than her daughter's, since she is at the end of her life and has to prepare herself for her ultimate departure. Like an emigrant who needs to go back to the native land to be able to abandon it again, Alice has to remember the events of her past to leave it for good.

Interestingly, as Loretta Baldassar explains in one of her essays on the phenomenon of emigration return, the emigrant's departure from the native soil has often been compared to death. This is why Cesare Pitto refers to the returnees as coming "once in a while from the other world" (Pitto 191). Thus, the act of returning, in this sense, has been often conceived as a sort of working-through a bereavement.

This is particularly evident in Alice's case. On the one hand, her decision to describe the most important events of her life in letters addressed to her daughter is a way to cope with her fear of death and to accept it. On the other hand, it serves as a means to rescue her memories from oblivion and to survive through them.

All these themes emerge in the novel from a series of flashbacks which shift the time of the narrative from the present to the past. After describing Beth's arrival in her family house, the author takes a leap back to the facts that occurred many months before, when Alice was not bedridden. In chapter III, the old woman begins to understand that she is gradually losing her memory and explicitly says she is deeply worried about it.

> Alice felt that she was dying in small steps. At first, it had seemed like an ordinary forgetfulness, like something being on the tip of your tongue, but the something had become more elusive than formerly. (Dunne 44)

As suggested by the passage above, the idea itself of death is immediately associated with that of "forgetfulness"—that is, with the loss of one's ability to remember. According to Luigi Lombardi Satriani:

> Life is possible because it is supported by memory; it guarantees the permanence of an individual's or a group's identity: in its name we can make sense of our behaviour, build a life, and by means of repetition rebuild it symbolically when it is at risk of being forever lost. (Lombardi Satriani 352)

The importance of memory, related to life and one's sense of identity, is well-known to the character herself:

> Old age is a terrible thing, she had once confided to James. [...] There was before she had seen the prospect of the oblivion which now yawned before her: physical infirmity she could take, she had no choice, but the obliteration of herself, her memories, filled her with terror. Much more than dying, she feared the incremental loss of the past and present lives which made up the person called Alice. That was now the nameless, formless future she felt condemned to. (Dunne 46-47)

The "incremental loss of the past" feared by Alice is manifested in many different ways. One of them is the difficulty of keeping words in mind. This problem, which may appear trivial, is very deeply connected with the wider idea of memory and with the world of affections enclosed in it. This is clearly proved by Alice's effort to remember the word "cherries":

> Suddenly, like a tiny explosion, it came to her: *cherries*. She had laughed out loud in relief [...]. And yet, it wasn't quite *remembering*; that didn't really describe it. It was more like searching for a sense

> of recognition. It was as though she had never seen cherries before; that even if she had remembered the word, it would no longer fit. She felt as a whole new language might need to be learned, with rules and grammar to suit the new strangeness of the previously familiar. (Dunne 45)

One term in particular, "recognition," reveals the existence, in the novel, of a more complex image of the relationship between Alice's memory and her life. Bruce Ross, in relation to pre-twentieth-century psychological studies, states:

> Recognition was the final step—a literal recognition—in subjectively identifying and perhaps categorizing an object. In this broader interpretation, the emphasis was on fitting the cognition of an object or an idea into previously obtained knowledge. Thus in this sense, the one emphasized by Aristotle, recognition was the terminal and uniquely human step in the memory cognition process. (Ross 20)

However, in Catherine Dunne's novel the achievement of "recognition" also leads the character to acknowledge that something has changed and needs a new language to be described. The word "cherries," even though it refers to a familiar object, sounds in fact unfamiliar. This is why Alice asks herself: "It was as though she had never seen cherries before; that even if she had remembered the word, it would no longer fit" (Dunne 45). Her return to the past is, therefore, an attempt to save her beloved memories (expressed by words and by the emotions they carry with them) from the passing of time. The letters written to Beth are, then, the way in which Alice tries to achieve this goal and to use language with the usual familiar meaning attached to it:

> The very simplicity of the idea delighted and startled her at first. She would write to them. While she still had a firm enough grasp of language, while she was still sharp and self-sufficient, she would write to her children. She didn't know how much longer she had before everything familiar was wiped out. (Dunne 47)

Each letter becomes, therefore, a journey back into the past and creates a digression in the narrative discourse. Alice, by recounting her own story, takes on the role of the narrator and makes a sort of "premise" to the reader whom she addresses—that is, to Beth. She thus explicitly asserts that the daughter's image she has in mind is still that of a child, and that, as a consequence, her letters can really be considered as coming from the past:

> I keep seeing you, but not as you are now—I see you as a tiny baby, or a toddler. And it's very strange, not being able to imagine when and where you, the grown-up, will hold these pages in your hands. It's a bit like posting letters from the past into the future—address unknown. (Dunne 50)

However, Alice herself does not recognise her own aspect as it is in the present, but still thinks of herself as she was in the past:

> Recently, when I've looked at the mirror, I've been startled to see the old, lined face that looks back at me. Sometimes, I wonder if it's really me. Inside, I feel much younger; I don't feel as though I've changed at all and it's been strange, looking out through my own eyes, not to recognize myself. (Dunne 52)

Despite this, she demands that her daughter should imagine her as she is now.

> I'd like to think that you'll remember me as I am, right this minute, sitting at the kitchen table. Can you see me? (Dunne 50)

As the text suggests, then, the physical aspect of the two women is subjected, like the events of their lives, to the transforming power of memory, which changes the outside world according to the inner perceptions and interpretations of the self. In the novel's context, this implies that the letters function as a mirror which reflects the characters' natures in the different stages of their lives: thus, Beth, is portrayed at the same time as a demanding child, a rebellious adolescent, a young woman. Alice addresses, therefore, the different voices of her daughter's soul and expresses her own way of being by mentally going back to her own many selves (the loving wife, the stern mother, the widow, the old woman).

Nevertheless, all these roles and identities converge on the written page and offer a more complete picture of the mother's and daughter's relationship. Thus, they help the characters to find a way to communicate. Again, in this regard, in Alice's writing the word "key" immediately appears figuratively to indicate the chance of understanding her past conflicts with Beth:

> Something tells me that these memories are very important—I have the feeling that there is a key somewhere in there, something to help me understand why you and I were never as close as we should have been, not real "mother-and-daughter" close. (Dunne 50)

But in order to find this key, Alice is aware that she has to retrace her own steps in life. As she confides:

> I've been thinking about those days a lot as I've been going through the old photographs, the one on the top of your wardrobe. It is, at times, quite painful. But I want to see it through to the end, because I'm learning things about myself, and beginning to feel more complete, somehow. (Dunne 20)

The need to become "more complete" is expressed symbolically, even in a dream in which she has to recollect all the scattered pearls of a broken necklace and hears an inner voice which seems to order her: "You must gather together all the pieces of yourself to become whole." Alice herself admits: "I feel that there are bits of me, fractured, all over the place—after your dad died, I blocked out so much of my life because it was too painful to remember" (Dunne 121).

The path towards the end of the journey back, however, is hard and marked by many obstacles. One of them is the sense of regret felt by Alice for lost opportunities. In particular, she recalls the image of a man, Arthur, who asked her to marry him after her husband's death and whom she refused out, of an unjustified sense of guilt and her concern for her children's happiness. Now, she asks herself:

> Should I have said yes? Wouldn't we all have been happier, less pressured as a family if I had agreed? Or is this just so much useless nostalgia? We were close, the three of us, weren't we? A real family? (Dunne 123)

These doubts and uncertainties are the means through which Alice understands that in the course of her life she has always silenced her emotions and true desires. However, she can achieve this awareness also thanks to her mental return to the events connected with Beth. By reasoning on her daughter's personality Alice actually comes to a better comprehension of her identity and even to a personal critique:

> I belonged too much to the old school, I think, where children had to be seen and not heard. You certainly didn't seem to be aware of that piece of old wisdom—you fought very hard indeed for your right to be heard. You were, I think, that word which I rarely hear applied to children nowadays—wilful. I'm sure now that it wasn't right to try and bend that will as much as I did. You insisted on being yourself, and I think you were right to do so. My generation understood a lot

about duty to others, and very little about duty to ourselves. (Dunne 119)

This mental return represents a real "anamnesis"—that is, a "process of remembering" (ana-, "back again"; -mneme, "memory"; -sis, "process"), associated also with the idea of rebirth. To quote "Autobiographical voices" by Françoise Lionnet: "In Catholic liturgy, it [the anamnesis] is a prayer in the Eucharistic service recalling the Passion, Resurrection and Ascension of Christ" (Lionnet 223). Although it may appear a paradox, the slow recollection of past events made by Alice before dying represents, then, a movement opposed to death and a sort of personal resurrection as well. It stands, in other words, for a resolution to exist fully, free from any kind of restrictions on identity, and with the awareness of belonging to a dimension wider than the individual one. This may explain why Alice admits in a letter:

> This is the first time in a long time I have felt so hopeless about what my life has meant, what it might continue to mean. I'm not just feeling sorry for myself, either—it's an entirely different feeling, as though I can see myself in terms of the vastness of the rest of the world. I feel very tiny and insignificant. It is rather a frightening feeling. (Dunne 128)

Before dying, the kind of experience she passes through can be compared to a sort of spiritual "awakening." As Carol Christ states:

> The experience of nothingness often precedes an *awakening*, similar to a conversion experience, in which the powers of being are revealed. A woman's awakening to great powers grounds her in a new sense of self and a new orientation in the world. (Christ 13)

However, the gaining of this "new sense of self" can be really meaningful for Alice only if it is communicated to Beth, who in fact comes to represent the very circumstance of continuity with her mother's life in and passage through this world.

The importance of writing for Alice lies, then, in the chance it gives her to reveal her deepest thoughts and to share them with Beth. Thus, written words become the means through which the two women can compare each other's natures. As Carol Christ again points out, speaking of women's quest for finding a new and freer identity:

> After a woman experiences the grounding of her quest in the powers of being, it is important for her to name her experience in words.

> When one woman puts her experiences into words, another woman who has kept silent, afraid of what others will think, can find validation. And when the second woman says aloud, "Yes, that was my experience too," the first woman loses some of her fear. "The dream of a common language," which Adrienne Rich has movingly depicted, is realized in the moment when two women acknowledge each other and themselves. (Christ 23)

Although this passage refers to a mystical search, the need to find a "common language" and to use words in order to "name experiences" is also felt by Catherine Dunne's characters in their metaphorical journey back to the past.

However, for Alice and Beth, the mutual communication achieved still remains a silent one and the very act of writing and reading the letters unites and divides them at the same time. Each is involved in a personal act of reconstruction of her life, which is carried on individually. As for Alice, she cannot learn anything about Beth's interpretations of the events she has written about in the letters. Only the daughter can compare her perspective with her mother's. However, Alice's purpose of communicating her memories to Beth and preserving them from the passing of time is fulfilled. Although their personal points of view and images of the past cannot be completely shared, the two women have nevertheless created a contact between them.

III. Conclusion

The theme of homecoming in *The Walled Garden* by Catherine Dunne plays a central role in the development of the whole story. The return of an emigrant to her native town is, in fact, the event which starts all the others in the novel and which leads, in particular, to the recollection of the past.

Like Rahel in *The God of Small Things* by Arundhati Roy, Beth is lead home by the need to see a loved one again. However, if in the case of Roy's heroine her desire to join her brother Estha is free from every sort of resentment, in the case of Dunne's heroine the encounter with her sick mother is imbued with a sense of fear and still painful incomprehension. The return experienced by Beth is not, therefore, a real "voluntary" one, for it is perceived as a duty to comply with.

Going back home, the young woman fears the ghosts of the past and, in particular, feels oppressed by the memory of the difficult relationship with her mother. This may recall a short story by the Canadian writer Caterina Edwards, "On a Platter," in which the main character, Fulvia, is terrified at the idea of leaving Canada to go back to Sicily, where she would have to readapt to the limited and restricted rules once imposed upon her by a too traditional society. Beth, too, fears that she may find herself again in the role of the oppressed daughter. Her homecoming can be therefore assimilated to that catalogued by Rosemarie Rogers in *Return Migration in Comparative Perspective* among the main reasons for abandoning the host country: "Migrants return because their families at home need them and they agree to follow their call" (Rogers 290).

However, to understand the sense of anguish felt by Beth at the moment of arrival in Dublin, we have to go back to her motivations for going away from home. More than from a real need to leave, her emigration arose from a gesture of rebellion against the strict education imposed by her mother. Like Gar O'Donnel in *Philadelphia, Here I Come!* by Brian Friel, Beth suffers for not identifying the place from which she comes from with a real "home." Both characters, furthermore, are disappointed by the difficulty of communicating with the parental figure (the father, in the case of Gar; the mother, in the case of Beth) and feel limited by the rules they have to respect in their native land. However, while Gar and his father never succeed in creating a contact between them (and do not share the memory of experiences lived together, keeping them enclosed and separate in their minds), Beth and her mother are finally united. Thanks to the mental journey back to the events of their past.

This is possible thanks to Alice's letters, which represent autobiographical pieces of writing. As in autobiographies, the past is in fact recreated by the individual perceptions of the author, who in this way can define her own self-portrait. By looking at this portrait, Beth is able to create her own. Back home, then, she can still be regarded as an emigrant who, metaphorically, holds on in her journey back to the native land in order to acquire a more complete knowledge of her nature. From this point of view, she can be in some way compared to a pilgrim in search of a personal truth. But this truth cannot be found by trusting the traditional notion of time and place. As Zygmut Bauman affirms: "For pilgrims through time, the truth is elsewhere: the true place is always some distance, some time away" (Bauman 20). The dimension in which Beth's search can continue is, thus, only that of memories, and her return can only occur ideally! in her mind by reading Alice's letters.

All the described aspects of the novel are, in conclusion, the consequence of homecoming. The theme of return itself, far from being the mere repetition of a journey back to the native country, appears as closely linked with the wider dimension of memory and with the potential for change and renovation of the self. Retracing one's steps and rethinking the past open up new perspectives and possibilities to the characters, marking a new start in their lives.

Works Cited

Baldassar, Loretta. Tornare al paese: territorio e identità nel processo migratorio. *Altreitalie* 23 (Jul.-Aug. 2001).

Baumann, Zygmunt. "From Pilgrim to Tourist—or a Short History of Identity." *Questions of Cultural Identity*. Ed. S. Hall and P. du Gay. London: Sage Publications, 1996. 18-36.

Christ, Carol. *Diving Deep and Surfacing. Women Writers on Spiritual Quest*. Boston: Beacon Press, 1980.

Connerton, Paul. *How Societies Remember*. Cambridge: Cambridge UP, 1989.

De Martino, Ernesto. *La fine del mondo*. Torino: Einaudi, 1977.

Dunne, Catherine. *The Walled Garden*. London: Picador, 2000.

Edwards, Caterina. "On a Platter." *Island of the Nightingales*. Toronto: Guernica, 2000. 102-09.

Friel, Brian. *Philadelphia, Here I Come!* London: Faber & Faber, 1965.

Lionnet, Françoise. *Autobiographical Voices: Race, Gender, Self-Portraiture*. Ithaca and London: Cornell UP, 1989.

Lombardi Satriani, Luigi Maria and Meligrana, Mariano. *Il ponte di San Giacomo*. Palermo: Sellerio, 1989.

Pitto, Cesare. *The Return of Immigrants to their Native Communities: Writers in Transition*. Proceedings of the First National Conference of Italian-Canadian Writers. Ed. Dino Minni, Anna Foschi Ciampolini. Montreal: Guernica Editions, 1990.

Rogers, Rosemarie. "Return Migration in Comparative Perspective." *The Politics of Return: International Return Migration in Europe*. Ed. D. Kuban. Staten Island: Center for Migration Studies, 1984. 277-98.

Ross, Bruce. *Remembering the Personal Past*. New York and Oxford: Oxford UP, 1991.

Roy, Arundhati. *The God of Small Things*. London: Flamingo, 1997.

Rubin, David. *Autobiographical Memory*. Cambridge: Cambridge UP, 1986.

Sayre, Robert F. *Autobiography and Images of Utopia*. *Salmagundi*. No 19. Saratoga Springs. NY: Skidmore College, 1972.

□

The Novel as a Game: Muriel Spark's *The Comforters*

Preeti Bhatt

Muriel Spark is a major contemporary writer who uses the art of fiction in strikingly original and powerful ways to convey serious truths. Her novels capture the dilemmas of the present age, facing a future in which religion and faith alone cannot sustain human beings. Through the focus on the dehumanisation of contemporary society, Spark explores in her fiction the various ontological conflicts and pressures besetting modern man.

Spark has written twenty-two novels so far, along with short stories, poetry, biographies and criticism. Her novels are unconventional, owing to her use of innovative narrative strategies to reflect the indeterminate nature of reality. Her first novel, *The Comforters* (1957), anticipates the postmodernist style of narration due to its experimental form. Spark uses the craft of novel-writing brilliantly in her very first novel to play games with the reader while raising subtly serious questions about the nature of truth and existence.

Critics have been tempted to analyse *The Comforters* as an expression of the semi-autobiographical nature of the protagonist Caroline's struggle to come to terms with her newly adopted Catholicism.[1] Elizabeth Dipple refers to "the confident, banal interpretations" given to Spark's "complexly peculiar novels," especially by the early critics, by "reducing her fiction to narrow dogmatic or theological stances" (Dipple 141). While the novel resonates with autobiographical nuances, Spark introduces many other complex issues in the narrative through the self-reflexivity of the plot and the rejection of the mimetic mode of narration. The present paper examines how the author underlines the constructed nature of the text through experimental strategies of narration, while drawing upon her personal spiritual experiences to foreground ontological dilemmas.

Reference to Spark's personal life would be of great relevance to the discussion of her first novel. Muriel Sarah Spark née Camberg (1918-) was born in Edinburgh of a Jewish father and Christian mother. Her mixed religious parentage influenced her deeply, as is revealed in one of her short stories, "The Gentile Jewess," and in the novel *The Mandelbaum Gate* (1965). Spark started writing poetry at the age of nine and was "deeply interested in poetry and imaginative writing of all kinds" (Spark, "Personal History" 77). At James Gillespie's Girls' School in Edinburgh she "was the school's Poet and Dreamer," and received the attention and encouragement which helped the budding writer (Spark, "What Images Return" 152).

Spark left for the then Rhodesia when she was nineteen and got married there. Many of her short stories are set in Africa. In 1944 she returned to England, her marriage having broken up. She tried her hands at a variety of writing tasks at the press offices of professional organisations including the British Intelligence Service. In 1948, Spark became editor of the magazine *Poetry Review* published by the Poetry Society, but was dismissed from the post due to her unconventional approach. She started publishing her own magazine *Forum* soon after, but had to discontinue its publication after two issues due to lack of funds.

In 1951, Spark entered a short-story competition organised by the *Observer* and won first prize for the story "The Seraph and the Zambesi," which, as its title indicates, was a combination of realistic, fantastic and supernatural strands. In 1952, her first book of poems appeared, *The Fanfarlo and Other Verse*. Spark also edited and collaborated with Derek Stanford on a number of critical works on nineteenth-century writers such as William Wordsworth, Mary Shelley and Emily Brontë during the early fifties. In 1953, her study of the works of the Poet Laureate John Masefield came out, and in 1957 an edited collection of John Henry Newman's letters was published.

During this period, Spark was also doing a lot of reading on spiritual and religious issues, which inspired her to convert to Catholicism. She was received into the Roman Catholic Church on 1 May 1954. In her autobiography she states: "I felt the Roman Catholic faith corresponded to what I had always felt and known and believed [...]" (Spark, *Curriculum Vitae* 202). Her creativity and literary talent were decidedly affected by her conversion. Her religious experience had a very releasing effect on her and helped her to find a writing voice.

This period was also one of physical and emotional suffering for Spark. Owing to financial constraints and wartime food rationing, she was undernourished. She had been taking appetite suppressants so that she would feel less hungry. She had also been trying to write something on the Book of Job, which was posing some problems to her. These factors and the religious conflict she was experiencing caused her to have hallucinations while reading. This confusing experience continued for three months. Spark writes in "My Conversion" that she was "ready for a breakdown." She says further, "I think it was the religious upheaval and the fact that I was trying to write and could not manage it" (Spark, "My Conversion" 50). This physical and psychological turmoil gave her a peculiar insight into hallucinations, the power of the imagination and an awareness of the inner self.

Spark decided at this time that she would write a novel "about my recent brief but extremely intense word-game experience" (Spark, *Curriculum Vitae* 205). Her use of this experience as a motif in *The Comforters* indicates that the writer wanted to bring in subjective psychical experiences in her fiction. It indicates that for her, events that seemed to be outside natural or physical laws were an essential part of reality. Spark's interest in the mystic and the spiritual and the recurrence of such incidents in her novels represent, in a way, a rejection of the rational view of existence. The realistic/mimetic mode of narration was entirely unsuitable for the kind of reality Spark wanted to represent in her fiction.

Spark's close examination of the style and technique used by nineteenth-century writers like Mary Shelley and Emily Brontë is a reflection of her own dissatisfaction with the realistic tradition. These writers had been innovative in their own ways and had made a creative use of imagination, intuition and fantasy in their writings. In *Frankenstein* (1818), Mary Shelley had disregarded the mimetic conventions of space, time and probability. She had utilised the resources of myth, legend and magic tales to produce an anti-realistic narrative. Emily Brontë's *Wuthering Heights* (1847), in its use of the shifting time-frame, metaphorical space and the juxtaposition of the supernatural with the natural, contrasted with the realistic novels of the nineteenth century.

The Comforters, Spark's first novel also moves between the realistic mode and Gothic fantasy. The writer uses the realistic mode to build up certain expectations of the reader, and then skilfully, through a clever playfulness, goes about shifting the form, the story and the characters in the novel. A number of surprises invert the meaning of the events, as the supernatural gradually starts intruding in the realistic narrative. The focus on the multiple levels of reality in Spark's novel makes the narrative complex and enigmatic, and forces the reader to question the plausibility of the events.

Judy Little places Muriel Spark in the category of "non mimetic writers," and points out that the non-realistic writer "may destroy the reader's expectations by rejecting chronology or letting characters argue with the author," instead of creating a complex world through rich details and inhabiting it with psychologically presented characters (Little 1). Spark violates the conventions of realism in *The Comforters* by introducing a character, Caroline Rose, who is aware of an authorial voice dictating and controlling her life and her fate. Caroline's search for faith, love and happiness in the narrative encourages the reader to identify with her. But the presence of another narrator in the story, who is invisible and whose supernatural presence disturbs Caroline, violates the illusion of reality.

The Comforters is a self-reflexive, self-begetting novel and conforms to the metafictional genre. Andrzej Gasiorek defines a metafictional text as one which offers "a double focus" since "it refers both to a reality outside the text and to the process by which that reality is fictionally constructed" (Gasiorek 13). While the identity of the narrator whose voice is heard by Caroline remains a mystery for most of the novel, it emerges towards the end that Caroline herself is the author of the book *The Comforters*. The author and the character coincide in Caroline and the novel thus becomes a story of its own birth. At the end of the text, the novel begets itself when the reader is told that Caroline is going to write a novel about "'Characters in a novel'" which will end with "'the death of the villain and the marriage of the heroine'" (Spark, *The Comforters* 202)[2]—in other words, how *The Comforters* ends. Caroline thus creates a story in the form of *The Comforters* and then herself becomes a part of it.

Spark's novel acquires a circular form due to its self-reflexivity, and encourages multiple readings. Alan Friedman refers to "the myth of openness," the means which the modern novelist adopts "to suggest at the end of his novel that these are the final pages of this particular rendering of experience [...] while at the same time he suggests that there is never a close to experience" (Friedman 180). In the concluding lines of the novel, Laurence, Caroline's boyfriend, tears up a letter he planned to give to her, the contents of which have been presented to the reader earlier. Laurence watches the scraps of paper as the breeze scatters them, "and he did not then foresee his later wonder, with a curious rejoicing, how the letter had got into the book" (*The Comforters* 204). Faith Pullin points out that "although in life he throws away his letter to Caroline, in fiction nothing is lost" (Pullin 79), and his letter is present in the novel which the reader has in hand. The author, by a metafictional reference to "the character called Laurence" (*The Comforters* 202) at the end of the novel, emphasises that Laurence figures as a character in Caroline's novel.

Steven G. Kellman says of the protagonist of Iris Murdoch's self-begetting novel *Under the Net*: "Jake's development as a novelist is inseparable from his growth as an individual. Both produce *Under the Net*" (Kellman, 89). Jake Donaghue's transformation from a translator of substandard fiction to an original writer of novels involves a long process of self-examination and a questioning of the reality of the world and its relationship with fiction. The same statement is applicable to Caroline Rose. Her experiences with the disembodied voices which predict her future, her interest in the art of fiction and the difficulties she faces when discussing realism in her book *Form in the Modern Novel* (*The Comforters* 57), the upheaval in her thoughts due to her recent conversion to Roman Catholicism, all these aspects of her life are directly interlinked. Once Caroline has come to terms with the unusual experiences with the narratorial voices, she is able to externalise her understanding of the relationship between the self, the world and the art of fiction in the form of the novel *The Comforters*. The development of Caroline as an individual coincides with the development of the novel in which she appears and which she is to write later.

A point of similarity can be discerned between *The Comforters* and Flann O'Brien's novel *At Swim-Two-Birds* (1939), in which the characters, as in Spark's novel, are aware of their status as characters in a novel. *At Swim-Two-Birds*[3] is a complex novel, the structure of which Robert S. Ryf describes as "wheels within wheels" (Ryf 322). It focuses primarily on the process of the creation of fiction and on the question of the autonomy of art. The novel involves layers of narratives, which at times intermingle and overlap with each other.[4] In keeping with a digression within the novel in which the narrator suggests that characters "should be allowed a private life, self-determination and a decent standard of living" (O'Brien 25), the characters try to control both narrator and narrative by ingenious means.

In *The Comforters*, Caroline tries to assert her freedom by commenting upon the invisible narrator in the middle of the narrative. While she is in hospital recovering from an accident, she states that the "Typing Ghost" has not described the hospital ward because he does not know how to do it. Caroline feels: "This interlude in my life is not part of the book in consequence" (*The Comforters* 161). The author goes on to comment: "It was by making exasperating remarks like this that Caroline Rose continued to interfere with the book." There follows a detailed and meticulous description of the hospital ward. Morroe Berger comments: "Intrusions and varieties of authorial omniscience" pervade the different levels of reality in Spark's novel (Berger 129). This kind of game-playing which goes on between the author and Caroline Rose takes on added significance when it is noted that by the end of the book Caroline herself takes over the role of the Typing Ghost. Who is narrating these lines then? Is this the work of Caroline or that of the author? Jennifer L. Randisi observes that "Caroline controls and is controlled by an agency both outside and inside the story. Both character and novelist are satirists, and the novel itself is a fictive hall of mirrors where illusion is reflected endlessly" (Randisi 141).

The Comforters is an unusual novel in which various novelistic sub-genres are intermingled. Yet Spark does not rigidly conform to the conventions of the different narrative modes that she takes up in the novel: those of the detective novel, the popular thriller, the preternatural fantasy or the mystery story. Ruth Whittaker sees *The Comforters* as having "a conspicuously overdramatic plot" in which the novelist satirises traditional expectations "while simultaneously fulfilling them by exploiting such novelistic devices as coincidence and happy endings" (Whittaker 94).

In this novel Muriel Spark exploits the conventions of different sub-genres to parody them and subvert the expectations of the reader. The mystery of the diamonds in the bread is resolved by Louisa herself, who later explains to Laurence how she managed to smuggle diamonds with the help of her gang (*The Comforters* 172-78), thereby deflating the genre of the detective novel. To create the atmosphere of a supernatural world, no scientific explanation is offered of the voices which Caroline hears. However, Caroline suggests and comes to believe towards the end of the novel that a novelist at another plane of existence is narrating a story in which Caroline herself figures as a character. Baron Stock's stories about Mervyn Hogg's diabolism and his "orgy of deliberate iconoclasm" (164) create a Gothic atmosphere, but later prove to be misleading when it is revealed that Mervyn used plaster statues to hide diamonds in for the smuggling. As in a supernatural fantasy, there are repeated references to Georgina Hogg being a witch, and descriptions of her mysterious disappearance: but at the end of the novel Georgina dies like a normal human being in an attempt to kill Caroline.

Muriel Spark plays with the idea of writing fiction in this novel. The author, the narrator and the characters, all at their own levels, weave elaborate tales so that different kinds of "fictions" are floated in the narrative. When some of these sub-stories are examined, it is revealed that they are pure fiction. Through these fictional stories the author draws attention to the constructed nature of the textual world and forces the reader to question the details presented before taking them at face value.

The sub-stories of Mervyn's diabolic activities (157-60, 163-66, 178-80) narrated by Baron Stock are a means to escape Caroline's suspicion of his involvement in Louisa Jepp's gang. Spark herself supports this perspective when she, the narrator, comments at one point in the narrative: "It is very much to be doubted if Mervyn Hogarth had ever in his life given any more than a passing thought to any black art or occult science" (157). Mervyn's regular visits to Catholic shrines with his handicapped son Andrew to pray for the latter's recovery are a pretext to smuggle diamonds through customs, by concealing them in plaster statues and rosary beads. Eleanor Hogarth has an innate talent for mimicry and she changes her personality like a fictional self to suit the occasion. But now her artificial demeanour dominates her real self: "soon one of them would stick, grotesque and ineradicable" (87). Spark creates an elaborate myth about the viciousness of Georgina Hogg through the speeches of other characters who are aware of her depravity. Her evil powers are given a physical dimension, for she is said to disappear as soon as others forget about her existence. Yet in the final mythical confrontation between Caroline and Georgina, good subdues evil when Georgina dies in the struggle.

Alain Robbe-Grillet, discussing the modern novel in his study *For A New Novel*, points out that in the search for new narrative techniques to represent the present world whose reality, rationality and stability has become questionable, the story-aspect of the novel has become very difficult to sustain. Yet he underlines the fact that in the novels of Proust, Faulkner and Beckett there are numerous story-lines, which become blurred due to the disruption of chronology or to the emphasis on the mental process of reconstruction of a past event. Robbe-Grillet reflects that in the modern novel "it is not the anecdote that is lacking, it is only its character of certainty, its tranquillity, its innocence" (Robbe-Grillet 33). He suggests that in the works of Beckett as well, the events and stories are not lacking, but they continuously destroy themselves by negating themselves. In *The Comforters* similarly, the stories being floated at different levels cannot be blindly taken to be true, for the element of certainty is missing in them. The narrator herself at various points in the narrative denies their truth, thereby negating what has just been stated.

The focus on the various false stories in the narrative makes the whole novel an elaborate, sustained game of artifice. Yet it is through the emphasis on the fictional aspect of her novel that Spark introduces profound issues. Caroline's interpretation of the mysterious voices: "'it is as if a writer on another plane of existence was writing a story about us'" (*The Comforters* 63), establishes a parallel between man's relationship with the Creator and that of the fictional character with the author of a work. *The Comforters* is thus a novel about another novel, which takes "the act of writing a novel as a paradigm for the workings of God's purposes in the world" (16).

By using the old analogy between the writer and God, Spark underlines the constructed nature of the textual world. In contrast to the mimetic representation of reality, wherein the artificiality of the text is camouflaged, here the author's role in the creation of the world within the narrative is foregrounded. As Brian McHale states regarding fictional works which draw on the idea of the author as God, the work "has become less the mirror of nature, more an artifact, visibly a *made* thing. As a corollary, then, to the artist's paradoxical self-representation, the artwork itself comes to be presented *as* an artwork" (McHale 30).

In her critical study of Mary Shelley's novels, *Child of Light*, Spark focuses on the roles of the creator and the created while discussing Shelley's *Frankenstein—Or, The Modern Prometheus*. Spark draws attention to the title of Shelley's novel and discusses the myth of Prometheus, who is said to have stolen fire from heaven in order to give it to mortals. Fernand Comte, in *The Wordsworth Dictionary of Mythology*, states that Prometheus, who harboured a passionate desire to rise to the stature of the gods, "symbolizes the revolt of man against the gods" (Comte 168). Another legend says that "Prometheus created man out of earth and water" (Smith 340). Spark concedes that Frankenstein the scientist initially is Prometheus, "the vital fire-endowing protagonist," for he creates the Monster out of the parts of the human body and breathes life into it (Spark, *Child of Light* 161). She adds that the Monster takes over the role of Prometheus as soon as he comes to life and the characters of the scientist and the Monster become complementary to each other. Spark comments that the basic issue underlying *Frankenstein* is "revolt against divine oppression, and indeed, against the concept of a benevolent deity" (*Child of Light* 162). Several characters in Spark's novels are aware of a divine agency or the author of the novel controlling and manipulating their actions, and try to exercise their freedom.

In *The Comforters*, Caroline questions the concept of free will. At one point she states: "I refuse to have my thoughts and actions controlled by some unknown, possibly sinister being. I intend to subject him to reason" (*The Comforters* 105). While Caroline intends to thwart the unseen author's plans for her as a character, she is also a human being presumably controlled by God. She states further, "I intend to stand aside and see if the novel has any real form apart from this artificial plot. I happen to be a Christian" (105). While Caroline rejects the predetermined form of the plot, her being a human being subjects her to the fate predestined by God for her. It is worth pointing out that Caroline is not successful in foiling the prophesies of the invisible author in spite of having tried her best. Does the author whose voices Caroline hears coincide with God? What is the status of the different characters, including Caroline and Laurence in the novel? Are they merely fictional creations, or real human beings? These connotations are woven in the complex structure of the novel, which gives it a philosophical depth. Glen Cavaliero notes that Spark's novel "combines an inquiry into the nature of fictive truth with an inquiry into the nature of supernatural reality" (Cavaliero 203). Through the self-conscious structure of this novel, Spark is able to examine theological and ontological issues that are an important part of her world-view.

In *The Comforters*, Spark alludes to the biblical myth of Job. The reference to Job occurs early in the novel, when Caroline is haunted by mysterious voices in the solitude of her flat in London, and finds no relief even in a religious retreat. The writer states at this point: "Brompton Oratory oppressed her when it was full of people [...]. As usual, when she entered, the line from the Book of Job came to her mind, 'Behold now Behemoth which I made with thee'" (100). Caroline discerns a similarity between her situation and that of Job: both feel they are being persecuted for no reason at all.

In *The Book of Job*, the tragic irony of the destiny of man is portrayed through the story of Job, a virtuous man who is made to experience physical and emotional distress in spite of his goodness. The accepted teachings of most religions profess that God blesses the good and punishes the wicked. But the writer of *The Book of Job* observes that good people suffer for no apparent reason, and he asks why. Francis Soundararaj lists some of the major issues raised by the writer of *The Book of Job*: "The nobility of patient resignation, the need for divine grace and fellowship, the hope of life after death, the love and awe of the created being for the Creator [...] and the spiritual value of suffering" (Soundararaj, xxiii).

In *The Comforters* the myth of Job is presented in the modern context through the extraordinary experiences of Caroline. Being a recent Catholic convert, she observes with surprise the spitefulness and hypocrisy of people like Georgina Hogg. She finds it difficult to be cordial to Georgina, as she is aware that her religiousness is only a farce, and that Georgina is full of evil. Caroline's aural hallucinations are a form of religious experience for her, for they cannot be explained on a rational basis, and they distance her from her friends. She realises that the disembodied voices discuss her thoughts and behaviour like an omnipotent god, and control her future. Her frantic attempts to change the course of events predicted by the invisible narrator meet with failure.

Caroline's suffering can be explained in existential terms, for it relates to the absurdity of human existence and to the limited understanding of man, a point also made in the myth of Job. The *Dictionary of The Bible* discusses the message implied in *The Book of Job* and states: "There is no solution to the mystery of existence, but God is God, infinite in wisdom. Man, his creature, is mortal and finite in understanding. To know that is to understand one's relationship to the living God" (120). Caroline, by the end of the novel, comes to terms with her unusual experiences, and realises the nature of the relationship between God and His created beings; and, being a writer herself, she also acquires an understanding of the complex relationship between a novelist and her characters.

In conclusion one can state that Spark experiments radically with plot, characterisation and narrative form in her very first novel. Through the innovative portrayal of the complex relationship between the writer, character and reader, *The Comforters* becomes a self-reflexive, self-begetting novel. The multiple levels of fictiveness and fabulation by the author, the narrator and the characters acquire significance in the narrative. Muriel Spark takes the reader for a ride by fabricating stories at different levels in this novel. It is observed that characters in *The Comforters* create stories and themselves become a part of them. Spark repeatedly subverts expectations of plot and story by employing different sub-genres, and deflating them at critical junctures in the story. The innovative strategies of foregrounding the element of fictionality and the playful, parodic, and ironic elements in *The Comforters* are a pointer to the kind of novels Spark would be interested in writing in the future. However, the focus on the complex relationship between the creator and the created in the novel brings out the moral concern of the writer, a deeper philosophical quest on her part through the mode of fiction.

Notes

1. See, for example: *The Faith and Fiction of Muriel Spark* (1982) by Ruth Whittaker, "Calvinism and Catholicism in Muriel Spark" by Allan Massie (in *Muriel Spark: An Odd Capacity for Vision*, ed. Alan Bold [1984]), and "Muriel Spark's Grammars of Assent" by Judy Little.
2. All quotations from *The Comforters* have been taken from the Penguin edition of the book (see Works Cited).
3. *At Swim-Two-Birds* was written by Brian O'Nolan under the pen-name of Flann O'Brien. Little notice was taken of the book when it was published in 1939, but it drew critical attention when it was reissued in 1960.
4. In Flann O'Brien's novel, the narrator who lives in Dublin is writing a novel about a writer called Trellis, who in turn is writing a novel praising virtue and condemning sin. Trellis has accommodated his characters in a hotel in order to keep an eye on them. But his control over them remains only while he is awake, and his characters keep him asleep for twenty hours a day in order to enjoy a free existence and assert their individual identities. Dissatisfied with the ways in which Trellis has been forcing them to behave, they eventually rebel against him and "write" him on trial before a jury they have constituted.

Works Cited

Berger, Morroe. *Real and Imagined Worlds: The Novel and Social Science.* Cambridge: Harvard UP, 1977.

Bold, Alan, ed. *Muriel Spark: An Odd Capacity for Vision.* London: Vision; Totowa: Barnes, 1984.

Cavaliero, Glen. *The Supernatural and English Fiction: From the Castle of Otranto to Hawksmoor*. Oxford: OUP, 1995.

Comte, Fernand. *The Wordsworth Dictionary of Mythology.* Wordsworth Reference. Ware: Wordsworth Editions, 1991.

Dictionary of the Bible. Brockhampton Reference. London: Brockhampton P, 1995.

Dipple, Elizabeth. "Muriel Spark and the Art of the Exclusive." *The Unresolvable Plot: Reading Contemporary Fiction.* New York: Routledge, 1988. 140-59.

Friedman, Alan. *The Turn of the Novel.* New York: OUP, 1966.

Gasiorek, Andrzej. *Post-War British Fiction: Realism and After.* London: Edward Arnold, 1995.

Kellman, Steven G. *The Self-Begetting Novel.* London: Macmillan, 1980.

Little, Judy. "Muriel Spark's Grammars of Assent." *The British and Irish Novel Since 1960.* Ed. James Acheson. New York: St. Martin's P, 1991. 1-16.

McHale, Brian. *Postmodernist Fiction.* London: Routledge, 1987.

O'Brien, Flann. *At Swim-Two-Birds.* 1939. New York: Penguin, 1967.

Page, Norman. *Muriel Spark.* Macmillan Modern Novelists. London: Macmillan, 1990.

Pullin, Faith. "Autonomy and Fabulation in the Fiction of Muriel Spark." In Bold, *Muriel Spark: An Odd Capacity*, 71-93.

Randisi, Jennifer L. "Muriel Spark and Satire." In Bold, *Muriel Spark: An Odd Capacity*, 132-46.

Robbe-Grillet, Alain. *For a New Novel: Essays on Fiction.* Trans. Richard Howard. 1963. New York: Freeport, 1970.

Ryf, Robert S. "Character and Imagination in the Experimental Novel." *Modern Fiction Studies* 20.3 (1974): 317-27.

Smith, William. *The Wordsworth Classical Dictionary.* Wordsworth Reference. Ware: Wordsworth Editions, 1996.

Soundararaj, Francis. Introduction. *The Book of Job.* Madras: Macmillan India, 1979. vii-xxiv.

Spark, Muriel. *Child of Light: A Reassessment of Mary Shelley.* 1951. Rpt. as *Mary Shelley.* London: Sphere Books, 1989.

——. *The Comforters.* 1957. London: Penguin, 1963.

——. *Curriculum Vitae.* London: Constable, 1992.

——. "My Conversion." *Twentieth Century* 170 (Autumn 1961): 58-63.

——. "Personal History: The School on the Links." *New Yorker* 25 Mar. 1991: 75-85.

——. "What Images Return." *Memoirs of a Modern Scotland.* Ed. Karl Miller. London: Faber & Faber, 1970: 151-53.

Whittaker, Ruth. *The Faith and Fiction of Muriel Spark.* London: Macmillan, 1982.

□

Shades of Grey: A Discussion of Pat Barker's *Regeneration*

Shari A. Koopmann

Introduction

In a review of Pat Barker's Booker-winning novel *The Ghost Road* that appeared in the *New Yorker*, Blake Morrison makes reference to the lamentation of the 1995 Booker Prize judge, the Member of Parliament George Walden, who remarked at the ceremony: "'So few of the Booker entries tackled modern England [...] [Nostalgia] is becoming our heavy industry'" (Morrison 80). Morrison refutes Walden's statement on the basis of Barker's modernisation of the language, (the officers in all three novels speak in "current idiom" rather than the more characteristic convoluted high language of the time), and the "candour" with which Barker deals with sexual content, Morrison fails to address the most obvious and compelling argument against Walden's philosophy, which is that Barker's trilogy actively employs its World War I setting as a periscope through which a critique of modern England becomes readily available (Morrison 80). It is my intention to examine the bridge between Barker's trilogy and the conception of the modern consciousness.

World War I provides a more than adequate framework to illustrate the prevailing characteristics of modern thought, or more specifically the intricate web of power-relationships which dominates Western civilisation. In *The Great War and Modern Memory,* Paul Fussell argues that the characteristic of World War I is a division and irony which has laid the foundation for the modern world's reliance on binary thinking:

> What we can call gross dichotomizing is a persisting imaginative habit of modern times, traceable, it would seem, to the actualities of the Great War [...]. We are all here on this side; 'the enemy' is over

> there. 'We' are individuals with names and personal identities; 'he' is a mere collective entity (Fussell 75).

It seems that this "model of modern political, social, artistic, and psychological polarisation" is exactly what Barker had in mind, for even the words that she chooses to employ at the close of the third novel of the trilogy are reminiscent of Fussell's passage quoted above:

> And I realize there's another group of words that still mean something. Little words that trip through sentences unregarded: us, them, we, they, here, there. These are the words of power, and long after we're gone, they'll lie about in the language, like the unexploded grenades in these fields, and anyone of them'll take your hand off (Barker, *The Ghost Road* 257).

These words of power and of destruction are words that distinguish, categorise, and designate difference, or more appropriately what Derrida calls *la différance*. And it is the longevity of these words that concerns Pat Barker.

Regeneration is framed by a seemingly innocuous description of the entrance hall of Craiglockhart. At the beginning of chapter III, Sassoon leads Graves into the hospital: "Graves picked up his bag and together they went up the steps, through the black and white tiled entrance hall on to the main corridor" (Barker, *Regeneration* 20). Following Sassoon's final salute after being "discharged to duty" by the Medical Board in the final pages of the novel, Rivers momentarily envisions the tortured Callan standing in Sassoon's place. That telling image fades, and Rivers' return to reality is described as follows: "Then the electrical room at Queen Square faded, and Rivers was back at Craiglockhart, on the black and white tiled floor, alone" (Barker 248).

The scope of Pat Barker's *Regeneration* expands beyond the constrictions of the genre of anti-war literature. Literally, the war plays only a minor role in the text; the only evidence of the experience in the trenches arrives in the form of cryptic dreams, hypnosis-induced memories, mysterious file folders (the authors of which remain unknown), and Rivers' interpretation of his patients' behavior (which ultimately falls victim to, not only his own scrutiny, but the reader's as well). Thus, *Regeneration* is a war novel of an unusual kind. Rather than focusing on the shots fired across "No Man's Land," the text explores the consequences of the wounds endured by those involved (the "No Man's Land" of the mind). It is a novel that is involved in the deconstruction of the two-dimensional package which serves as the foundation upon which society builds and orders reality. The argument present in the text is that the soldier is the victim of such an oversimplified view of the world. He does not fit into any of the available moulds, and thus, is rendered invisible—forced inside the grouting between the black and white tiles of perception.

It is appropriate, therefore, that the story is framed between the black and white floor tiles that decorate the entrance hall of Craiglockhart because central to the text are the many shades of *grey* that define the victims of the war. It is also appropriate, therefore, that the reader's first image of the war arrives in the form of "lines of men with *grey* muttering faces clambering up the ladders to face the guns" (Barker 5, italics added for emphasis).

In fact, the colour *grey* appears frequently in the text. Graves is initially awed by the "massive yellow-*grey* facade of Craiglockhart," and Sarah, while waiting for Prior who never arrives, watches "the *grey* trickle of tea creep up the sides of her cup" (Barker 20, 109 italics added for emphasis). During Burns' Medical Board, "there was a great deal of light, it seemed to him [Burns], floods of silver-*grey* light filtered through white curtains that stirred in the breeze, and the insistent buzzing of an insect, trapped" (Barker 132). Perhaps the most baffling scene in the text—the episode during which Burns leaves the hospital and climbs the hill to the trees with dead animals as fruit—is also riddled with grey imagery. At the opening of the scene, Burns is looking out of the window: "Rain had blurred the landscape, dissolving sky and hills together in a wash of *grey*" (Barker 37 italics added for emphasis). And on his voyage of discovery, Burns meets with an obstacle—a wire fence blocking his passage: "A tuft of *grey* wool had caught on one of the barbs" (Barker 37; italics added for emphasis). This description seems too well placed not to have been an intentional play on the white / black dichotomy. We can address these scenes in greater depth only after we have established the parameters for defining the perception of reality that the black and white tiles symbolise. So, let us pause briefly to consider the dichotomies which are being systematically deconstructed.

In *Regeneration,* Barker challenges the accepted interpretations and associations of the following binaries: masculine/feminine, dominant/submissive, doctor/patient, verbalisation/silence, sight/blindness, fact/fiction, mobility/immobility, sanity/insanity, and freedom/enslavement. All of these dichotomies revolve around issues of control, power, and sexuality. And it seems that Barker is arguing that the war perverts such cultural distinctions as those mentioned above, causing a conflict to arise within the soldier, manifesting itself in dual personalities that are irreconcilable. Ultimately these inner conflicts result in a breakdown of mind and body. The novel seems to be arguing against the inflexibility of such strict binaries as the gender dichotomy, and instead argues for the *greys* of perception.

For organisational reasons, I have broken this discussion into three parts: the first will identify and discuss the ways in which the novel suggests the existence of these conflicts within the soldier; the second will discuss the reasons why such conflicts prevent the soldier's metaphoric return regardless of the attempted "cure;" and the final section will then explore the significance of the grey.

Part I—Loss of the Sabre

"But then in a war nobody is a free agent."—Rivers (Barker 238)

The novel appropriately opens with Sassoon's declaration, in which he, speaking "on behalf of soldiers," declares his position "against the political errors and insecurities for which the fighting men are being sacrificed" (Barker 3). The term "sacrifice" reminds one of the reference to the biblical sacrifice of Isaac that appears a little later in the text. Below a "flag-draped altar," which implies the mingling of politics and religion, is a scene depicting Abraham about to sacrifice his son:

> The bargain, Rivers thought, looking at Abraham and Isaac. The one on which all patriarchal societies are founded—If you, who are young and strong, will obey me, who am old and weak, even to the extent of being prepared to sacrifice your life, then in the course of time you will peacefully inherit, and be able to exact the same obedience from your sons [...]. Only we're breaking the bargain Rivers thought. All over northern France, at this very moment in trenches and dugouts and flooded shell-holes, the inheritors were dying, not one by one, while old men, and women of all ages, gathered together and sang hymns [hymns which praised God for working in 'mysterious ways'] (Barker 149).

In Genesis: 22, God asks Abraham to sacrifice his son, and Abraham complies. However, at the moment when Abraham is about to kill Isaac God supplies a ram as a substitute. There is no reason given in Genesis for the idea of the sacrifice—no reason offered to explain why God asks

Abraham to kill his beloved son; rather, the emphasis is placed on Abraham's *obedience* to God. Thus, the story is somewhat analogous to World War I. The soldiers are asked to sacrifice their lives, and just as with Abraham, the reason for the sacrifice is not given. Thus, the soldier necessarily experiences an inner conflict between a need to justify his own as well as others' deaths—a human need to end suffering, and a desire to serve and to carry out his duty to his country—to be an Abraham, who, for his righteous and unquestioning obedience, was rewarded with a divine blessing.

Sassoon's declaration expresses at least the first half of this conflict: "I believe that the purposes for which I and my fellow soldiers entered upon this war should have been so clearly stated as to have made it impossible to change them [...] now I make this protest against the deception which is being practised on them [the soldiers]" (Barker 3). The *deception* to which Sassoon refers is the lack of a reason or a justification for the many deaths and wounds that have been incurred. It is Rivers' job, on the other hand, to convince Sassoon that it is his *duty* to return to the battlefield and that this duty defies reason.

Rivers expresses anxiety over Sassoon's case: "he was finding it difficult to examine the evidence impartially" (Barker 8). His inability to be objective is due to the fact that he is also troubled by this inner conflict between duty to one's county and freedom of one's individual conscience: "'You realize, don't you, that it's my *duty* to [...] to try to change that [Sassoon's anti-war neurosis]?'" Rivers asks Sassoon, whose "glance took in both their uniforms" (Barker 15 italics added for emphasis). It is also interesting to note that when Sassoon explains that although he realised the futility of his protest, (the throwing of the MC ribbon into the Mersey), "'It still had to be done. You can't just acquiesce,'" Rivers responds by quickly and significantly attempting to close their conversation: "'Look, I think we've [...] we've got about as far as we can get today. You must be very tired'" (Barker 15). Perhaps the reason why Rivers silences this specific subject is because he realises the paradox between his agreement with Sassoon's protest against the senseless slaughter necessitated by the war, and his position as an instrument of that senselessness; he "cures" the soldiers so that they may return to the slaughterhouse. As one critic noteș: "However benevolent, he [Rivers] was part of the military machine. His job was to get these chaps fighting—fit again" (Morrison 78). In fact, it is his job, his duty, to convince these men to, like Rivers himself, *acquiesce.* When Sassoon remarks "'It suits [Graves] to attribute everything I've done to to to to [...] a state of mental breakdown, because then he doesn't have to ask himself any awkward questions. Like why he agrees with me about the war and does nothing about it,'" Rivers hesitates for a moment, as he did in the previous example, and then blatantly changes the subject: "'I know Richard Dadd was a painter. What else did he do?'" (Barker 34). Rivers is essentially avoiding the realisation that this is as true of himself as it is for Graves; for it is revealed earlier in the text that he also "wanted Sassoon to be ill" because "he'd be a lot less trouble" if he were (Barker 8).

This conflict between the freedom of the individual's conscience and the enslavement of duty is just one of the many interpretations of Burns' statement "'it's a joke'" (Barker 19). This is only one of the many causes of the fracturing that occurs within those individuals involved in the war experience (and we have already established with the example of Rivers that the compass of this experience extends outside of the trenches). Another dichotomy that we have yet to explore is masculine/feminine.

In an interview with Donna Perry, Pat Barker remarked: "I find the analysis of men's dependency and their lack of autonomy in that war, a study of why they suffered from hysterical symptoms rather than paranoia is a feminist analysis [...]. They were helpless—just floating along till whatever might happen did, feeling that they couldn't control it" (Perry, *Backtalk* 52).

The men have changed significantly because of the war experience: "He'd [Sassoon] have given anything to be out there, away from the stuffiness of the carriage, the itch and *constriction* of his uniform" (Barker 6 italics added for emphasis). The uniform, the position, is constraining or repressing the men—eliminating certain aspects of their pre-war personalities and in their stead preparing to fill the hollowness with a new hybrid of man—the feminised soldier—"neither fish nor fowl" (Barker 57).

Although the war promised adventure and manliness (bravery, courage), it delivered something quite the opposite. As Prior explains: "Oh, all right, I was in love with it once. Shall I tell you something about that ['big glorious cavalry'] charge? Just as it was about to start an officer saw three men smoking. He thought that was a bit too casual, so he confiscated their sabres and sent them into the charge unarmed. Two of them were killed" (Barker 66). Thus, the war was actually quite an emasculating experience, in the sense that these men were murdered by an officer's blatant abuse of power. There was nothing brave or courageous about their deaths. And the act of stripping the men of their sabres implies castration; the sabre, in this instance, has phallic connotations.

However, just as the officer serves as the metaphorical castrator, he also represents a mother-figure. As one critic notes:

> It was one of the ironies of the war that the disordered minds of [Rivers'] patients would frequently display symptoms that had previously been identified as belonging to hysterical women. The officers' duties, too—disciplining and caring for their men, providing food and comfort—were curiously domestic, like those of mothers rather than warriors. (Birch 22)

Thus, it is appropriate that when Sarah becomes lost in the hospital, and comes across "notices" that "refer to [each areas] [...] use before the war," she finds herself staring into a room marked "maternity," in which were beds full of wounded officers (Barker 92).

Interestingly, Rivers also represents a mother-figure. He recalls a patient named Layard: "What was it he'd said? 'I don't see you as a *father*, you know.' Looking up from the rug in front of the fire. Laughing. 'More a sort of [...] male mother.' He was like Prior. The same immensely shrewd eyes. X-ray eyes. The same outrageous frankness" (Barker 107). The officers, being responsible for the lives of their men, became motherly, in the sense that they were forced not only to provide food, shelter, and protection for these much younger soldiers (innocent, like children, unaware of the horrors into which they had been plunged) but had also to care for these men—and care very deeply: "This most brutal of conflicts [...] [sets] up a relationship between officers and men that was [...] domestic. Caring. As Layard would undoubtedly have said, maternal [...]. The war had promised so much in the way of 'manly' activity had actually delivered 'feminine' passivity, and on a scale that their mothers and sisters had scarcely known. No wonder they broke down" (Barker 109). Rivers in Craiglockhart is in a very similar position to the officers at the front; the situation demands that his emotions become entangled in the lives of his patients. And the very act of psychoanalysis, getting the men to discuss their feelings, is culturally defined as a motherly quality.

Rivers is also, however, like the officer, in the sense that he is the castrator. He strips the men of their freedom, by systematically forcing them back into the societal moulds which they had previously rejected. Essentially, his duty is to control and manipulate his patients' emotions in order to get them to agree to sacrifice their lives:

> A bit. An instrument of control. Obviously he and Yealland were both in the business of controlling people. Each of them fitted young men back into the role of warrior, a role they had—however unconsciously—rejected [...]. But then in a war nobody is a free agent. He and Yealland were both locked in, every bit as much as their patients were [...] so, in an infinitely more gentle way, he silenced his patients; for the stammerings, the nightmares, the tremors, the memory lapses of officers were just as much unwitting protest as the grosser maladies of the men. (Barker 238)

It is fitting then that Rivers connect his nightmare in which he imagines himself in Yealland's position with "an oral rape," because the dream action, which serves as a metaphor for his chosen method of treatment, is very much like a rape (Barker 236). Rivers acknowledges experiencing "a momentary spasm of satisfaction" while running a spoon along the back of Prior's throat, which caused a "choking reflex" (Barker 237). One can only assume then that Rivers, at least to some extent, enjoys his control. And perhaps it is important to note that when Willard, in a wheelchair which is significantly being pushed by his wife, meets the obstacle of a steep slope, Rivers jumps to take control. The matron, who quite obviously disapproves of the way in which Rivers handles the situation, remarks "'You could have sent an orderly down to push the chair, Captain Rivers'" (Barker 119). Rivers' name is hardly ever preceded by his title, *Captain*; the Matron in calling our attention to Rivers' rank is also significantly emphasising his position of power—and thus, his abuse of power. Hence, Rivers, in this scenario, becomes the castrator. He acknowledged the fact that Willard was made furious by his predicament, and is somehow delighted by this information: "He felt Willard's fury at being stranded like this, impotent. Good. The more furious the better" (Barker 119). And it is at that point that he offers Willard help, perhaps knowing that this offer will only serve to frustrate Willard to a greater degree than before. One can only assume that Willard found all of this to be quite humiliating; it is, at least symbolically, an emasculating experience. The description of Willard's face after he arrives safely at the top of the hill supports this analysis: "Willard's face would have curdled milk" (Barker 119). Perhaps Willard feels very much like Prior had felt when he was being examined by the medical doctor: "He had a picture of himself driving his knee into the man's groin"—a desire to emasculate the man that is emasculating him, and thereby, to reclaim one's power and one's status as a man (Barker 162).

The war instilled in the men attributes commonly associated with femininity, while the women took over the masculine positions in society to replace the men who had gone to the front. All of the residents of Craiglockhart (at least those with whom the reader shares some level of intimacy) can be characterised as having both masculine and feminine tendencies. As one critic notes: "[The soldiers'] symptoms included nightmares, mutism, immobility, insomnia, anxiety, and depression brought about by a sense of having failed to be 'real men'" (Morrison 78). Anderson's dream clearly symbolises the feminisation of the soldier. Perhaps it would be beneficial to list some of the characteristics associated with the term feminisation: passivity, objectification, loss of control, weakness, sensitivity, emotionalism, and hysteria. Anderson describes the dream to Rivers in a session. He begins by explaining the shame he felt upon realising his nakedness in the presence of his wife and a few of her female companions. He had been wearing a uniform: thus, the feelings are directly associated with his position in the war. He then describes being chased by his father-in-law who is waving a big stick with a snake wound around it,—the phallic implications are obvious. When he is caught, his hands are tied, symbolising a loss of control, with "a pair of lady's corsets" (Barker 28). He is thrown into a grave-like enclosure, where he meets Rivers "wearing a post-mortem apron and gloves" (Barker 28). One could argue that the dream is an expression of Anderson's anxiety over his feminine side—or, more appropriately, over his lack or loss of attributes commonly associated with masculinity. Similarly Burns, when peering down at his naked body within the circle of what he perceives to be dead moles, "cupped his genitals in his hands, not because he was ashamed, but because they looked incongruous, they didn't seem to belong with the rest of him" (Barker 37).

The men are systematically rendered impotent by the war. And thus, it is appropriate that Prior uses war metaphors to describe an inability to perform in a sexual encounter: "the first time was almost always a disappointment. Either stuck at half mast or firing before you reached the target" (Barker 130). After years of being "backhanded" by one's father for "coming in crying," perhaps it is not completely absurd that Anderson and the other men are having nightmares about being chased with sticks and leading lives that Rivers describes as "completely inconsistent" (Barker 56, 76). One must remember that these men had "been trained to identify emotional repression as the essence of manliness" (Barker 48). As Rivers observes:

> Men who broke down, or cried, or admitted to feeling fear, were sissies, weaklings, failures. Not *men* […]. And yet in advising his young patients to abandon the attempt at repression and to let themselves feel the pity and terror their war experience inevitably evoked, he was excavating the ground he stood on. (Barker 48)

Rivers is literally standing on the black and white floor tiles of Craiglockhart, and he is metaphorically excavating the gender dichotomy which those tiles symbolise.

While the men were emasculated by the war experience, the women were at least temporarily freed from their positions in the gender—power dichotomy. It is appropriate, therefore, that Prior "didn't know what to make" of Sarah; he felt somewhat "out of touch" with women: "They seemed to have changed so much during the war, to have expanded in all kinds of ways, whereas men in the same period had shrunk into a smaller and smaller space" (Barker 90). It is also appropriate that Sarah exhibit many of the attributes associated with masculinity. She not only works in a munitions factory but "she was tall for a woman, and they [she and Prior] fitted together, shoulder and hip. He hardly had to shorten his stride […]. He guessed she more usually wore boots" (Barker 92). And as one critic notes: "The women at home were freeing themselves from the worst tyrannies of domestic service, often earning high wages in the munitions factories, and finding some degree of the freedom that the men at the front had lost (Birch 22). This notion that the war was a freeing experience for the women is supported by the fact that some of the female characters in *Regeneration* express enjoyment of the war. For example Ruth Head remarks: "'the air raids are my guilty secret.'" And she explains her guilty secret as follows:

> 'I enjoy them. It's a terrible thing to say, isn't it? All that damage. People killed. And yet every time the siren goes, I feel this immense sense of exhilaration. I'd really like to go out and run about in it.' She laughed, self-deprecatingly. 'I don't of course. But I get this feeling that the […] the *crust* of everything is starting to crack.' (Barker 164)

And as Barker herself remarks in an interview with Donna Perry: "I wanted to bring out how women enjoyed the war. They adored it" (Perry, *Literary Review* 240). In a sense, Ruth Head is right. *The crust of everything is starting to crack*—the strict binaries are beginning to unravel. As a result of the war, the gender dichotomy has, in a manner of speaking, begun to come undone. The tiles are dislodging, and the grey grouting is beginning to shine through.

Rivers responds appropriately to Ruth Head's statement: "'I'm just not sure we're going to like what's under the crust'" (Barker 164). To acknowledge the grey is to acknowledge the full spectrum of individual cases outside of the strict binaries that define notions of gender, race, class, and power. It is to face reality in all of its glory and all of its horror. It is much safer to hide behind *a faith that ignores the facts*—to chalk everything up to the glory of *God's mysterious ways*. If one chooses to face the truth and to look under that crust, she will see Burns covered in the entrails of another soldier, and herself as the one who metaphorically dropped the shell that caused his predicament. She will be forced to face the culturally—uncomfortable notion of homosexuality, of bisexuality, and of an "intermediate sex" (Barker 54). She will be forced to look into the blue eyeball that triggers Prior's breakdown. And like Prior, she will break down "because the boundaries of what he [she] has been taught to expect can't contain what he [she] has seen," just as Rivers' story on one of the Solomon Islands indicate (Birch 22):

> Nobody was making those sounds, and yet we all heard them. You see, the rational explanation for that is that we'd allowed ourselves to be dragged into an experience of mass hypnosis, and I don't for a moment deny that that's possible. But what we'd been told to expect was the swish of paddles. Nobody'd said anything about whistling. (Barker 188)

Barker is arguing that society's perception of reality is limited, and its limited scope is due to the fact that it is based on comfort rather than on truth. It is Barker's intention to present her readers with that truth.

Part II—What Blows Up Must Come Down

"Language ran out on you in the end." (Barker 90)

Regeneration suggests that the war machine perverts the "natural" order, which is symbolised by the all-too-common World War I literary image of the "two hands sticking up out of a heap of pocked and pitted chalk, like *the roots of an overturned tree*" (Barker 16; italics added for emphasis). I have deliberately written the word *natural* in quotation marks, because, as I mentioned previously, it seems to me that it is Barker's intention to point out the very *unnaturalness* of this manner of ordering reality. The "natural" order is "sanity" as it is defined by English society and culture: "We—the patients are *like* Antaeus in the sense that we've been ungrounded by the war. And the way back to health is to reestablish the link between oneself and the earth, but understand 'earth' to mean society as well as nature" (Barker 123). This notion of sanity is an impossibility for the sufferers of war.

The "natural" order, or the system of power dichotomies which we have been discussing, is not interpreted as "safe" by the returning soldier. In fact, the war itself offers the only notion of safety that is available to him: "A few days of *safety*, and all the *clear spirit* of the trenches was gone" (Barker 44; italics added for emphasis). The war is the only place where the returning soldier can feel some sense of belonging—of safety,—because the world outside of the trenches denies his very existence. Sassoon, at the very beginning of the novel, remarks: "'I think the army's probably the only place I've ever really belonged'" (Barker 36). He finds it difficult to sleep away from the trenches: "He tossed and turned, thinking how stupid it was not to be able to sleep here, in safety and comfort, when in France he'd been able to sleep anywhere. If he could sleep on a firestep in drenching rain, surely he could sleep now" (Barker 143). And Prior explains why he wants to return to the front as follows: "'When all this is over, people who didn't go to France, or didn't do well in France—people of my generation, I mean—aren't going to count for anything. This is the Club to end all Clubs'" (Barker 135). In fact, the war creates two exclusive clubs. The first consists of those who have experienced the war either first-hand in the trenches, or second-hand by hearing the truth through the mouths of the abovementioned. The second club is populated by the rest of society, those who either have no knowledge of the war experience or refuse to acknowledge the truth. The exclusiveness of these clubs is evident in the following quotation:

> They don't want the truth. It's like letters of condolence. 'Dear Mrs. Bloggs, Your son had the side of his head blown off by a shell and took five hours to die. We did manage to give him a decent Christian burial. Unfortunately that particular stretch of ground came under heavy bombardment the day after, so George—or Johnny—or whatever

> his name was, died a quick death and was given a decent send off.' He said deliberately, 'Yesterday, at the seaside I felt as if I came from another planet.' (Barker 134)

And indeed, in a sense, he is from a different planet—a planet whose inhabitants are alien and therefore unrecognisable to the inhabitants of *this* planet (and here, of course, I am referring to society). Society *is* the "*Shuttered* windows, like *blind* eyes, [which] watched from either side;" society is the real wearer of the "rather badly fitting mask" which Sarah removes in order to shake the yellow dust off of her face (Barker 234, 201; italics added for emphasis).

Perhaps, the reference to the Apostles at Pentecost is significant to our discussion. According to J.R. Porter, the "Descent of the Spirit at Pentecost" has been "interpreted as the moment when the old Jewish Law was replaced by a new spiritual revelation for all humanity" (Porter 216). The spirit gave the Apostles the ability to speak in other languages. The scene of Rivers' last dinner at Craiglockhart before going on leave is perhaps a parody of the scene at Pentecost; it is almost as if each man at the table is speaking a different language:

> "Even at this distance you could distinguish Brock's high, reedy voice, MacIntyre's broad Glaswegian, Bryce's Edinburgh, Ruggles's American, and Rivers, who, when he got excited in a discussion, as he often did, sounded rather like a sodawater syphon going off [...]. Fothergill [...] had started to complain about the soup. 'Nay, verily,' he said. 'A man knoweth not what manner of thing he eateth.' [...] Sassoon, marooned between two particularly bad stammers," was silent. (Barker 140)

There is only one important piece missing from the equation. According to Rivers "the gift of Pentecost had made the Apostles *comprehensible* in all known languages" (Barker 153). This is the reason the men can never reestablish their feet on those black and white tiles. They are incomprehensible to the world at large—they are to all intents and purposes invisible. And for the soldier, therefore, returning to his pre-war life is as inconceivable as forging a future in a world in which he no longer belongs. Rivers, like the men he treats, "can't imagine going back to the same way of life" (Barker 241).

As Rivers himself observes: "What you will never find is that mythical creature, half caterpillar, half butterfly, a fit emblem of the human soul" (Barker 184). The cocoon is the line that divides these two worlds; there exists no in-between—that is, like the half caterpillar half butterfly, the soldier functioning in society is the stuff of myths. The irony, of course, is that society expects these men to have no trouble easing back into its comfortable world, after they have come face to face with the reality which blew society's walls apart—the reality that cannot fit into the strict binaries available to them. As one critic notes: "Shattered men may be rebuilt here, but not *necessarily* along the lines of their original construction" (Pierpont 74). I would push the point further and remove the disclaimer: the returning soldier cannot step into his pre-war skin and zip it up—he doesn't fit into that uniform any more.

After Sassoon is "discharged to duty," he experiences "exactly the same feeling he had had on board ship going to France, watching England slide away into the mist. No doubts, no scruples, no agonising, just a straightforward, headlong *retreat* towards the front" (Barker 248; italics added for emphasis). England, here, represents the "natural" order—the reality that fits snugly into the black and white squares. It is appropriate therefore that England slides away "into the mist;" these squares, these black and white lines become indistinguishable as he nears the *clear spirit* of the trenches—perhaps, it is not inappropriate to assume that this mist is grey. Sassoon describes his voyage back to the trenches as a "retreat." He is running away from the brand of comfort that defines the tightly knit fabric of binaries which make up English society and culture, the quilt of which every square denies his existence and denies the truth; he is retreating into the mist.

Rivers' epiphany moment on the mission boat is the closest to authorial intent the reader can get:

> 'And I suddenly saw that their reaction to my society were neither more nor less valid than mine to theirs. And do you know that was a moment of the most *amazing* freedom. I lay back and I closed my eyes and I felt as if a ton weight had been lifted […] the *Great White God* de-throned, I suppose. Because we did, we quite unselfconsciously *assumed* we were the measure of all things. That was how we approached them. And suddenly I saw not only that we weren't the measure of all things, but that there was no measure […]. Nothing changed *in England.* And I don't know why. I think partly just the sheer force of other people's expectations. You know you're walking around with a mask on, and you desperately want to

take it off and you can't because everybody else thinks it's your face.' (Barker 242)

The fact that Rivers realises the possibility of a multitude of equally valid interpretations supports my claim that the novel is arguing for the greys of perception. Similarly Rivers' statement that we have incorrectly assumed ourselves to be *the measure of all things*, when in fact there is *no measure*, challenges the pretensions of society in establishing these strict binaries and expecting everything and everyone to have a place in that system. The dethroning of the Great White God implies that there no longer exists, for Rivers at least, a system of binaries into which everything is categorised. This notion of reality which we have donned like masks, like uniforms in fact will constrict him no longer. Rivers is undeniably the protagonist of the text. And thus, the enlightenment that Rivers experiences is the enlightenment that the author hopes the reader will also experience. In other words, Barker's argument is essentially that we should take off our own masks, and think critically about the system of which we are an integral part.

Part III—Season of Mists: Conclusion

The appearances of grey in the text ironically symbolise moments of clarity—the *clear spirit* of the trenches. The grey is the measureless, limitless, and boundary-less truth that necessarily eludes dichotomous construction. Let us consider the scene in which Burns leaves the hospital. The scene opens with Burns staring through the rain blurred window: the sky and hills had dissolved "together in a wash of grey" (Barker 37). He is listening to people talking "about the war the war the war," and feels the growing need to escape to the outdoors, to the grey (Barker 37). However, he pauses at the main gates "because he'd been inside so long, the possibilities seemed endless" (Barker 37). Perhaps, his trepidation is analogous to English society, which has been trapped so long within the system of power dichotomies, that, if it were to dismantle that system, the possibilities for a multitude of contradictory but equally valid truths would be limitless. Burns does not like "the contact or the smell" of the crowds of people on the bus with him, implying that he is exceedingly discomfited by society outside of the trenches—the society of which he is no longer a member (Barker 37).

The description of his voyage up the hill seems to duplicate the conditions of the battlefield: his path is blockaded by a barbed wire fence; he is dressed in full khaki uniform and "mud-encumbered" boots; he listens "for the whine of shells"; he struggles through thick mud which "dragged at him, [causing him to] [...] slow to a walk;" and his final destination is an open "field," similar to that of "No Man's Land" (Barker 38). The muddy earth is described as "sucking" him in. One might argue that this detail is an ironic twist of the story of Antaeus; Burns is being metaphorically grounded by the war, this symbolising perhaps that the battlefield, the war itself, grounded these men in a reality far more honest than the black and white squares of a faith not based in fact. The visibility increases as he climbs, perhaps indicating that he is nearing *the clear spirit* of the trenches for which Sassoon had pined. He is climbing without a clear destination as if driven by some external force. And as he reaches the top of the hill, overcoming the struggle with nature (the thick mud and the rain), his mind is described as being "incapable of making comparisons," perhaps implying that his struggle was in fact with the "natural" order—the system of binaries (Barker 38). Comparison is what this system of binaries is based on; thus, his victory over this struggle lies in his inability to make distinctions, or to perceive the world in dichotomies.

He arrives at a cluster of trees: "Looking up, he saw that the tree he stood under was laden with dead animals. Bore them like fruit. A whole branch of moles in various stages of decay" (Barker 38). A mole is an animal that burrows underground. Thus, it is not inappropriate to assume that the dead moles hanging from the branches of the tree represent the trench soldiers, and the fact that they exist in various stages of decay is perhaps reminiscent of the mythical creature—half caterpillar and half butterfly—the returning wounded soldier functioning within the framework of English society. However, moles are not the only fruits on the tree: there was also "a ferret, a weasel, three magpies, [and] a fox" (Barker 38). The ferret, the weasel, and the fox are all flesh-eating mammals, and like the mole, could simply represent trench soldiers; however, the magpie sets up a different set of assumptions. The magpie is a bird related to the jay that is black and white in colouring. Perhaps, the significance of the animals lies in their colouring. For example, the magpie could symbolise the dichotomies that define English society and culture, and the mole, which is frequently grey in colour, would symbolise not only the soldier, but the truth that the soldier represents. Perhaps the tree represents the tree of knowledge and the fruit that it bears is the fruit of wisdom. The acknowledgement of the brutality and the horror of the war with its "bloodied teeth," and the awareness of the black and white dichotomies of English culture, therefore, become the first step in the path toward enlightenment (Barker 38). Burns begins releasing the animals by untying their wings. The fact that their wings are tied implies that these soldiers were controlled, manipulated into a passive position (very much like Anderson in his dream—tied with corsets). Burns arranges the corpses on the ground in a circle around himself: "Now they could dissolve into the earth *as they were meant to do*" (Barker 39; italics added for emphasis). Perhaps this action implies that he is attempting to return the metaphorical soldiers to some natural state prior to the slaughter—he is grounding them.

It is significant that he places his clothes outside of the circle, (remember he is wearing his full uniform); thus, he is ridding the circle of all evidence of the war, and returning it to a more natural state (hence, his nakedness): "Then he folded his clothes carefully and put them outside the circle. He sat down again with his back to the tree and looked up through the tracery of branches at *grey* and scudding clouds" (Barker 39; italics added for emphasis). However, looking down at his naked body, he "cupped his genitals in his hands, not because he was ashamed but because they looked incongruous, they didn't seem to belong with the rest of him" (Barker 39). He fails in his attempt to return his circle into a pre-war state because he has inherently changed as a result of his experience in the war—he has become feminised. And that change is irreversible and permanent. He can cover it up as he does later in the text by choosing not to receive newspapers, by surrounding himself with childhood books, by taking an interest in meaningless hobbies and local gossip, but in the end it proves inescapable, as the scene in the watchtower indicates. The soldier cannot return into a society that has no method to comprehend his experience—a society whose very language is an intricate system of traps set up to trip those that don't seem to fit into its available moulds.

Regeneration argues that we should look critically at a system that defines insanity as anything beyond our limited perspective. Barker is arguing that a more honest perception of reality is one that allows for the inclusion of even the most horrific experiences like Burns', one that provides a haven for people who fall somewhere outside of gender, class, and power dichotomies, and one that does not limit our comprehension of the diverse truths that exist in the world. In essence, *Regeneration* argues for a method of perception that includes the many shades of grey.

Works Cited

Barker, Pat. *Regeneration.* New York: Penguin, 1993.

——. *The Ghost Road.* New York: Penguin, 1996.

Birch, Dinah. "Invalided Home." *London Review of Books* 15.20 (1993): 22.

Fussell, Paul. *The Great War and Modern Memory.* New York: OUP, 1975.

Morrison, Blake. "War Stories: What Booker Prize Winner Pat Barker Sees in Soldiers." *The New Yorker* LXXI.45 (1996): 78-80.

Perry, Donna. "Going Home Again: An Interview with Pat Barker." *The Literary Review* 34.2 (1991): 235-44.

Perry, Donna. *Backtalk: Women Writers Speak Out: Interviews by Donna Perry.* New Brunswick, New Jersey: Rutgers UP, 1993. 43-62.

Pierpont, Claudia Roth. "English Lessons." *The New Yorker* 68.25 (1992): 74-79.

Porter, J.R. "The Descent of the Spirit." *The Illustrated Guide to the Bible.* New York: OUP, 1995. 216-17.

□